The **I Found It!** *Series*

POWER
AND
PRAYERS

To DESTROY THE
MEANS OF THE WICKED

*Understanding And Dismantling
Every Demonic Attack*

JOSHUA TEMITAYO OBIGBESAN

To the God of all grace who, in choosing me
as His battle axe and weapon of war,
has allowed me to see the grace in His eyes.

Acknowledgments

The writing of this book was born out of my love for people and my desire for those held captive in any form of bondage to be set free. To this end, I have received input and encouragement which must be acknowledged.

The Holy Spirit is the initiator of my desire. He enabled me to preach and teach all the topics in this book, and He is the power behind all the prayer guides offered herein. To Him I give glory and honor.

To my blessed wife, Marion Bose Obigbesan, who has urged me on and been my stalwart support during the preparation of the manuscript, I express much thanks.

To my prayer partners and associate pastors of Christ Liberty Restoration Ministries, David Adedoyin Abraham and Ray Shiffer, I express my gratitude for their unwavering commitment to the work of the ministry at all times.

To my friends and dedicated members of Christ Liberty Restoration Ministries, William and Nora Cole, and Jim and Angelica Vogel, I sincerely appreciate your financial support for the publication of this book.

My sincere appreciation also goes to my divinely-connected editor, Donna Scuderi, who through much patience edited and organized this book into this remarkable form.

Contents

Introduction

The Bible says "Many are the afflictions of the righteous: but the Lord delivereth him out of them all" (Ps. 34:19). God's Word is telling us that even the righteous experience affliction, but God delivers the righteous from *all* their troubles. The very next verse emphatically states that the Lord "keepeth all his [the righteous person's] bones: not one of them is broken" (Ps. 34:20). In other words, the righteous person's affliction will not damage his physical frame.

Praise the Lord! The righteous receive all these benefits because the Lord God is faithful.

So, what is affliction? It is adversity, a state of misery, hardship, or misfortune in which one can become "infested" with calamity. Because affliction brings great grief and distress, the righteous are aware when it comes. Although they know that affliction is assigned by the devil and his agents, they might not recognize the forms in which affliction comes. (Or perhaps I should say that the righteous are often careless in seeking to understand the means of the wicked.)

The wicked one assigns affliction in many ways. Let me say, dear reader, that although some affliction is intended to produce death, some leads only to misery and suffering. The devil and his agents have specific goals in assigning affliction: to steal, kill, or destroy.

The Nature of the Wicked

Affliction reflects the wickedness of its author, whose general nature is revealed in Psalms chapter 10. Verse 2 explains that in his arrogance, the wicked oppresses the poor. Verse 3 says he is boastful and supports what the Lord abhors. Verses 4 through 8 show that he does not reverence God, and instead does grievous things without regard for God's judgment. The wicked one's heart is fixed on doing evil; his mouth is full of cursing, deceit, and fraud. He is also a murderer!

Many believers know something about the wicked one (Satan), but are not aware of the means by which he operates. This understanding is critical, because when his means are destroyed, he is rendered powerless. The coming chapters will expose him *and* his means of operation—and will teach you how to destroy his methods using Holy-Spirit-inspired prayers!

1

Understanding Power Delegations

Power is defined as "physical strength or force exerted or capable of being exerted."[1] It is "the ability…to exercise control."[2] Power is given so it can be exercised. Whether it is used properly, misused, or abused depends upon the intent of the one to whom it is entrusted.

Divine power is delegated to produce godly outcomes. When Jesus addressed the seventy disciples who returned from an evangelism trip, He described the power He had given them to overcome Satan's power:

> *Behold, I give unto you power to tread on serpents and*
> *scorpions, and over all the power of the enemy: and*
> *nothing shall by any means hurt you* (Luke 10:19).

First, Jesus gave His disciples the power to trample on demonic entities. Second, He equipped them to overpower the master of demonic entities, which is Satan himself. Third, Jesus promised to protect His disciples. This divine protection is guaranteed to every believer through the Holy Spirit.

Many believers are either unaware of the power delegated to them or are unclear as to its use. As we continue this study, you will see the divinely appointed means of the righteous. For now, it is important to know that such power is available and was intended for righteous use.

Satanic power is delegated to oppose God's will in His Creation. In Luke 10:19, Jesus attested to Satan's power, which the wicked one delegates to his cohorts. Unfortunately, many believers are unaware of Satan's power. Therefore, they are ignorant of when and how it operates.

The example set by the Lord Jesus Christ should quell any ignorance in this regard. Immediately after He was baptized in the Jordan, Jesus was led into the wilderness by the Holy Spirit. During Jesus' testing, Satan's deceptive words bore witness to one truth: that the wicked one can delegate power:

> *The devil, taking him* [Jesus] *up into a high mountain, shewed unto him all the kingdoms of the world in a moment of time. And the devil said unto him, All this power will I give thee, and the glory of them: for that is delivered unto me; and to whomsoever I will I give it* (Luke 4:5-6).

Every Christian must understand that Satan has and delegates power to his wicked helpers. In Exodus, for example, we see Satan's minions producing counterfeit miracles:

> *Moses and Aaron went in unto Pharaoh, and they did so as the Lord had commanded: and Aaron cast down his rod before Pharaoh, and before his servants, and it became a serpent. Then Pharaoh also called the wise men and the sorcerers: now the magicians of Egypt, they also did in like manner with their enchantments. For they cast down every man his rod, and they became serpents: but Aaron's rod swallowed up their rods* (Exod. 7:10-12).

Clearly, Satan possesses the power to deceive people. But the Lord's power is mighty to override all demonic demonstrations. The drama in Pharaoh's palace proves that only God has total power. Praise the Lord!

The Power of Death

Remember that one of Satan's roles is that of murderer (see John 10:10). A conversation between God and Satan reveals that Satan possesses the power of death:

> *The LORD said unto Satan, Behold, all that he hath is in thy power; only upon himself put not forth thine hand. So Satan went forth from the presence of the LORD* (Job 1:12).

God clearly permitted Satan to exert the power of death against whatever belonged to Job and whomever was dear to him. However, God commanded that Job's life be spared. Had God permitted it, Satan would have killed Job also.

Satan cannot create anything. The power of death was given to him by Almighty God. At an appointed time, the Almighty Father made a way for man to resist the power of death used against him by Satan: the way was made through the death and resurrection of our Lord Jesus Christ!

Times, Places, and Violence

The Bible reveals that Satan delegates evil power to those who want to be his agents. This power is used in accordance with Satan's intended purpose, in the time of his choosing.

> *Woe to them that devise iniquity, and work evil upon their beds! When the morning is light, they practise it, because it is in the power of their hand* (Mic. 2:1).

In this verse, a curse is pronounced against evil people who plan iniquity at nighttime and implement their plans by day. Darkness is advantageous to (and compatible with) demonic activity. Therefore, much witchcraft and occultic operation occurs while most people are asleep.

13

The Bible clearly shows that the wicked have the power (including the resources, evil "wisdom," and often the legal grounds) to perform wickedness. Therefore, the believer must disgrace the wicked by dispossessing them of this power.

This requires vigilance. The wicked are specific in their timing and in other details (the who, what, where, and how) of their work:

> *They covet fields, and take them by violence; and houses, and take them away: so they oppress a man and his house, even a man and his heritage* (Mic. 2:2).

Satanists and other evildoers have violence in their blood. They do not know the way of peace; their only goal is to steal, kill or destroy. Their violence is not always overt, however. They also seek to confound God's people and set them at each other's throats. They do this simply by generating envy and strife:

> *For where envying and strife is, there is confusion and every evil work* (James 3:16).

> *Let us walk honestly, as in the day; not in rioting and drunkenness, not in chambering and wantonness, not in strife and envying* (Rom. 13:13).

> *Ye are yet carnal: for whereas there is among you envying, and strife, and divisions, are ye not carnal, and walk as men?* (1 Cor. 3:3).

God's people must be wise, discerning, and skilled in resisting the works of darkness! The wicked know only the way of violence; therefore, believers must heed this message of our Lord Jesus Christ: "From the days of John the Baptist until now the kingdom of heaven suffereth violence, and the violent take it by force" (Matt. 11:12). Our mandate as believers is clear: we must exercise holy violence against the wicked and repossess all that the enemy has stolen from God's people.

The Divine Plan to Receive "All Power"

The Bible reveals that our Lord Jesus was incarnated to reverse Satan's evil works. We can rest assured that Satan's wickedness will be exposed, and the power of the revealed Messiah will prevail.

> *He that committeth sin is of the devil; for the devil sin-*
> *neth from the beginning. For this purpose the Son of*
> *God was manifested, that he might destroy the works*
> *of the devil* (1 John 3:8).

Our mighty God made perfect provision for us. How blessed we are to be so loved by Him! Hear what His Word says about His desire to comfort His people:

> *So I returned, and considered all the oppressions that*
> *are done under the sun: and behold the tears of such*
> *as were oppressed, and they had no comforter; and*
> *on the side of their oppressors there was power; but*
> *they had no comforter* (Eccles. 4:1).

This verse attests to the oppressors' power; but it also reveals God's great love. the Lord made available a higher power to override that of the devil and his agents. Remember that the believer must know about this power *and* must learn to access and use it.

Shortly before He was taken up to heaven, Jesus told His disciples, "All power is given unto me in heaven and in earth" (Matt. 28:18). His statement reveals that He alone has the power to rule and overrule. Centuries earlier, the Holy Spirit revealed this power to the prophet Daniel:

> *I saw in the night visions, and, behold, one like the*
> *Son of man came with the clouds of heaven, and*
> *came to the Ancient of days, and they brought him*
> *near before him. And there was given him dominion,*
> *and glory, and a kingdom, that all people, nations,*
> *and languages, should serve him: his dominion is an*

15

everlasting dominion, which shall not pass away, and his kingdom that which shall not be destroyed.

I Daniel was grieved in my spirit in the midst of my body, and the visions of my head troubled me. I came near unto one of them that stood by, and asked him the truth of all this. So he told me, and made me know the interpretation of the things.

These great beasts, which are four, are four kings, which shall arise out of the earth. But the saints of the most High shall take the kingdom, and possess the kingdom for ever, even for ever and ever (Daniel 7:13–18).

Daniel saw that the saints of the Lord would receive and possess the kingdom forever and ever. Luke 10:19 reveals that Jesus delegated the power by which they would accomplish their mission. He now shares this power with all who join themselves to Him and submit to His authority. He also He tells them, "Come unto me all ye that labor and are heavy laden, and I will give you rest." (Matt. 11:28). Only this "all power" can guarantee rest—rest from the hard labor that yields little or no results, and rest from unending physical and spiritual battles.

This "all power" can be received only one way:

Ye shall receive power, after that the Holy Ghost is come upon you: and ye shall be witnesses unto me both in Jerusalem, and in all Judea, and in Samaria, and unto the uttermost part of the earth (Acts 1:8).

This is the divine arrangement. Isaiah 40:29 says that God "giveth power to the faint; and to them that have no might he increaseth strength." He is a good God, and He looks after His own!

Endnotes

1. *American Heritage® Dictionary of the English Language, 5th Edition,* 2011, s.v. "power," accessed February 4 2016, http://www.thefreedictionary.com/power.

2. Ibid.

2

Weapons of the Believer's Warfare

Those who choose to destroy the means of the wicked must know and understand the weapons that are available to them in spiritual warfare. It is also important to understand the weapons used by the Lord to achieve His purposes and oppose the wicked. The weapons covered here will add to your understanding; the corresponding scriptures can also be used in prayer. In addition, individual prayer guides will demonstrate practical applications of the concepts.

The Name of Jesus Christ

There is power in Jesus' name. It is not to be taken in vain and it must be used only in accordance with His will.

- **At the name of Jesus Christ, every knee should bow.**

> *At the name of Jesus every knee should bow, of things in heaven, and things in earth, and things under the earth* (Phil. 2:10).

> **Application and Prayer Guide:** In the name of Jesus Christ, I command all wickedness standing against the fulfillment of my destiny to crumble.

At the mention of the name *Jesus Christ*, the entire universe must bow in worship, surrendering to His superiority,

18

authority, and power. Anything standing in opposition to the divine will must acquiesce when His name is invoked.

- **In the name of Jesus Christ, demons must be cast out.**

Paul, being grieved, turned and said to the spirit, I command thee in the name of Jesus Christ to come out of her. And he came out the same hour (Acts 16:18).

> **Application and Prayer Guide:** In the name of Jesus Christ, I bind and cast out all demons operating in my environment to hinder or prevent me.

In Mark 16:17, Jesus said that believers would cast out devils in His name. In Thyatira, the apostle Paul cast out the demon of divination from a young lady. This power was not for Paul only, but is for all who believe in Jesus Christ.

- **Healing is accomplished in the name of Jesus Christ.**

Then Peter said, Silver and gold have I none; but such as I have give I thee: In the name of Jesus Christ of Nazareth rise up and walk (Acts 3:6).

When healing prayer is offered in the name of Jesus Christ, the dynamic power in that name flows through the infirmed body and wholeness is restored. The apostle Peter understood that Jesus' name was mighty to heal.

> **Application and Prayer Guide:** In the name of Jesus Christ, I command healing in my body, now!

■ **In the name of Jesus Christ, the gospel is preached.**

Barnabas took him, and brought him to the apostles, and declared unto them how he had seen the Lord in the way, and that he had spoken to him, and how he had preached boldly at Damascus in the name of Jesus (Acts 9:27).

Jesus Christ said, "Go ye therefore, and teach all nations" (Matt. 28:19a). This instruction can only be carried out in His name.

Application and Prayer Guide: I command every anti-gospel spirit in this place to be bound now, in the name of Jesus Christ.

■ **In the name of Jesus Christ, we are justified.**

Such were some of you: but ye are washed, but ye are sanctified, but ye are justified in the name of the Lord Jesus, and by the Spirit of our God (1 Cor. 6:11).

To be justified in His name means that we are forgiven based on His merits and not our own. No corrupt charge can be brought against those who have been washed and sanctified by His blood. Acts 13:39 says they "are justified from all things."

Application and Prayer Guide: No legal ground shall stand against me, for I am justified in the name of Jesus Christ.

■ **Thanksgiving is offered in the name of Jesus Christ.**

Giving thanks always for all things unto God and the Father in the name of our Lord Jesus Christ (Eph. 5:20).

The first step in spiritual warfare is to thank Jesus for all things. The hosts of darkness understand what Colossians 1:16 declares: "By him were all things created, that are in heaven, and that are in earth, visible and invisible, whether they be thrones, or dominions, or principalities, or powers: all things were created by him, and for him...." Therefore, this step is effective.

Application and Prayer Guide: Lord, in the name of Jesus Christ, I thank You for Your wonderful care of me.

- **All things must be done in the name of Jesus Christ.**

Whatsoever ye do in word or deed, do all in the name of the Lord Jesus, giving thanks to God and the Father by him (Col. 3:17).

Those who ask, seek, or knock must do so in the name of Jesus Christ (see Matt. 7:7). This is because He owns everything, as His statement in Matthew 11:27 reveals: "All things are delivered unto me of my Father...."

Application and Prayer Guide: Father Lord, open to me the door of spiritual breakthrough, in the name of Jesus Christ.

- **We tread upon the wicked through the name of Jesus Christ.**

Through thee will we push down our enemies: through thy name will we tread them under that rise up against us (Ps. 44:5).

Application and Prayer Guide: In the name of Jesus Christ, I decree confusion in the camp of the wicked who have collaborated against my success.

When prayer warfare is conducted in the name of Jesus Christ, the wicked are quickly subdued and destroyed. A holy decree can also be issued in Jesus' name to shatter unity among wicked forces.

The Blood of Jesus Christ

The Lord's precious blood was spilled so that we might be cleansed. The power of His blood is eternal. Poured out two thousand years ago, the blood remains effectual today.

- **The blood of Jesus Christ cleanses from all sins.**

If we walk in the light, as he is in the light, we have fellowship one with another, and the blood of Jesus Christ his Son cleanseth us from all sin (1 John 1:7).

And from Jesus Christ, who is the faithful witness, and the first begotten of the dead, and the prince of the kings of the earth. Unto him that loved us, and washed us from our sins in his own blood (Rev. 1:5).

Only the blood of Jesus Christ can wash away the pollution that comes through our sins. When we appropriate His blood, our prayer warfare is effective in destroying the legal ground from which Satan inflicts affliction and hindrance.

Application and Prayer Guide: In the name of Jesus Christ, let the blood of Jesus Christ cleanse me from the sins of my youth.

- **The blood of Jesus Christ has redeemed us unto God the Father.**

Who hath delivered us from the power of darkness, and hath translated us into the kingdom of his dear Son: in whom we have redemption through his blood, even the forgiveness of sins (Col. 1:13-14).

22

Believers were purchased for God by the blood of Jesus. His blood paid the price for our sin, which was eternal punishment. In spiritual warfare, His blood can be applied against the claims of ancestral spirits and against ancient curses prevailing in a life, family, or community.

Application and Prayer Guide: Let the blood of Jesus Christ redeem my life from the dominion of satanic deceptions, in the name of Jesus Christ.

- **The blood of Jesus Christ appeases divine justice.**

  Almost all things are by the law purged with blood; and without shedding of blood is no remission (Heb. 9:22).

  All have sinned, and come short of the glory of God; being justified freely by his grace through the redemption that is in Christ Jesus: whom God hath set forth to be a propitiation through faith in his blood, to declare his righteousness for the remission of sins that are past, through the forbearance of God (Rom. 3:23-25).

  Our God, who created the heavens and the earth, is utterly faithful. He says, "When I see the blood, I will pass over you." When we appropriate Jesus' blood, in faith, against sins and iniquities, He is faithful to this covenant promise!

Application and Prayer Guide: Father, because Christ's blood has marked me, release me from the punishment due me because of my ancestors' sins.

- **The blood of Jesus Christ procures God's eternal covenant for believers.**

  Now the God of peace, that brought again from the dead our Lord Jesus, that great shepherd of the sheep, through the blood of the everlasting covenant, make you perfect in every good work to do his will, working in you that which is wellpleasing in his sight, through Jesus Christ; to whom be glory forever and ever. Amen (Heb. 13:20-21).

By the blood that was shed on the cross of Calvary, believers were forgiven their sins and made holy.

Application and Prayer Guide: By the blood of Jesus Christ, I receive the everlasting covenant promise to reign with Him.

- **The blood of Jesus Christ gives life.**

Then Jesus said unto them, Verily, verily, I say unto you, Except ye eat the flesh of the Son of man, and drink his blood, ye have no life in you (John 6:53).

This is the spiritual eating of the flesh and the spiritual drinking of the blood of Jesus Christ, by faith. The drinking of His blood brings healing and deliverance, and thereby gives life. Hallelujah!

Application and Prayer Guide: As I drink the blood of Christ, let healing and deliverance begin, in Jesus' name.

- **The blood of Jesus Christ brings us close to God.**

Now in Christ Jesus ye who sometimes were far off are made nigh by the blood of Christ (Eph. 2:13).

The Lord told the Israelites that they must be holy, for He is holy (see Lev. 11:45). The filthiness caused by our sins pushes us away from Him. But through the cleansing blood of Jesus Christ, we are brought close to our God, to commune freely with Him.

Application and Prayer Guide: By Jesus Christ's blood, and in His name, I have access to God's throne of mercy, and I experience breakthrough in my spiritual life.

- **The blood of Jesus Christ provides entrance into the holiest of God.**

    Having therefore, brethren, boldness to enter into the holiest by the blood of Jesus... (Heb. 10:19).

    "The holiest" is the spiritual location of the mysteries of God. We can enter and receive from this place only because the blood of Jesus Christ has cleansed us and made us qualified.

Application and Prayer Guide: By the cleansing blood of Jesus Christ, and in His name, I enter into the holiest place of God and am empowered.

- **Jesus Christ's sacrificial blood speaks better things than the shed blood of Abel.**
    The following verse reveals the secret of the efficacy of Jesus' blood in the court of heaven:

    And to Jesus the mediator of the new covenant, and to the blood of sprinkling, that speaketh better things than that of Abel (Heb. 12:24).

    The blood of Abel spoke of vengeance. The blood of the Savior speaks of healing, deliverance, forgiveness, peace, restoration, and redemption. The above verse reveals the secret of the efficacy of Jesus' blood in the court of heaven. Hallelujah!

Application and Prayer Guide: Let the sacrificial blood of Jesus Christ arise and speak deliverance and healing to my spirit, soul, and body now, in the name of Jesus Christ.

- **Satan is defeated by the blood of Jesus Christ.**

They overcame him by the blood of the Lamb, and by the word of their testimony; and they loved not their lives unto the death (Rev. 12:11).

Jesus Christ shed His blood to destroy the devil, who has the power of death. In spiritual warfare, when the blood of Jesus Christ is held up in faith against Satan's purposes, those purposes are countered and destroyed.

Application and Prayer Guide: I overcome every satanic attack with the precious blood of Jesus Christ.

- **The blood of Jesus purchased the Church.**

Take heed therefore unto yourselves, and to all the flock, over the which the Holy Ghost hath made you overseers, to feed the church of God, which he hath purchased with his own blood (Acts 20:28).

Application and Prayer Guide: Lord Jesus, arise and protect this church by Your blood, which You shed to obtain it.

The Glory of God

- **The glory of God is the power behind the resurrection of Jesus.**

We are buried with him by baptism into death: that like as Christ was raised up from the dead by the glory of the Father, even so we also should walk in newness of life (Rom. 6:4).

As Jesus linked Lazarus' restored life to the glory of God (see John 11:40), the Holy Spirit (through the apostle Paul) links the resurrection of Jesus Christ to the glory of God. The glory of God is divine; it can fall on a dead place and revive it.

Application and Prayer Guide: Glory of God, overshadow me and revive any dead or dying bodily organs, in the name of Jesus Christ.

- **The glory of God brings the dead to life.**

After identifying Himself as the resurrection, and before raising Lazarus from the dead, Jesus asked Lazarus' sister Martha the following question, thereby linking the resurrection of the dead man with God's glory:

Said I not unto thee, that, if thou wouldest believe, thou shouldest see the glory of God? (John 11:40).

Application and Prayer Guide: Glory of God, overshadow and revive my glory now, in the name of Jesus Christ.

- **The glory of God gives light.**

The city had no need of the sun, neither of the moon, to shine in it: for the glory of God did lighten it, and the Lamb is the light thereof (Rev. 21:23).

Having the glory of God: and her light was like unto a stone most precious, even like a jasper stone, clear as crystal (Rev. 21:11).

The glory of God can shine as light. Therefore, we can pray for the glory of God to remove darkness from a place or a life.

Application and Prayer Guide: Glory of God, arise, shine, and be a light as I pass through the dark places of this world, in the name of Jesus Christ.

- **The glory of God is powerful.**

  The temple was filled with smoke from the glory of God, and from his power; and no man was able to enter into the temple, till the seven plagues of the seven angels were fulfilled (Rev. 15:8).

  And, lo, the angel of the Lord came upon them, and the glory of the Lord shone round about them: and they were sore afraid (Luke 2:9).

  The power of God's glory can generate smoke, as fire does. Tapping into this power in spiritual warfare brings confusion and fear into the enemy's camp.

Application and Prayer Guide: Let the glory of God arise and bring confusion to the enemies of my breakthrough, in the name of Jesus Christ.

- **The glory of God defends.**

  And said unto him, Run, speak to this young man, saying, Jerusalem shall be inhabited as towns without walls for the multitude of men and cattle therein: for I, saith the LORD, will be unto her a wall of fire round about, and will be the glory in the midst of her. (Zech. 2:4-5).

  All the congregation bade stone them with stones. And the glory of the LORD appeared in the tabernacle of the congregation before all the children of Israel (Num. 14:10).

The glory of the Lord defended Joshua and Caleb as the Israelites attempted to stone them. In spiritual warfare, we can prayerfully ask for His glory to defend us.

> **Application and Prayer Guide:** Lord, let Your glory arise and defend me against satanic accusations and attacks, in the name of Jesus Christ.

- **The glory of God makes to shine.**

  Behold, the glory of the God of Israel came from the way of the east: and his voice was like a noise of many waters: and the earth shined with his glory (Ezek. 43:2).

  Wherever the glory of God appears, the wonders of God must occur. When a place shines because of God's glory, it is blessed and must prosper. When we pray for God's glory to come upon a situation, destiny, or life, it must shine. When it does, it will do great exploits.

> **Application and Prayer Guide:** I will arise and shine, for the glory of the Lord is over me, in the name of Jesus Christ.

The Whirlwind of the Lord

- **The whirlwind of the Lord attacks and destroys the wicked.**

  Behold, a whirlwind of the LORD is gone forth in fury, even a grievous whirlwind: it shall fall grievously upon the head of the wicked (Jer. 23:19).

Behold, the whirlwind of the Lord goeth forth with fury, a continuing whirlwind: it shall fall with pain upon the head of the wicked (Jer. 30:23).

The whirlwind of the Lord is a great weapon that can be used against the wicked and their tools. We can pray for the Lord's whirlwind to dismantle any witchcraft coven. Although the dismantling will occur in the spirit realm, manifestation in the physical realm will follow.

Application and Prayer Guide: By the anointing of the Holy Spirit, I command the Lord's whirlwind to go forth and rout all of the wicked's operating bases in my environment, in the name of Jesus. Christ.

- **The whirlwind of the Lord scatters.**

Thou shalt fan them, and the wind shall carry them away, and the whirlwind shall scatter them: and thou shalt rejoice in the Lord, and shalt glory in the Holy One of Israel (Isa. 41:16).

I scattered them with a whirlwind among all the nations whom they knew not. Thus the land was desolate after them, that no man passed through nor returned: for they laid the pleasant land desolate (Zech. 7:14).

The whirlwind of the Lord can be invoked spiritually by the steadfast prayer warrior and sent to scatter evil gatherings.

Application and Prayer Guide: Let the whirlwind of the Lord arise now and scatter the satanists who have gathered because of me, in the name of Jesus Christ.

- ## The whirlwind of the Lord uproots.

Yea, they shall not be planted; yea, they shall not be sown: yea, their stock shall not take root in the earth: and he shall also blow upon them, and they shall wither, and the whirlwind shall take them away as stubble (Isa. 40:24).

We can pray to the Lord to release His whirlwind, removing any evil being generated against us from particular locations and uprooting the wicked ones behind it.

> **Application and Prayer Guide:** Agents of darkness causing trouble in this environment, I command the whirlwind of the Lord to dismantle you now, in the name of Jesus Christ.

The Holy Spirit

- ## The Holy Spirit empowers.

Jesus returned in the power of the Spirit into Galilee: and there went out a fame of him through all the region round about (Luke 4:14).

Then he answered and spake unto me, saying, This is the word of the LORD unto Zerubbabel, saying, Not by might, nor by power, but by my spirit, saith the LORD of hosts (Zech. 4:6).

Truly I am full of power by the spirit of the LORD, and of judgment, and of might, to declare unto Jacob his transgression, and to Israel his sin (Mic. 3:8).

The Holy Spirit is the source of great spiritual accomplishment. When we ask God the Father, through God the Son, for God the Holy Spirit, He comes and empowers us as He dwells within.

> **Application and Prayer Guide:** Spirit of God, arise now and empower me to overcome, spiritually and physically, in the name of Jesus Christ.

- **The Holy Spirit brings signs and wonders.**

I will not dare to speak of any of those things which Christ hath not wrought by me, to make the Gentiles obedient, by word and deed, through mighty signs and wonders, by the power of the Spirit of God; so that from Jerusalem, and round about unto Illyricum, I have fully preached the gospel of Christ (Rom. 15:18-19).

When the Holy Spirit comes to indwell the believer, He empowers that person for great physical and spiritual exploits.

> **Application and Prayer Guide:** O Lord, by the Holy Spirit, empower my calling for signs and wonders, in the name of Jesus Christ.

The Word of God

- **The Word of God is quick and powerful.**

The word of God is quick, and powerful, and sharper than any twoedged sword, piercing even to the dividing asunder of soul and spirit, and of the joints and marrow, and is a discerner of the thoughts and intents of the heart (Heb. 4:12).

The Word of God is alive and forceful. When spoken, it can penetrate and deal decisively, wherever it is sent. Jesus said,

"The words that I speak unto you, they are spirit, and they are life" (John 6:63).

> **Application and Prayer Guide:** The Word of the Lord declares that no weapon formed against me shall prosper (see Isa. 54:17). Therefore, in the name of Jesus Christ, I command the wickedness that is set against me to be made null and void.

When we understand Jesus' statement, we are compelled to confess what the Word says, at all times.

> **Application and Prayer Guide:** The Word of God says it shall be well with the righteous (see Isa. 3:10). Therefore, I declare that no matter what the enemy does, it shall be well with me, in the name of Jesus Christ.

■ **The Word of God creates.**

By the word of the LORD were the heavens made; and all the host of them by the breath of his mouth (Ps. 33:6).

Through faith we understand that the worlds were framed by the word of God, so that things which are seen were not made of things which do appear (Heb. 11:3).

For this they willingly are ignorant of, that by the word of God the heavens were of old, and the earth standing out of the water and in the water (2 Pet. 3:5).

Psalms 33:9 says, "He [the Lord] spake, and it was done; he commanded, and it stood fast." When the Word of God is spoken in faith, its dynamic power brings the stated request into manifestation.

> **Application and Prayer Guide:** In the name of Jesus Christ and by the anointing of the Holy Spirit, I decree that new, healthy organs are being formed to replace damaged ones in the body of (insert name).

- **The Word of God heals and delivers.**

  He sent his word, and healed them, and delivered them from their destructions (Ps. 107:20).

  Whenever it is confessed in faith, the Word of God heals and delivers. Confess the above verse and thank Him for your healing and deliverance. It shall be so! Declare God's Word saying, "By His stripes I was healed" (see 1 Pet. 2:24). Satan cannot contest your declaration. Hallelujah!

> **Application and Prayer Guide:** In Jesus' name, I am healed and I overcome all evil plots against me by the blood of the Lamb of God.

> **Application and Prayer Guide:** Isaiah 48:22 says there is no peace for the wicked. Therefore, I decree that trouble and restlessness shall be the portion of those on evil assignments against me, in the name of Jesus Christ.

The Finger of God

- **The finger of God casts out devils.**

  If I with the finger of God cast out devils, no doubt the kingdom of God is come upon you (Luke 11:20).

  The finger of God is a spiritual weapon to oust satanic hosts from their strongholds. The power of the Almighty flows through His finger to deal with all wicked powers.

> **Application and Prayer Guide:** In the name of Jesus Christ and by the finger of God, I cast out every demon that is secretly operating against me in my workplace.

- **The finger of God writes commandments, statutes, and laws.**

  He gave unto Moses, when he had made an end of communing with him upon mount Sinai, two tables of testimony, tables of stone, written with the finger of God (Exod. 31:18).

  The LORD delivered unto me two tables of stone written with the finger of God; and on them was written according to all the words, which the LORD spoke with you in the mount out of the midst of the fire in the day of the assembly (Deut. 9:10).

  The same finger of God that writes commandments, statutes, and laws can be spiritually and prayerfully employed to write righteous decrees regarding us and our loved ones.

> **Application and Prayer Guide:** O Lord, let Your finger arise now and write decrees of deliverance for my life, in the name of Jesus Christ.

- **The finger of God disgraces evil power and brings deliverance.**

  Then the magicians said unto Pharaoh, This is the finger of God: and Pharaoh's heart was hardened, and he hearkened not unto them; as the LORD had said (Exod. 8:19).

  When the finger of God is raised against them, wicked acts will not stand. We can ask God to raise His finger against any projected wickedness and muzzle it.

> **Application and Prayer Guide:** O God, my Father, raise up Your finger against the works of evil in my life and destroy them, in the name of Jesus Christ.

- **The finger of God writes decrees of judgment.**

   In the same hour came forth fingers of a man's hand, and wrote over against the candlestick upon the plaster of the wall of the king's palace: and the king saw the part of the hand that wrote (Dan. 5:5).

   The finger of God writes His judgments against evildoers. Therefore, this weapon can be used to stop the wicked acts and schemes of satanists.

> **Application and Prayer Guide:** Let the finger of God write woes to the wicked spirits troubling my life, in the name of Jesus Christ.

The Voice of the Lord

- **The voice of the Lord is powerful and majestic.**

   The voice of the LORD is powerful; the voice of the LORD is full of majesty (Ps. 29:4).

   As He prepared to endure the cross, Jesus heard the Lord's voice comforting and assuring Him that He would be glorified.

   The voice of the Lord also speaks peace to His saints (see Ps. 85:8). In spiritual warfare, we can pray to hear and be comforted by the Lord's voice.

> **Application and Prayer Guide:** O voice of the Lord, arise and speak courage to my soul, in the name of Jesus Christ.

- **The voice of the Lord thunders and does wonders.**

After it a voice roareth: he thundereth with the voice of his excellency; and he will not stay them when his voice is heard (Ps. 29:4).

God thundereth marvelously with his voice; great things doeth he, which we cannot comprehend (Job 37:5).

When the voice of the Lord is employed in prayer against evil gatherings (including those called to "gang up" on God's people), great scatterings and confusion will be unleashed in the camp of the wicked.

> **Application and Prayer Guide:** Let the camp of those who oppose my peace be scattered now by the voice of the Lord, in the name of Jesus Christ.

- **The voice of the Lord dismantles obstacles.**

The voice of the LORD breaketh the cedars; yea, the LORD breaketh the cedars of Lebanon (Ps. 29:5).

The Lord's voice removes obstacles. Believers can ask for the voice of the Lord to dismantle any demonic hindrances that have been set against them.

> **Application and Prayer Guide:** O Lord, in the name of Jesus Christ, speak by Your voice to overthrow all wicked resistance to my progress.

■ **The voice of the Lord produces hailstones and coals of fire.**

The voice of the LORD divideth the flames of fire
(Ps. 29:7).

*The LORD also thundered in the heavens, and the
Highest gave his voice; hail stones and coals of fire*
(Ps. 18:13).

The Bible is very clear about what the voice of the Lord does:
it releases hailstones and coals of fire upon the wicked and
their tools — and they must be consumed!

Application and Prayer Guide: In the name of Jesus Christ,
O voice of the Lord, release hailstones and coals of fire on
those who vow not to eat or drink until they have killed me.

■ **The voice of the Lord shakes off dryness, emptiness, and
lack (represented by "the wilderness").**

*The voice of the LORD shaketh the wilderness; the
LORD shaketh the wilderness of Kadesh* (Ps. 29:8).

When the voice of the Lord speaks against them, evil attach-
ments such dryness, emptiness, and lack can be disconnected
from lives and destinies.

Application and Prayer Guide: Let the voice of the Lord
shake loose from my life all dryness, emptiness, and lack, in
the name of Jesus Christ.

■ **The voice of the Lord brings forth life and reveals.**

*The voice of the LORD maketh the hinds to calve, and
discovereth the forests: and in his temple doth every
one speak of his glory* (Ps. 29:9).

When the enemy schemes to delay blessing or disguise truth, believers can war in the Spirit. The weapon of God's voice will undo these schemes.

> **Application and Prayer Guide:** Let the voice of the Lord uncover all truth and call forth my blessings from all demonic cages, in Jesus' name.

- **The voice of the Lord strikes His enemies with dismay and terror.**

Through the voice of the LORD shall the Assyrian be beaten down, which smote with a rod (Isa. 30:31).

The voice of the Lord renders recompense to His enemies (see Isa. 66:6). We can ask in prayer for His voice to repay our enemies justly.

> **Application and Prayer Guide:** Let the voice of the Lord generate terror in my enemy's camp, and let them flee before me, in Jesus' name.

The Arm of the Lord

- **The arm of the Lord sets captives free.**

Wherefore say unto the children of Israel, I am the LORD, and I will bring you out from under the burdens of the Egyptians, and I will rid you out of their bondage, and I will redeem you with a stretched out arm, and with great judgments (Exod. 6:6).

When the Lord stretches out His arm against enemies that rejoice at a believer's captivity, deliverance and freedom result.

> **Application and Prayer Guide:** O Lord arise, stretch out Your arm, and release me from demonic captivity (of fear, lack, sickness, etc.) in the name of Jesus Christ.

- **The arm of the Lord paralyzes the wicked.**

   Fear and dread shall fall upon them; by the greatness of thine arm they shall be as still as a stone; till thy people pass over, O LORD, till the people pass over, which thou hast purchased (Exod. 15:16).

   The arm of the Lord is a spiritual power that believers can use to paralyze the wicked and all their wickedness. Believers can pray for the arm of the Lord to work in their behalf.

> **Application and Prayer Guide:** Let the arm of the Lord arise and oppose the enemies of my breakthrough, in the name of Jesus Christ.

- **The arm of the Lord delivers from bondage.**

   Remember that thou wast a servant in the land of Egypt, and that the LORD thy God brought thee out thence through a mighty hand and by a stretched out arm: therefore the LORD thy God commanded thee to keep the sabbath day (Deut. 5:15).

> **Application and Prayer Guide:** O Lord, by Your outstretched arm, deliver me from the bondage of alcohol and all addictions, in the name of Jesus Christ.

- **The arm of the Lord destroys wicked spirits.**

   Awake, awake, put on strength, O arm of the LORD; awake, as in the ancient days, in the generations of old. Art thou not it that hath cut Rahab, and wounded the dragon? (Isa. 51:9)

The spiritual weapon of the arm of the Lord can be used against the hosts of wicked spirits.

Application and Prayer Guide: Let the arm of the Lord arise in its full strength and destroy any environmental spirit attacking my destiny, in the name of Jesus Christ.

- **The arm of the Lord strengthens.**

  With whom my hand shall be established: mine arm also shall strengthen him (Ps. 89:21).

  Here is a revelation from the Lord: His arm strengthens! Therefore, believers can pray for Him to strengthen them with His arm.

Application and Prayer Guide: O Lord, by Your arm, arise and strengthen me now, in the name of Jesus Christ.

- **The arm of the Lord gathers.**

  He shall feed his flock like a shepherd: he shall gather the lambs with his arm, and carry them in his bosom, and shall gently lead those that are with young (Isa. 40:11).

Application and Prayer Guide: O Lord, let Your arm gather to me the blessings of this environment, in the name of Jesus Christ.

Application and Prayer Guide: O Lord, let Your arm gather prayer helpers in this church, in the name of Jesus Christ.

The Thunder of God

- ## The thunder of God discomfits the wicked.

As Samuel was offering up the burnt offering, the Philistines drew near to battle against Israel: but the LORD thundered with a great thunder on that day upon the Philistines, and discomfited them; and they were smitten before Israel (1 Sam. 7:10).

A prayer warrior besieged by great forces of evil can pray that the Lord will release His thunder to discomfit them.

Application and Prayer Guide: Father Lord, arise now in the name of Jesus Christ and discomfit with Your thunder the demonic hosts that are attacking my progress.

Application and Prayer Guide: Let the thunder of God attack the habitation of the wicked spirits hindering my progress, in the name of Jesus Christ.

- ## The thunder of God breaks adversaries to pieces.

The adversaries of the LORD shall be broken to pieces; out of heaven shall he thunder upon them: the LORD shall judge the ends of the earth; and he shall give strength unto his king, and exalt the horn of his anointed (1 Sam. 2:10).

The spiritual weapon of God's thunder is powerful and renders the wicked powerless.

Application and Prayer Guide: Arise O Lord and let Your thunder break to pieces the wicked weapons of my enemies, in Jesus' name.

- **The thunder of God casts away.**

  At thy rebuke they fled; at the voice of thy thunder they hasted away (Ps. 104:7).

  Assigned powers of wickedness are put to flight as the thunder of God is released against them in battle.

Application and Prayer Guide: Let the sound of God's thunder chase evil far from me, in the name of Jesus Christ.

The Hornets of God

- **The hornets of God drive away the wicked.**

  I will send hornets before thee, which shall drive out the Hivite, the Canaanite, and the Hittite, from before thee (Exod. 23:28).

  Moreover the LORD thy God will send the hornet among them, until they that are left, and hide themselves from thee, be destroyed (Deut. 7:20).

  The hornets of God are spiritual weapons of divine judgment. When employed in spiritual warfare against established evils, they bring unbearable pain, forcing the wicked to flee.

Application and Prayer Guide: In the name of Jesus, I command the hornets of God to attack the demonic powers that are resisting my advancement.

The Fire of God

- ## The fire of God gives justice.

Behold, the LORD will come with fire, and with his chariots like a whirlwind, to render his anger with fury, and his rebuke with flames of fire. For by fire and by his sword will the LORD plead [i.e., decide, judge, give justice] *with all flesh: and the slain of the LORD shall be many* (Isa. 66:15-16).

The fire of God is a spiritual weapon of divine judgment that can be used in spiritual warfare to remedy injustices.

> **Application and Prayer Guide:** O Lord, arise by fire and defend Your interest in me, as you did for Elijah at Mount Carmel, in Jesus' name.

- ## The fire of God devours.

Thus hath the Lord GOD shewed unto me: and, behold, the Lord GOD called to contend by fire, and it devoured the great deep, and did eat up a part (Amos 7:4).

There went up a smoke out of his nostrils, and fire out of his mouth devoured: coals were kindled by it (Ps. 18:8).

As the fire of the Lord devoured the burnt sacrifice (including the wood, stones, and dust), and licked up the water in the trench dug by the prophet Elijah on Mount Carmel (see 1 Kings 18:38), so will His fire fall on your behalf.

> **Application and Prayer Guide:** Let the fire of God fall upon the habitation of the wicked in my environment and consume it, in Jesus Christ's name.

44

The Sword of the Lord

- ## The sword of the Lord destroys evils.

The spoilers are come upon all high places through the wilderness: for the sword of the LORD shall devour from the one end of the land even to the other end of the land: no flesh shall have peace (Jer. 12:12).

The sword of the Lord avails much against evil. Isaiah 31:8 (NIV) distinguishes between the Lord's sword and man's, saying, "Assyria will fall by no human sword; a sword, not of mortals, will devour them. They will flee before the sword and their young men will be put to forced labor."

> **Application and Prayer Guide:** O Lord, by Your sword, rip out the strength of Leviathan that is troubling my life, in Jesus Christ's name.

- ## The sword of the Lord cuts off the wicked.

O thou sword of the LORD, how long will it be ere thou be quiet? put up thyself into thy scabbard, rest, and be still (Jer. 47:6).

How can it be quiet, seeing the LORD hath given it a charge against Ashkelon, and against the sea shore? there hath he appointed it (Jer. 47:7)

Therefore thus saith the Lord GOD; Behold, I will bring a sword upon thee, and cut off man and beast out of thee (Ezek. 29:8).

The LORD discomfited Sisera, and all his chariots, and all his host, with the edge of the sword before Barak; so that Sisera lighted down off his chariot, and fled away on his feet (Judg. 4:15).

The Lord can set His sword against people or objects to destroy them. This sword is spiritual, but the physical manifestations will be destruction and defeat.

Application and Prayer Guide: O Lord, with Your sword, arise and fight my battle for me, in the name of Jesus Christ.

The Arrows of the Lord

■ **The arrows of the Lord scatter wicked gatherings.**

Yea, he sent out his arrows, and scattered them; and he shot out lightnings, and discomfited them (Ps. 18:14).

Application and Prayer Guide: Father, send Your arrows into the midst of the demonic powers that oppose me and scatter them, in Jesus' name.

■ **The arrows of the Lord destroy wickedness.**

Cast forth lightning, and scatter them: shoot out thine arrows, and destroy them (Ps. 144:6).

In the spirit realm, arrows are like bullets or missiles fired to destroy a target and the wickedness that is established to oppress or kill.

Application and Prayer Guide: Let the arrows of the Lord destroy anything that has been assigned to destroy me, in the name of Jesus Christ.

The Lightning of the Lord

■ **The lightning of the Lord discomfits and scatters.**

Yea, he sent out his arrows, and scattered them; and he shot out lightnings, and discomfited them (Ps. 18:14).

Cast forth lightning, and scatter them: shoot out thine arrows, and destroy them (Ps. 144:6).

Scripture suggests that the Lord used His lightning to discomfit the five kings of Amorites and the king of Jerusalem before Joshua and the men of Gibeon (see Josh. 10:10). Therefore, this weapon is available in spiritual warfare.

Application and Prayer Guide: In the name of Jesus Christ, let the lightning of God strike and scatter those who have gathered to destroy me.

Brimstone and Fire

■ **Brimstone and fire from the Lord overthrow wickedness.**

Upon the wicked he shall rain snares, fire and brimstone, and a horrible tempest: this shall be the portion of their cup (Ps. 11:6).

Then the LORD rained upon Sodom and upon Gomorrah brimstone and fire from the LORD out of heaven (Gen. 19:24).

Application and Prayer Guide: Father Lord, arise now and rain brimstone and fire upon the place from which evil is being generated against me, in the name of Jesus Christ.

The Anger of God

- **The anger of God destroys evil habitations and makes them desolate.**

  They have sown wheat, but shall reap thorns: they have put themselves to pain, but shall not profit: and they shall be ashamed of your revenues because of the fierce anger of the LORD (Jer. 12:13).

  The peaceable habitations are cut down because of the fierce anger of the LORD (Jer. 25:37).

  Demonic powers love to position themselves for optimal "success" in wickedness. Believers can invoke the anger of God to come against such positions and destroy these powers.

Application and Prayer Guide: Father, arise in Your anger and destroy the habitation of witchcraft in this city, in the name of Jesus Christ.

The Power of God

- **The power of God subdues the wicked.**

  The power of God subdues the wicked. Say unto God, How terrible art thou in thy works! Through the greatness of thy power shall thine enemies submit themselves unto thee (Ps. 66:3).

  God exercises His power in many ways, and no opposition can withstand it. Because Jesus Christ died and rose again to make it available, believers can tap into that power. Hallelujah!

> **Application and Prayer Guide:** In the name of Jesus Christ, I receive the power of God to subdue my enemies.

- ### The power of God delivers from oppression.

Moses besought the LORD his God, and said, LORD, why doth thy wrath wax hot against thy people, which thou hast brought forth out of the land of Egypt with great power, and with a mighty hand? (Exod. 32:11)

By His power, God delivered the Israelites from the oppression of Pharaoh. God stands ready to exercise that power on behalf of those who know and understand how to tap into it.

> **Application and Prayer Guide:** O Lord, arise today and deliver me from the wicked forces of oppression arrayed against me, in the name of Jesus Christ.

- ### The power of God is the power that no principalities, rulers of the darkness of this world, etc. can withstand.

[Jehoshaphat] *said, O LORD God of our fathers, art not thou God in heaven? and rulest not thou over all the kingdoms of the heathen? and in thine hand is there not power and might, so that none is able to withstand thee?* (2 Chron. 20:5).

God's power is a highly dynamic weapon of spiritual warfare that can be used to arrest and immobilize great forces of darkness.

> **Application and Prayer Guide:** Let the power of God pursue, immobilize, and destroy any local demon that is hindering the spread of the gospel in this land, in the name of Jesus Christ.

- **The power of God is against those who turn away from Him.**

  I was ashamed to require of the king a band of soldiers and horsemen to help us against the enemy in the way: because we had spoken unto the king, saying, The hand of our God is upon all them for good that seek him; but his power and his wrath is against all them that forsake him (Ezra 8:22).

  Application and Prayer Guide: Father Lord, uphold me by Your Holy Spirit and let not Your power turn against me, in the name of Jesus Christ.

- **The power of God scatters.**

  Slay them not, lest my people forget: scatter them by thy power; and bring them down, O Lord our shield (Ps. 59:11).

  God's power is invisible, but mighty to disband wickedness.

  Application and Prayer Guide: By the power of God, I command all storms of affliction and tragedy conjured against me to scatter, in the name of Jesus Christ.

The Rod of God

- **The rod of God breaks evils in pieces.**

  Thou shalt break them with a rod of iron; thou shalt dash them in pieces like a potter's vessel (Ps. 2:9).

  A rod can be used to punish, fight, rule, or walk. As we use rods in the physical realm, God uses His rod in the spiritual. Jeremiah declared, "I am the man that hath seen affliction by the rod of His wrath" (Lam. 3:1). Jeremiah spoke here of the rod that punishes.

Application and Prayer Guide: Let the rod of the Lord defend me and break evil in pieces, in the name of Jesus Christ.

Application and Prayer Guide: O Lord, let the rod of Your anger strike the satanic agents that conjure storms of tragedy against my family, in the name of Jesus Christ.

The Rebuke of the Lord

- **At the Lord's rebuke, Satan will flee.**

The LORD said unto Satan, The LORD rebuke thee, O Satan; even the LORD that hath chosen Jerusalem rebuke thee: is not this a brand plucked out of the fire? (Zech. 3:2)

Yet Michael the archangel, when contending with the devil he disputed about the body of Moses, durst not bring against him a railing accusation, but said, The Lord rebuke thee (Jude 9).

Dear reader, the rebuke of the Lord is one of the most powerful weapons in God's arsenal. The archangel Michael addressed it in contending with the devil over Moses' body (see Jude 9). When righteously and faithfully invoked, this weapon is effective against Satan or any other principalities or powers.

Application and Prayer Guide: Satan, the Lord rebuke you. Depart from me now, in the name of Jesus Christ.

- **At the rebuke of the Lord, devourers are silenced.**

I will rebuke the devourer for your sakes, and he shall not destroy the fruits of your ground; neither shall your vine cast her fruit before the time in the field, saith the LORD of hosts (Mal. 3:11).

Devourers are evil spirits that secretly destroy blessings, breakthroughs, and prosperity. They work underground, escaping victims' awareness until the collapse is made evident. Devourers work toward the same goal but from different directions. The rebuke of the Lord, in the name of Jesus, will destroy them.

> **Application and Prayer Guide:** O Lord, arise and rebuke the devourers for my sake, in the name of Jesus Christ.

Empowered for Effectual Prayer

It is the spirit that quickeneth; the flesh profiteth nothing: the words that I speak unto you, they are spirit, and they are life (John 6:63).

Here Jesus explained the essence of His words (He is The Word). Consider your prayers as arrows fired into spiritual realms. When God's Word is the bow that launches your prayer arrows, the result is always dynamic. But how far the prayer arrow goes depends upon the freedom with which God's power operates through the one who is praying. This freedom comes in three ways:

1. **Through the Word of God**
   The word of God is quick, and powerful, and sharper than any twoedged sword, piercing even to the dividing asunder of soul and spirit, and of the joints and marrow, and is a discerner of the thoughts and intents of the heart (Heb. 4:12).

2. Through the Holy Spirit

John answered, saying unto them all, I indeed baptize you with water; but one mightier than I cometh, the latchet of whose shoes I am not worthy to unloose: he shall baptize you with the Holy Ghost and with fire (Luke 3:16).

3. Through the holy fire of God

The believer who is immersed in God's Word and submits to the ministry of the Holy Spirit will pray effectively. The effective pray-er must also be empowered by the holy fire of God. The apostles received the holy fire of God and experienced great spiritual successes in their ministries.

There appeared unto them cloven tongues like as of fire, and it sat upon each of them (Acts 2:3).

3

Legal Grounds in Spiritual Warfare

To destroy the means of the wicked, believers must understand the importance and function of legal grounds in any dispute or confrontation. Simply stated, legal grounds are the lawful, legitimate reasons or justifications for taking a position or performing an action.

- Legal grounds substantiate a chosen action.
- Legal grounds provide permission to act.
- The opposite of legal grounds is *groundlessness* ("baselessness"), which delegitimizes an action.
- A groundless case lacks reason or cause.
- A case (including a spiritual attack) can be based on multiple legal grounds.

Satan is a legalist. He takes full advantage of any legal grounds we offer him and rests his "case" upon them, even if we yielded them inadvertently.

Jesus mentioned legal grounds when He said, "Hereafter I will not talk much with you: for the prince of this world cometh, and hath nothing in me" (John 14:30). What Jesus meant was that the devil found no legal ground from which to steal from, kill, or destroy Jesus. The next verse explains why no legal ground existed:

> *But that the world may know that I love the Father; and **as the Father gave me commandment, even so I do** (John 14:31).*

Jesus Christ was obedient only to His Father. He laid down his life; that was what the Father sent Him to do. In submitting to death on the cross, he did not create legal grounds for attack; he fulfilled His purpose.

Proverbs 26:2 provides further clarification: "As the bird by wandering, as the swallow by flying, so the curse causeless shall not come." The *International Standard Version* interpretation says, "Like a fluttering sparrow or a swallow in flight, a curse without cause will not alight." In other words, a groundless curse *will not stand.*

The legal ground Satan sought but could not find in Jesus was sin. Jesus did no evil, nor was any corruption found in Him. Therefore, Satan had no legal power against Him.

God's people have long understood this principle. Hear what the children of Israel said in Nehemiah's day:

> *Behold, we are servants this day, and for the land that thou gavest unto our fathers to eat the fruit thereof and the good thereof, behold, we are servants in it: and it yieldeth much increase unto the kings whom thou hast set over us **because of our sins**: also they have dominion over our bodies, and over our cattle, at their pleasure, and we are in great distress* (Neh. 9:36-37).

The sins of disobedience and wickedness were the legal grounds by which evil powers won dominion over Israel and brought them great distress.

How Legal Ground Is Ceded

The following are some common ways in which we cede legal ground to Satan, empowering him to hinder or even destroy us:

1. **Sin**

   God's commands are given to protect us. Sin opens our "territory" to enemy advances. To mitigate our sin and revoke the legal ground it creates, we must ask the Lord for forgiveness and plead His blood, which covers us.

Thou hast forgiven the iniquity of thy people, thou hast covered all their sin. Selah (Ps. 85:2).

Sin clothes us with filthy spiritual "garments." Joshua, the high priest, learned this firsthand:

He answered and spake unto those that stood before him, saying, Take away the filthy garments from him [Joshua]. *And unto him he said, Behold, I have caused thine iniquity to pass from thee, and I will clothe thee with change of raiment* (Zech. 3:4).

The Lord forgave the high priest's sins, thereby stripping away his filthy garments. (My book, *Power and Prayers to Prevail over Spiritual Garments of Hindrance*, addresses this issue more fully. It is available at Amazon.com.)

2. Unfulfilled vows, promises, or agreements

The Word of God says we must *not* defer (postpone) paying our vows or fulfilling our promises to the Lord. We must keep our word, as the psalmist explains:

Vow, and pay unto the LORD your God: let all that be round about him bring presents unto him that ought to be feared (Ps. 76:11).

If a man vow a vow unto the LORD, or swear an oath to bind his soul with a bond; he shall not break his word, he shall do according to all that proceedeth out of his mouth (Num. 30:2).

When thou vowest a vow unto God, defer not to pay it; for he hath no pleasure in fools: pay that which thou hast vowed. Better is it that thou shouldest not vow, than that thou shouldest vow and not pay. Suffer not thy mouth to cause thy flesh to sin; neither say thou before the angel, that it was an error: wherefore should God be angry at thy voice, and destroy the work of thine hands? (Eccles. 5:4-6).

I have sworn, and I will perform it, that I will keep thy righteous judgments (Ps. 119:106).

Broken vows give the accuser (the devil) legal ground from which to strike. People often back out carelessly from the promises they make, without regard to the physical and spiritual repercussions. Ecclesiastes 5:5-6 explains that the work of a person's hands can be destroyed when a vow is broken.

3. Ignorance

Ignorance is a lack of knowledge that can lead to pain, sorrow, failure, and even destruction. Often, we sin because we are ignorant of God's Word. The devil wants believers to remain ignorant, especially of the consequences related to what they do or fail to do.

Our ignorance does not excuse our sin. Always, repentance is essential to being restored and to recovering the ground we surrendered.

The priest shall make an atonement for the soul that sinneth ignorantly, when he sinneth by ignorance before the Lord, to make an atonement for him; and it shall be forgiven him (Num. 15:28).

The times of this ignorance God winked at; but now commandeth all men every where to repent (Acts 17:30).

The ramifications of ignorance are revealed in Jesus' words: "If you have not been faithful in that which is another man's, who shall give you that which is your own?" (Luke 16:12).

When we fail to take good care of other people's belongings, we give the enemy legal ground from which to block our future blessings.

4. Destructive (evil) covenants

Generally speaking, covenants are binding agreements to perform, or refrain from performing, certain acts. Each covenant is made between two or more parties and is marked by an attached sign, which the Bible calls a *token*.

Laban and Jacob entered into a covenant, which Laban said would stand as a witness between them. This means that if either man violated it, the covenant would bear witness against him and appropriate judgment would be dispensed.

The token attached to this covenant was a heap of stones:

Now therefore come thou, let us make a covenant, I and thou; and let it be for a witness between me and thee. And Jacob took a stone, and set it up for a pillar. And Jacob said unto his brethren, Gather stones; and they took stones, and made an heap: and they did eat there upon the heap. (Gen. 31:44-46).

The most well-known covenant token was a rainbow: God said [to Noah], *This is the token of the covenant which I make between me and you and every living creature that is with you, for perpetual generations: I do set my bow in the cloud, and it shall be for a token of a covenant between me and the earth* (Gen. 9:12-13).

Scripture warns: "Have respect unto the covenant: for the dark places of the earth are full of the habitations of cruelty" (Ps. 74:20). We must tread prayerfully when entering into agreements. Covenants entered into by ungodly means are destructive or evil covenants (evil binding agreements) that stand against God's divine purposes and against the parties involved. Consider the following examples:

- Occult covenants: These are forbidden by God, who said, "Thou shalt make no covenant with them, nor with their gods" (Exod. 23:32). One of the occult methods for ensuring secrecy is the making of evil covenants. When such covenants are broken, the token attached to the covenant is invoked against the person who defaulted.
- Blood covenants: Man-made covenants involving the exchange of blood are forbidden by God. Jesus said, "Let your communication be Yea, yea; Nay, nay: for whatsoever is more than these cometh of evil" (Matt. 5:37). In exchanging blood, covenant parties enter into strong agreement that goes beyond words. They cut their flesh and drink blood from each other's wounds. Because blood is involved, this practice can result in grave spiritual and physical consequences.
- Ungodly soul-tie covenants: Men and women who become sexually yoked outside of marriage form ungodly soul-tie covenants that keep both parties bound, even after the relationship has ended. The covenant formed then attacks new relationships. This is a major cause of tumult in modern relationships. The Bible clearly says, "What? know ye not that he which is joined to a harlot is one body? For two, saith he, shall be one flesh" (1 Cor. 6:16). When one sexual relationship ends and another begins, three or more become one flesh. This is contrary to the divine design: two (one man and one woman) becoming one flesh.
- Covenants with God's enemies: A biblical example is the covenant between Judah's King Asa and Syria's king, Ben-hadad (see 2 Chron. 16:1-14). When believers form alliances with practitioners of abomination, they inadvertently open the door to God's wrath and may be handed over to Satan for destruction.

5. **Bad foundations**

In life, a good foundation guarantees a better future. Sadly, foundations and roots have been widely underestimated and even ignored, bringing unnecessary hardship, pain, and sorrow into countless lives.

Are you struggling to achieve success? Have you performed every necessary step with all tact and wisdom, yet still see no tangible results? Do you sense that your present state defies the divine intent?

Do you wonder why your parents, grandparents, and great grandparents lived and died under unfavorable or painful conditions like those you are now experiencing?

Your present predicament may be traced to your foundation. This includes your ancestral foundation and the foundations you yourself have laid. Ask the Holy Spirit to uncover any foundations that are corrupt, bewitched, or built upon untruths.

Psalms 11:3 says, "If the foundations be destroyed, what can the righteous do?" This spiritual question demands a spiritual response: the righteous and wise must rebuild any faulty foundations. The following passage gives just one example:

*Charge them that are rich in this world, that they be not highminded, nor trust in uncertain riches, but in the living God, who giveth us richly all things to enjoy; that they do good, that they be rich in good works, ready to distribute, willing to communicate; laying up in store for themselves **a good foundation against the time to come**, that they may lay hold on eternal life* (1 Tim. 6:17-19).

Paul explained that the wealthy can lay up for themselves "a good foundation" that would directly affect their future and even their eternity. Pride and the hoarding of riches ensure a bad foundation.

How Godly Legal Grounds Are Established

We continually build our foundations and determine the legal grounds that affect our lives. Jesus provided powerful insights into avoiding evil foundations and building godly ones:

> *He that is faithful in that which is least is faithful also in much: and he that is unjust in the least is unjust also in much. If therefore ye have not been faithful in the unrighteous mammon, who will commit to your trust the true riches? And if ye have not been faithful in that which is another man's, who shall give you that which is your own?* (Luke 16:10-12)

To be blessed with our own possessions we must handle justly that which belongs to others. The Lord watches to see whether we have laid the foundation of good service to others. If not, no one will be there to serve us.

Jesus was very clear about the good foundation of forgiveness:

> *If ye forgive men their trespasses, your heavenly Father will also forgive you: but if ye forgive not men their trespasses, neither will your Father forgive your trespasses* (Matt. 6:14-15).

Jesus said those who forgive can be forgiven because they have laid a foundation for it. If we do not forgive, we lay an evil foundation and build our future upon it.

Often we learn to do right by understanding what "wrong" looks like. Esau's story shows what *not* to do in laying a foundation for the future. Esau possessed the powerful blessing of the firstborn, and squandered it, giving the devil legal ground from which to work against him:

> *Jacob sod pottage: and Esau came from the field, and he was faint: and Esau said to Jacob, Feed me, I pray thee, with that same red pottage; for I am faint: therefore was*

his name called Edom. And Jacob said, Sell me this day thy birthright. And Esau said, Behold, I am at the point to die: and what profit shall this birthright do to me? And Jacob said, Swear to me this day; and he sware unto him: and he sold his birthright unto Jacob. Then Jacob gave Esau bread and pottage of lentiles; and he did eat and drink, and rose up, and went his way: thus Esau despised his birthright (Gen. 25:29-34).

Eventually, Esau would regret the foundation he laid, and would beg to restore the blessing he forfeited. But when his father, Isaac, was dying, Esau's loss was made permanent.

Isaac his father said unto him [Esau], *Who art thou? And he said, I am thy son, thy firstborn Esau. And Isaac trembled very exceedingly, and said, Who? where is he that hath taken venison, and brought it me, and I have eaten of all before thou camest, and have blessed him? yea, and he shall be blessed. And when Esau heard the words of his father, he cried with a great and exceeding bitter cry, and said unto his father, Bless me, even me also, O my father. And he said, Thy brother came with subtilty, and hath taken away thy blessing* (Gen. 27:32-35).

Esau's ungodly attitude gave his younger brother legal ground to rule over him as the Lord had already said he would:

The LORD said unto her [Rebekah], *Two nations are in thy womb, and two manner of people shall be separated from thy bowels; and the one people shall be stronger than the other people; and the elder shall serve the younger* (Gen. 25:23).

Making an oath for the sake of a meal, Esau transferred his valuable birthright to Jacob. Unlike Esau, Jacob valued the birthright, and won it! Remember that "as the bird by wandering, as the swallow by flying, so the curse causeless shall not come" (Prov. 26:2). Esau brought a curse upon himself by establishing legal ground for it. However, Jacob laid a good foundation for his future and for God's people.

How to Dissolve Evil Legal Grounds

Because of the work of Calvary, you can be delivered from the consequences of unfavorable legal grounds—if you are diligent. The following steps are essential:

1. **Confess all known personal and ancestral sins.** Confession must be done in such a way that the demons assigned to enforce punishment must depart. Confess each sin one by one. For example, you can say, "Lord, I confess that I stole my friend's Bible sometime in 1999. Have mercy and forgive me, O Lord, for I did it in ignorance." Then move on to another sin, saying, "Lord, I confess my fornication with (insert name). Father, forgive me now as I did this ignorantly, not understanding the consequences of this wicked act. Have mercy on me and forgive me, in the name of Jesus Christ." Confess as many sins as the Holy Spirit brings to your mind, no matter how long it takes.

2. **Appropriate the blood of Jesus Christ to neutralize the confessed sin.** For each sin, you can appropriate the blood of Jesus Christ by saying, "Blood of Jesus Christ, arise now and cover the stealing and fornication I just confessed, in the name of Jesus Christ."

3. **Rebuke any demon connected to the confessed sins.** Demons originate sins and demons are assigned to enforce punishment for sin. After confessing your sins and appropriating the blood of Jesus Christ, rebuke the demons connected with each sin. For example, you can say, "You demons assigned to afflict my life and destiny because of my stealing and fornication, I have confessed my sins and appropriated the blood of Jesus Christ. So now, the Lord rebuke you. Depart from me, in the name of Jesus Christ. Amen." I tell

you the truth, in Jesus Christ's name: they must depart and you shall have your freedom restored.

4. **Make restitution where possible.** If for example, you took someone's Bible and you still have it, be bold enough to return it, if the person is still alive and in a known location.

5. **Search by the Spirit to find any legal ground that exists in your life.** This step is ongoing. Ask the Holy Spirit to reveal any legal ground the enemy might have to resist your deliverance from any unresolved spiritual or physical problem.

6. **Identify the areas of your life (marriage, relationships, finances, etc.) where legal grounds have opened the door to affliction.** The psalmist wrote, "Before I was afflicted I went astray: but now have I kept thy word" (Ps. 119:67). He understood that his going astray gave the devil legal ground from which to afflict him. Most of our afflictions and problems are directly or indirectly linked to sin. May the Lord grant us the wisdom to pursue spiritual knowledge and understanding, in the name of Jesus Christ.

7. **Cry out to the Lord for solutions.** In spiritual warfare, we must be willing and able to persevere long in prayer. When fasting is added, the human spirit is energized to pray till breakthrough is achieved.

ಜ ಜ ಜ

The means of the wicked are destroyed by the godly means of the righteous. Prayer is essential! You have already been given individual prayer guide examples. Here and throughout the remaining chapters and the Appendix of this book, we will cover many prayer categories, each with Bible Prayer Links, a Prayer Focus, and Prayer Guides to help you pray effectively.

✞ PRAYERS TO REMOVE LEGAL GROUNDS GENERATED BY DESTRUCTIVE COVENANTS

BIBLE PRAYER LINKS

Asa...sent to Ben-hadad king of Syria, that dwelt at Damascus, saying, There is a league between me and thee, as there was between my father and thy father... go, break thy league with Baasha king of Israel, that he may depart from me. And Ben-hadad hearkened unto king Asa, and sent the captains of his armies against the cities of Israel....At that time Hanani the seer came to Asa king of Judah, and said unto him, Because thou hast relied on the king of Syria, and not relied on the LORD thy God, therefore is the host of the king of Syria escaped out of thine hand....Herein thou hast done foolishly: therefore from henceforth thou shalt have wars (2 Chron. 16:2-5, 9b).

The eyes of the LORD run to and fro throughout the whole earth, to shew himself strong in the behalf of them whose heart is perfect toward him (2 Chron. 16:9a).

PRAYER FOCUS
- To keep my eyes fixed on God's covenant with me, thanking Him for all His promises
- To uncover and renounce all evil covenants

PRAYER GUIDES
1. Father Lord, I thank You for my deliverance, which You made possible by the shedding of Your Son's blood.
2. Blood of Jesus Christ, redeem my life (my destiny, marriage, etc.) from any destructive covenant made unconsciously. I ask this in the name of Jesus Christ.
3. Every destructive covenant bearing witness against me, break and loose your hold now, by the blood of Jesus Christ.

4. *Place all your fingers on your navel and declare*: Any destructive covenant operating in my father's or mother's family line, be severed. Release me now, in the name of Jesus Christ.

5. By the blood of Jesus Christ, I disconnect myself from any destructive covenant that runs in my family.

6. All soul ties and evil covenants established between me and any ex-boyfriends/ex-girlfriends including (<u>name them</u>), be broken. Loose your hold upon my life now, by the blood of Jesus Christ.

7. All soul ties and evil covenants established with any places I have lived before, break now. Loose your hold upon my life, by the blood of Jesus Christ.

8. All soul ties and evil covenants established between me and any agent of darkness, break now. Loose your hold upon my life and destiny, by the blood of Jesus Christ.

9. *Place your hands on your head as you declare*: All forms of misfortune rooted in evil covenants, I cast you away today, by the blood of Jesus Christ.

10. All conscious and unconscious destructive covenants that oppose my progress (my healing, prosperity, relationships, etc.) be canceled now, by the blood of Jesus Christ.

11. *Place your right hand on your forehead and your left hand on your chest as you pray*: Any destructive covenants responsible for spiritual or physical problems in my life, break now. Loose your binding power, by the blood of Jesus Christ.

12. Thank You, Jesus, for answering my prayers. Amen.

Records Create Legal Grounds

To record something is to preserve it in writing or by some other permanent means. Some records are physical, such as the record found in Exodus 17:13-14:

> *Joshua discomfited Amalek and his people with the edge of the sword. And the LORD said unto Moses, Write this for a memorial in a book, and rehearse it in the ears of Joshua: for I will utterly put out the remembrance of Amalek from under heaven* (Exod. 17:13-14).

God instructed Moses to make a permanent record of the war between Israel and the Amalekites, including the victory achieved through Moses' prayer and Joshua's sword. Moses' physical record also generated a record in the realm of the spirit.

Nonphysical records are invisible to our physical eyes. They are pronouncements recorded, not on paper, but within the material of the earth, sun, moon, stars, oceans, and so forth. Examples of a physical and a nonphysical recording are found in Joshua 24:

> *Joshua wrote these words in the book of the law of God, and took a great stone, and set it up there under an oak, that was by the sanctuary of the LORD. And Joshua said unto all the people, Behold, this stone shall be a witness unto us; for it hath heard all the words of the LORD which he spoke unto us: it shall be therefore a witness unto you, lest ye deny your God* (Josh. 24:26-27).

Joshua's writings were physically recorded in the book of God's law. But his testimony was also recorded by setting a stone under the oak tree. This record was not captured in words seen by the human eye; yet the message was understood by the human heart.

Both physical and nonphysical records can be either good or bad, divine or evil. A well-known nonphysical record was issued and later physically recorded in the Pentateuch:

> *I have set before thee this day life and good, and death and evil; in that I command thee this day to love the LORD thy God, to walk in his ways, and to keep his commandments and his statutes and his judgments, that thou mayest live and multiply: and the LORD thy God shall bless thee in the land whither thou goest to possess it. But if thine heart turn away, so that thou wilt not hear, but shalt be drawn away, and worship other gods, and serve them; I denounce unto you this day, that ye shall surely perish, and that ye shall not prolong your days upon the land, whither thou*

passest over Jordan to go to possess it. I call heaven and earth to record this day against you, that I have set before you life and death, blessing and cursing: therefore choose life, that both thou and thy seed may live (Deut. 30:15-19).

Moses registered God's pronouncements in the earth and in the heavens; they remain binding on the Jews to this day, because people, the earth, and the heavens heard him. Clearly, when an individual registers blessings or curses into the earth or heavens against an individual, community, or race, both the heavens and Earth keep the record. The effectiveness, however, is dependent upon these factors:

1. Whether the target of the curse or blessing qualifies for fulfillment of the blessing or curse pronounced
2. The spiritual foundation of the individual making the pronouncement

When individuals, communities, cities, races, tribes, nations, or continents commit abominations, divine judgments can be recorded against them. Moses recorded such a judgment:

Gather unto me all the elders of your tribes, and your officers, that I may speak these words in their ears, and call heaven and earth to record against them (Deut. 31:28).

Moses' words were not baseless. Notice also the authoritative manner in which he registered his pronouncement in the heavens and the earth, saying, "Give ear, O ye heavens, and I will speak; and hear, O earth, the words of my mouth" (Deut. 32:1).

Centuries later, the following divine record was made concerning the new heaven and new earth:

He that sat upon the throne said, Behold, I make all things new. And he said unto me, Write: for these words are true and faithful. And he said unto me, It is done. I am Alpha and Omega, the beginning and

the end. I will give unto him that is athirst of the foun-
tain of the water of life freely.... And the city lieth four-
square, and the length is as large as the breadth: and
he measured the city with the reed, twelve thousand
furlongs. The length and the breadth and the height
of it are equal (Rev. 21:5-6, 16).

Whether the record is divine or evil, a set time, period, season, or cycle is attached to it. Such records have agendas to build or destroy, to lift up or cast down, to cause to excel or fail, to move forward or make stagnant, to establish a glorious destiny or a perverted one, to bless or curse. This "programming" pulls the subject of the record toward achieving what was recorded.

Records can be transferred or inherited, and binding upon generations as yet unborn. A divine record concerning Abraham's seed had a certain timing attached to it:

He said unto Abram, Know of a surety that thy seed
shall be a stranger in a land that is not theirs, and
shall serve them; and they shall afflict them four hun-
dred years (Gen. 15:13).

This message came to Abram before his son Isaac was even born. God's agenda was recorded, and everything in heaven and on Earth that was necessary in bringing it to pass was set in motion at the time of the recording.

Another record, this time concerning the rebuilding of the city of Jericho was similarly set in motion when Joshua made this pronouncement:

Cursed be the man before the LORD, that riseth up and
buildeth this city Jericho: he shall lay the foundation
thereof in his firstborn, and in his youngest son shall
he set up the gates of it (Josh. 6:26).

The city heard and recorded Joshua's words. When Hiel tried to rebuild Jericho, Joshua's proclamation came to pass:

In his days did Hiel the Bethelite build Jericho: he laid the foundation thereof in Abiram his firstborn, and set up the gates thereof in his youngest son Segub, according to the word of the LORD, which he spoke by Joshua the son of Nun (1 Kings 16:34).

The curse that had been spoken took effect in Hiel's family.

✟ PRAYERS TO DESTROY THE POWER OF EVIL RECORDS

BIBLE PRAYER LINK

No weapon that is formed against thee shall prosper; and every tongue that shall rise against thee in judgment thou shalt condemn. This is the heritage of the servants of the LORD, and their righteousness is of me, saith the LORD (Isa. 54:17).

PRAYER FOCUS
- To discover, by the Spirit, any evil records pronounced against me
- To erase all evil records

PRAYER GUIDES
1. Father God, You said You would be gracious to whom You choose to be gracious. Today, be gracious to me and deliver me from any satanic hold upon my spiritual and physical advancement, in the name of Jesus Christ.
2. Father God, You said You would show mercy to whom You choose to show mercy. Be merciful to me today and erase all evil records that are troubling my life, in the name of Jesus Christ.
3. With the resurrection power of the Lord Jesus Christ, I come against all evil pronouncements recorded in my foundation.
4. In Jesus' name, I hold the blood of Christ against any recorded ancestral sins that are holding my breakthroughs in bondage.

70

5. In Jesus' name, I hold the blood of Christ against any recorded ancestral covenants that are denying me my divine position in life.

6. In Jesus' name, I hold the blood of Christ against every demon assigned to afflict my destiny because of evil records in my foundation.

7. Evil assignment programmed into the earth to make me a nonentity, come out and die, in the name of Jesus Christ.

8. By the authority of Calvary, I remove all evil pronouncements registered by the sun, moon and stars against my advancement, in the name of Jesus Christ.

9. By the blood of Jesus, I cancel every witchcraft curse projected into the heavens against my life, in the name of Jesus Christ.

10. Hindrances in my spiritual and physical life resulting from my ancestors' sins, give way by the blood of Jesus Christ.

11. In the name of Jesus Christ, let the thunder of God scatter all warfare coming against my life from within the waters, rivers, or seas.

12. Every curse registered in the cycle of the moon and afflicting my health, be nullified by the blood of Jesus Christ.

13. Every curse registered in the cycle of the moon and afflicting my childbearing potential, be nullified by the blood of Jesus Christ.

14. Every curse registered in a menstrual cycle and afflicting my marital destiny, be nullified, by the blood of Jesus Christ.

15. Every curse registered in a cycle or period of time, and afflicting my glory, be nullified by the blood of Jesus Christ.

16. I stand on the authority of Calvary and I command every affliction generated against my life from any witchcraft coven and registered in the cycle of a season to be destroyed now, in Jesus Christ's name.

17. With the blood of Jesus Christ and in His name, I revoke every ancestral covenant that gives legal ground to any ancestral spirit in pursuit of any destructive agenda for my life.

18. Glory of God, overshadow my life and release me from every demonic hold, in the name of Jesus Christ.

19. Let the blood of Jesus nullify every record of untimely death against me, in the name of Jesus Christ.
20. Wicked practices recorded in the heavenlies against my family lineage and affecting my life: be erased by the blood of Jesus Christ. Release me!
21. Thank You, Father Lord, for answering my prayers. Amen.

✝ Prayers to Establish Divine Records of Victory over the Enemy

Bible Prayer Links

> *Joshua discomfited Amalek and his people with the edge of the sword. And the Lord said unto Moses, Write this for a memorial in a book, and rehearse it in the ears of Joshua: for I will utterly put out the remembrance of Amalek from under heaven. And Moses built an altar, and called the name of it Jehovah-nissi: for he said, Because the Lord hath sworn that the Lord will have war with Amalek from generation to generation* (Exod. 17:13-16).

> *Joshua said unto all the people, Behold, this stone shall be a witness unto us; for it hath heard all the words of the LORD which he spake unto us: it shall be therefore a witness unto you, lest ye deny your God* (Josh. 24:27).

Prayer Focus
- To proclaim the power of God's divine record on my behalf
- To declare victory over all evil records

Prayer Guides
1. Thank You, Lord Jesus Christ! With Your blood You have redeemed me from the curse of the law (see Gal. 3:13).
2. Father Lord, let the glory of divine liberty be seen on me today and forever, in the name of Jesus Christ.

3. Thank You, Lord Jesus Christ, that Your blood stands as the divine record of victory. It overcomes and cancels all wickedness recorded by the earth and the heavens against my family lineage and my life and destiny, in the name of Jesus Christ.

4. I bring the blood of Jesus Christ to bear upon every record of my ancestral sins that is standing against my progress and prosperity, in the name of Jesus Christ.

5. Lord Father, Your Word records that, through the work of Calvary, the Lord Jesus Christ nullified every destructive record registered in my foundation to generate problems in my life and destiny, in the name of Jesus Christ.

6. Let the divinely-recorded blood of Jesus Christ come against and cancel all recorded ancestral sins that hold my blessings in bondage, and all ancestral covenants that are denying me of my divine position in life, in the name of Jesus Christ.

7. I call to record the blood of Jesus Christ that comes against and cancels all hindrances in my spiritual, physical, and financial life resulting from my ancestors' sins.

8. Thank You, Lord, that the work of Calvary bears witness against and destroys every curse recorded and registered in the cycle of the moon to afflict my health.

9. Thank You, Lord, for the divine record declaring that the work and authority of Calvary overcome every affliction generated against my life and destiny from any witchcraft coven and registered in the cycle of a season. These evils are destroyed now, in the name of Jesus Christ.

10. Let the blood of Jesus Christ recorded in heaven nullify every record of untimely death against me and members of my household, in the name of Jesus Christ.

11. Demonic embargo imposed upon the glory of my divine liberty, be lifted now by the decree of Almighty God, in the name of Jesus Christ.

12. O Lord, I declare that if my journey in this life has been altered through demonic interference, Your record of the work of Calvary stands against it and You are powerful to correct it, in the name of Jesus Christ.

13. O Lord, send forth Your rebuke against any demonic embargo imposed upon my healing, blessings, breakthrough, success, progress, etc. Let the glory of divine liberty manifest now in my life, in the name of Jesus Christ.
14. Thank You, Jesus Christ, for answering my prayers. Amen.
15. As you pray daily, continue to ask the Holy Spirit to expose any evil records opposing your life and progress and to reveal the divine record that bears witness against the devil's schemes.

4

The Power and Kinds of Prayer

Prayer is a foundational weapon for believers. A person who chooses to destroy the means of the wicked must know and distinguish between different kinds of prayers and their uses.

Hopeless Prayers

Effective, godly prayer assumes the element of hope. Prayers lacking this fundamental ingredient cannot bear the intended fruit. Following are some characteristics of hopeless prayers.

1. Hopeless prayers lack determination and persistency.

> *Jacob was left alone; and there wrestled a man with him until the breaking of the day. And when he saw that he prevailed not against him, he touched the hollow of his thigh; and the hollow of Jacob's thigh was out of joint, as he wrestled with him. And he said, Let me go, for the day breaketh. And he said, I will not let thee go, except thou bless me* (Gen. 32:24-26).

Determined and persistent, Jacob wrestled in prayer warfare. You can wrestle with God by praying to Him all night, refusing to sleep or to stop praying unless He blesses you and grants your petitions. God sees your heart and answers according to your faith. Determination and persistency are products of faith.

2. Hopeless prayers lack desperation and specificity.

Bartimaeus, a blind man, was begging by the highway when Jesus came by. The man boldly called out to Jesus, asking for mercy. The crowd attempted to silence him, but he continued, and got Jesus' attention.

Jesus answered and said unto him, What wilt thou that I should do unto thee? The blind man said unto him, Lord, that I might receive my sight. And Jesus said unto him, Go thy way; thy faith hath made thee whole. And immediately he received his sight, and followed Jesus in the way (Mark 10:51-52).

Your desperate, specific cry will get the Lord's attention, as it did for Bartimaeus—and He will harken to your plea!

Note that when Jesus Christ responded, Bartimaeus did not enumerate his problems. He simply made his specific request known. This contributed to his healing.

3. Hopeless prayers are prayed with idols in the heart.

Then came certain of the elders of Israel unto me, and sat before me. And the word of the Lord came unto me, saying, Son of man, these men have set up their idols in their heart, and put the stumblingblock of their iniquity before their face: should I be enquired of at all by them? Therefore speak unto them, and say unto them, Thus saith the Lord God; Every man of the house of Israel that setteth up his idols in his heart, and putteth the stumblingblock of his iniquity before his face, and cometh to the prophet; I the Lord will answer him that cometh according to the multitude of his idols myself (Ezek. 14:1-4).

76

Certain elders sought answers from Ezekiel. God saw that their hearts were not pure, but centered on idols, whether of greed, self-centeredness, or pride. A prayer offered with idols in the heart is doomed to failure.

4. Hopeless prayers are prayed without faith.

If any of you lack wisdom, let him ask of God, that giveth to all men liberally, and upbraideth not; and it shall be given him. But let him ask in faith, nothing wavering. For he that wavereth is like a wave of the sea driven with the wind and tossed. For let not that man think that he shall receive any thing of the Lord. A double minded man is unstable in all his ways (James 1:5-8).

Doubt in the heart of the petitioner prevents any positive response from the Lord.

5. Hopeless prayers lack intensity.

Being in an agony he [Jesus] *prayed more earnestly: and his sweat was as it were great drops of blood falling down to the ground. And when he rose up from prayer, and was come to his disciples, he found them sleeping for sorrow, and said unto them, Why sleep ye? rise and pray, lest ye enter into temptation* (Luke 22:44-46).

When prayer becomes casual or occasional, it is also ineffective. Our Lord Jesus Christ prayed wholeheartedly to God the Father as the time of His sacrifice approached.

6. Prayers from a fragmented soul are hopeless prayers.
A fragmented soul is a fractured soul that contains a confused mind and an intellect that is unable to reason. Such a soul lacks understanding and cannot pray effectively. A prayer without understanding is a hopeless prayer. Hopeless prayers

are not prayed only by unbelievers; even Christians can pray this way without being aware of it.

✞ Praying Hopeful Prayers

Bible Prayer Link

Be careful for nothing; but in every thing by prayer and supplication with thanksgiving let your requests be made known unto God. And the peace of God, which passeth all understanding, shall keep your hearts and minds through Christ Jesus (Phil. 4:6-7).

Prayer Focus
- To pray in agreement with the Spirit of truth
- To remove all forms of hopelessness in prayer

Prayer Guides
1. Spirit of truth and wisdom possess me now, in the name of Jesus Christ.
2. Spirit of divine knowledge and understanding, guide my prayers, in the name of Jesus Christ.
3. Anointing of the Holy Spirit, guide me in praying rightly, in the name of Jesus Christ.
4. Holy Spirit, guide my thoughts, step into the affairs of my life, and bring Your glory as I pray, in the name of Jesus Christ.
5. Holy Spirit, empower me with divine understanding as I pray, in the name of Jesus Christ.
6. I bind every spirit of doubt in my prayer life, in the name of Jesus Christ.
7. I bind the spirit of lukewarmness in my prayer life, in the name of Jesus Christ.
8. Thank You, Lord, for answering my prayers. Amen.

Living Prayers

Unlike hopeless prayers, living prayers are active and productive. They are abiding appeals or pleas to the Lord God, and they get His attention.

1. **Living prayers are anointed and spoken in the Spirit.**
   As the apostle Paul wrote: "Praying always with all prayer and supplication in the Spirit, and watching thereunto with all perseverance and supplication for all saints..." (Eph. 6:18).

   The following are anointed prayers: the first was prayed by Jesus for the Church; the second by Eli, over Hannah.

   I pray for them: I pray not for the world, but for them which thou hast given me; for they are thine....And now I am no more in the world, but these are in the world, and I come to thee. Holy Father, keep through thine own name those whom thou hast given me, that they may be one, as we are....I pray not that thou shouldest take them out of the world, but that thou shouldest keep them from the evil....Sanctify them through thy truth: thy word is truth (John 17:9, 11, 15, 17).

   Then Eli answered and said, Go in peace: and the God of Israel grant thee thy petition that thou hast asked of him. And she said, Let thine handmaid find grace in thy sight. So the woman went her way, and did eat, and her countenance was no more sad (1 Sam. 1:17-18).

2. **Living prayers are "strong crying and tears" prayers (see Heb. 5:7).**

   She [Hannah] *was in bitterness of soul, and prayed unto the* LORD, *and wept sore. And she vowed a vow, and said, O* LORD *of hosts, if thou wilt indeed look on the affliction of thine handmaid, and remember me, and not forget thine handmaid, but wilt give unto thine handmaid a man child, then I will give him unto the* LORD *all the days of his life, and there shall no razor come upon his head* (1 Sam. 1:10-11).

Being in an agony he [Jesus] *prayed more earnestly: and his sweat was as it were great drops of blood falling down to the ground* (Luke 22:44).

Who in the days of his flesh, when [Jesus] *had offered up prayers and supplications with strong crying and tears unto him that was able to save him from death, and was heard in that he feared* (Heb. 5:7).

As Hannah prayed, her spirit, soul, and body were completely, harmoniously, and emphatically engaged. In both examples of Jesus' praying, He appealed to His Father with strong emotion and fervency.

3. **Living prayers are backed with purposeful fasting.**
When prayers are backed with purposeful fasting, immediate answers are more common. Jesus Christ told His disciples, "This kind can come forth by nothing, but by prayer and fasting" (Mark 9:29). When extraordinary problems manifest, extraordinary levels of prayer will resolve them, as happened in Queen Esther's day:

Then Esther bade them return Mordecai this answer, Go, gather together all the Jews that are present in Shushan, and fast ye for me, and neither eat nor drink three days, night or day: I also and my maidens will fast likewise; and so will I go in unto the king, which is not according to the law: and if I perish, I perish (Esther 4:15-16).

4. **Living prayers are prophetic.**
God has always used His people to speak His will.

The elders of the Jews builded, and they prospered through the prophesying of Haggai the prophet and Zechariah the son of Iddo. And they builded, and finished it, according to the commandment of the God of Israel, and according to the commandment of Cyrus, and Darius, and Artaxerxes king of Persia (Ezra 6:14).

To make decrees is to pray prophetically. The Lord says that we shall decree a thing and it shall be established unto us (see Job 22:28). Ezekiel prayed this way in the valley of the dry bones—and the dry bones came back together again with flesh and life (see Ezek. 37).

The following prophetic prayers were prayed by Jesus and Elisha, respectively:

I [Jesus] say also unto thee, That thou art Peter, and upon this rock I will build my church; and the gates of hell shall not prevail against it. And I will give unto thee the keys of the kingdom of heaven: and whatsoever thou shalt bind on earth shall be bound in heaven: and whatsoever thou shalt loose on earth shall be loosed in heaven (Matt. 16:18-19).

And he [Elisha] said, Call her. And when he had called her, she stood in the door. And he said, About this season, according to the time of life, thou shalt embrace a son. And she said, Nay, my lord, thou man of God, do not lie unto thine handmaid. And the woman conceived, and bare a son at that season that Elisha had said unto her, according to the time of life (2 Kings 4:15-17).

81

5. Living prayers are serious and intense.

Being in an agony he prayed more earnestly: and his sweat was as it were great drops of blood falling down to the ground (Luke 22:44).

Living prayers are often prayed when life itself is at stake, and are often charged with agony. Because He knew what He was about to suffer, Jesus Christ suffered such agony, with a heavy weight bearing on His soul. The degree to which you pray is the extent to which you receive the Lord's mercy to answer your prayer.

6. Living prayers are on-time prayers.

These prayers are said at just the right time—the acceptable time in which the Lord wills them. It is the time of His grace and mercy. Blind Bartimaeus prayed an on-time prayer. As Jesus departed from Jericho, Bartimaeus prayed aloud: "Jesus, thou son of David, have mercy on me" (Mark 10:47). Jesus stood still and answered his prayer.

Thus saith the LORD, In an acceptable time have I heard thee, and in a day of salvation have I helped thee: and I will preserve thee, and give thee for a covenant of the people, to establish the earth, to cause to inherit the desolate heritages (Isa. 49:8).

Seek ye the LORD while he may be found, call ye upon him while he is near (Isa. 55:6).

7. Living prayers have ultimate authority and power.

When the sons of Korah rebelled, Moses prayed that God would not punish all of Israel. Moses then prophesied the offenders' demise:

Moses said, Hereby ye shall know that the LORD hath sent me to do all these works; for I have not done them of mine own mind. If these men die the common death of all men, or if they be visited after the visitation of all men; then the LORD hath not sent me. But if the LORD make a new thing, and the earth open her mouth, and swallow them up, with all that appertain unto them, and they go down quick into the pit; then ye shall understand that these men have provoked the LORD. And it came to pass, as he had made an end of speaking all these words, that the ground clave asunder that was under them: and the earth opened her mouth, and swallowed them up, and their houses, and all the men that appertained unto Korah, and all their goods. They, and all that appertained to them, went down alive into the pit, and the earth closed upon them: and they perished from among the congregation (Num. 16:28-33).

8. Living prayers are radical.

Elijah the Tishbite, who was of the inhabitants of Gilead, said unto Ahab, As the LORD God of Israel liveth, before whom I stand, there shall not be dew nor rain these years, but according to my word (1 Kings 17:1).

By the Spirit, Elijah declared a drought, and a persistent drought resulted. This kind of prayers brings revolutionary and immediate change.

9. Living prayers are overcoming prayers.
Elijah later prayed to end the very drought his prayer declared. The long drought promptly ended.

And Elijah said unto Ahab, Get thee up, eat and drink; for there is a sound of abundance of rain. So Ahab went up to eat and to drink. And Elijah went up to the top of Carmel; and he cast himself down upon the earth, and put his face between his knees, and said to his servant, Go up now, look toward the sea. And he went up, and looked, and said, There is nothing. And he said, Go again seven times. And it came to pass at the seventh time, that he said, Behold, there ariseth a little cloud out of the sea, like a man's hand. And he said, Go up, say unto Ahab, Prepare thy chariot, and get thee down that the rain stop thee not. And it came to pass in the meanwhile, that the heaven was black with clouds and wind, and there was a great rain. And Ahab rode, and went to Jezreel (1 Kings 18:41-45).

10. Living prayers are explicit and definite prayers.

[Jesus] *asked him, saying, What wilt thou that I shall do unto thee? And he said, Lord, that I may receive my sight* (Luke 18:40-41).

When asked what he wanted from Jesus Christ, blind Bartimaeus went straight to the point. Living prayers are unambiguous; they state the request directly and plainly.

11. Living prayers are challenging prayers.

It came to pass at the time of the offering of the evening sacrifice, that Elijah the prophet came near, and said, LORD God of Abraham, Isaac, and of Israel, let it be known this day that thou art God in Israel, and that I am thy servant, and that I have done all these things at thy word (1 Kings 18:36).

Living prayers put God in remembrance of His promises. Elijah challenged God to protect His interest in the prophet and the prophet's assignment. Elijah needed God's grace to complete his mission, so he prayed in a confrontational, expectant manner.

12. Living prayers are defiant.

Elijah answered and said to the captain of fifty, If I be a man of God, then let fire come down from heaven, and consume thee and thy fifty. And there came down fire from heaven, and consumed him and his fifty. Again also he sent unto him another captain of fifty with his fifty. And he answered and said unto him, O man of God, thus hath the king said, Come down quickly. And Elijah answered and said unto them, If I be a man of God, let fire come down from heaven, and consume thee and thy fifty. And the fire of God came down from heaven, and consumed him and his fifty (2 Kings 1:10-12).

Elijah was under threat. He did not cower, but instead called the living fire of God to come down and consume his would-be arresters. God answered by doing what Elijah asked. Defiant prayers will neutralize enemy operations.

Success in Prayer

To be successful in prayer, we must be trained and equipped. Let's explore some of the elements needed for our prayers to succeed:

1. **Strength to pray**

   When weakness is permitted to keep us from prayer, the battle is already lost. When prayer sessions are postponed for a "better time," weakness increases and the flesh gets stronger. Press into prayer regardless of how you feel, and you will grow stronger in prayer.

2. **Vision to pray**

   If you have no vision (goal) of where you are headed, the engine (the issue that propels you to pray) remains dormant and the enemy continues his assault. The wicked count on robbing you of vision. They then rejoice in the fulfillment of their dark, expected ends. Remember that the intent of the wicked is to steal, kill, and destroy. Rest assured that if you do not pray, the enemy's assault will continue.

3. **The knowledge of how to pray specifically**
   To be successful in prayer, you must be accurate and diligent. God is not a God of ambiguity. Pray according to His will and your specific needs.

   First address the inherent, ongoing issues in your life, so you can be strengthened and equipped to pray for bigger and/or more universal issues.

We cannot be silent and expect to receive of the Lord. Our words establish our requests. Once you know how to pray specifically, then state your case before God.

The Laws of Living Prayer

Just as our earthly lives are governed by laws that ensure an orderly society, certain spiritual laws govern and guide the art of prayer. It is incumbent upon us to understand these laws and other aspects of prayer.

The Welsh evangelical Jessie Penn-Lewis said, "Prayer fulfills some law which enables God to work, and makes it possible for Him to accomplish His purpose."[1] The Lord put laws in place to ensure that our prayers would be living and active, not null and void. When we abide by His laws, He divinely connects us to the Helper who brings the answers to pass.

Here are some guidelines to keep your prayers alive:

1. **Pray to God the Father, in the name of Jesus Christ.**
   Every prayer must be prayed in the name of Jesus Christ. God wills that we come and ask in His Son's name. To ignore this rule is to nullify our prayers.

   At that day ye shall ask in my name: and I say not unto you, that I will pray the Father for you (John 16:26).

When we ask in Jesus' name, we will receive, because He is forever interceding for us before His Father (see Heb. 7:25).

2. Everything has ears.

Joshua...took a great stone, and set it up there under an oak, that was by the sanctuary of the LORD. And Joshua said unto all the people, Behold, this stone shall be a witness unto us; for it hath heard all the words of the LORD which he spake unto us: it shall be therefore a witness unto you, lest ye deny your God (Josh. 24:26-27).

Any object that the wicked use against us can be spoken to. Therefore speak in the name of Jesus Christ to the thing that is contrary. It will hear you and it will change.

Give ear, O ye heavens, and I will speak; and hear, O earth, the words of my mouth (Deut. 32:1).

Natural substances have a voice; God said that Abel's blood spoke when he was murdered:

The LORD said unto Cain, Where is Abel thy brother? And he said, I know not: Am I my brother's keeper? And he said, What hast thou done? the voice of thy brother's blood crieth unto me from the ground. And now art thou cursed from the earth, which hath opened her mouth to receive thy brother's blood from thy hand (Gen. 4:9-11).

That everything has an ear is a spiritual understanding unknown to many. According to Joshua, the stone placed under an oak tree heard all the words which the Lord spoke to His people. So the stone has ears (see Josh. 24:26-27).

3. **Spirits are behind contrary spiritual and physical situations.**

Then said he unto me, Fear not, Daniel: for from the first day that thou didst set thine heart to understand, and to chasten thyself before thy God, thy words were heard, and I am come for thy words. But the prince of the kingdom of Persia withstood me one and twenty days: but, lo, Michael, one of the chief princes, came to help me; and I remained there with the kings of Persia (Dan. 10:12-13).

Daniel's difficulty was not random. The spirit of the Prince of Persia willfully opposed Daniel's prayers and delayed the answer. Demon interference has direct bearing on spiritual and physical issues. For example, a sick person with spiritual understanding will pray to cut off the evil spirit that is feeding or reinforcing the sickness. Therefore, that person will proceed to recovery.

4. **There is power in commanding and decreeing.**
Words are powerful. Jesus spoke to a fig tree and it obeyed Him. His disciples were amazed, so He explained the law of commanding and decreeing (see Matt. 21:21). When understood, this law makes your prayers living, active, and able to remove hindrances.

Speaking to Job, the Lord made reference to His own acts of commanding and decreeing:

Hast thou commanded the morning since thy days; and caused the dayspring to know his place; that it might take hold of the ends of the earth, that the wicked might be shaken out of it? (Job 38:12-13).

We, too, can command and decree, expecting our words to be fulfilled.

Thou shalt also decree a thing, and it shall be established unto thee: and the light shall shine upon thy ways (Job 22:28).

5. **Prayer requires persistence.**
To be persistent is to be tenacious, determined, tireless, steadfast, unrelenting, constant, enduring, and continual. These traits are necessary in overcoming opposition.

He [Jesus explained]*...that men ought always to pray, and not to faint; saying, There was in a city a judge, which feared not God, neither regarded man: And there was a widow in that city; and she came unto him, saying, Avenge me of mine adversary. And he would not for a while: but afterward he said within himself, Though I fear not God, nor regard man; yet because this widow troubleth me, I will avenge her, lest by her continual coming she weary me. And the Lord said, Hear what the unjust judge saith. And shall not God avenge his own elect, which cry day and night unto him, though he bear long with them? I tell you that he will avenge them speedily. Nevertheless when the Son of man cometh, shall he find faith on the earth?* (Luke 18:1-8).

Do not be slack in your prayer life. There is an order in prayer that enables you to receive from the Lord: Start your prayer time in praise and worship. Follow with thanksgiving. Proceed with your prayers of asking, or supplication. And finally, close with a prayer of thanksgiving to the Lord that reflects your belief that your prayers have been answered.

6. **Overcoming requires perseverance.**
To persevere is not only to persist, but also to continue, to stick to, to insist on, to endure and to proceed. While persistency is an attitude or mind-set, persevering is a way of life.

*But the prince of the kingdom of Persia withstood me
one and twenty days: but, lo, Michael, one of the chief
princes, came to help me; and I remained there with
the kings of Persia* (Dan. 10:13).

Perseverance was a characteristic of Daniel's life. He not only
persisted in his prayers; he also persevered until the answer
came. That is a key to success in life and in prayer.

Focus is an important part of perseverance. Do not focus on
your shortcomings (to do so is to assist the devil. Instead,
train your spiritual eyes on the Lord Jesus Christ and His
perfection.

7. **Understand the importance of binding and loosing.**
   Apply the law of binding evil and loosing the power of the
   Holy Spirit in your life—and understand which is which!
   When you bind and loose according to God's will, you silence
   the enemy's taunts.

   *Verily I say unto you, Whatsoever ye shall bind on
   earth shall be bound in heaven: and whatsoever
   ye shall loose on earth shall be loosed in heaven*
   (Matt. 18:18).

   What you bind in the earthly realm is bound from working
   against you in the heavenlies. When you loose the Holy Spirit
   to work in your life, heaven's resources are made available
   to meet your needs and fulfill your purpose. In John 11:44,
   Jesus said, "Loose him, and let him go." These words were
   spoken to complete the deliverance of Lazarus from the hold
   of the spirit of death.

8. **Use the power of agreement, and use it wisely.**
   As a believer, it is imperative to pray with at least one person
   who agrees with your request. This is especially important
   if you have been struggling alone in a particular situation.

Be certain, however, that the person you enlist is true and trustworthy. Sound prayers of agreement touch the throne of grace and mercy.

Again I say unto you, That if two of you shall agree on earth as touching anything that they shall ask, it shall be done for them of my Father which is in heaven (Matt. 18:19).

9. **Engage in corporate or collective prayer.**
   When the children of God join their voices in corporate prayer, they make a wonderful melody for the Lord's ears. Corporate prayer is one of the great benefits of fellowship among believers.

   For where two or three are gathered together in my name, there am I in the midst of them (Matt. 18:20).

These are powerful truths about prayer. As your understanding increases, your prayer life will become more fruitful and your life will be transformed. Use the following prayer guides to strengthen your journey, beginning with the prayer of thanksgiving.

✞ Praying the Prayer of Thanksgiving

Bible Prayer Link

Enter into his gates with thanksgiving, and into his courts with praise: Be thankful unto him, and bless his name (Ps. 100:4).

Prayer Focus
- To acknowledge the faithfulness of God
- To assume a posture of thankfulness

PRAYER GUIDES

1. Thank You, Jesus Christ, for being my shelter and strong tower from the enemy (see Ps. 61:3).
2. Thank You, Jesus Christ, for loading me with benefits every day (see Ps. 68:19).
3. Father Lord, I thank You for not giving me as prey to the teeth of the enemy (see Ps. 124:6).
4. Father Lord, I thank You for the wonderful things you have done in my life (see Ps. 72:18).
5. Father God, I thank You for blessing me with all spiritual blessings in the heavenly places in Christ (see Eph. 1:3).
6. Father God, I thank You for giving me victory over oppressive forces, through Jesus Christ (see 1 Cor. 15:57).

✟ PRAYERS TO BRING BREAKTHROUGH

BIBLE PRAYER LINKS

Take the helmet of salvation, and the sword of the Spirit, which is the word of God: praying always with all prayer and supplication in the Spirit, and watching thereunto with all perseverance and supplication for all saints (Eph. 6:17-18).

The Spirit also helpeth our infirmities: for we know not what we should pray for as we ought: but the Spirit itself maketh intercession for us with groanings which cannot be uttered (Rom. 8:26).

PRAYER FOCUS
- To pray living, effective, Spirit-led prayers
- To prayerfully seek progress, blessing, and breakthroughs

PRAYER GUIDES
1. Father God, where there seems to be no way, arise today and make a way for me, in the name of Jesus Christ.

2. My destiny is attached to God. Therefore, I decree that I shall neither fall nor fail nor be in want, in the mighty name of Jesus Christ.
3. In the name of Jesus, I declare that my tomorrow is blessed in Christ Jesus, therefore, no satanic deception will divert me from the will of God.
4. By the Word of the Lord, God shall make me an eternal excellency and a joy of many generations, in the mighty name of Jesus Christ (see Isa. 60:15).
5. Showers of blessings and breakthrough, begin to fall upon my life, destiny, finances, etc., in the name of Jesus Christ.
6. O Lord, refresh me now with Your blessings and breakthroughs, in the name of Jesus Christ. (When the Lord refreshes you, dryness is rebuked in every area of concern.)
7. Thank You, Lord, for answering my prayers. Amen.

✟ PRAYERS TO THE GOD OF MERCY, GRACE, AND POWER

BIBLE PRAYER LINKS

O give thanks unto the LORD; for he is good; for his mercy endureth for ever (1 Chron. 16:34).

The God of peace shall bruise Satan under your feet shortly. The grace of our Lord Jesus Christ be with you. Amen (Rom. 16:20).

He giveth power to the faint; and to them that have no might he increaseth strength (Isa. 40:29).

Therefore let us not sleep, as do others; but let us watch and be sober (1 Thess. 5:6).

PRAYER FOCUS
- To rest prayerfully in the mercy and grace of God
- To affirm the power of God on behalf of the believer
- To dismantle all works of the spirit of slumber

Prayer Guides

1. I thank You, Lord, for opening the door of Your mercy and grace to me, in the name of Jesus Christ.
2. O God of mercy and grace, visit me now and glorify Your name in my life, in the name of Jesus Christ.
3. By the grace of God, I shall not miss my divine connection, in the name of Jesus Christ.
4. By the grace of God and in the name of Jesus Christ, all satanic connections assigned to pull me down shall be cut off from me.
5. Father Lord, if I have missed my divine connection, arise in the power of Your mercy and grace and reconnect me now, in the name of Jesus Christ.
6. Father Lord, if I have missed my divine connection, empower me to recover now by the power of the Holy Spirit, in the name of Jesus Christ.
7. Every blocker spirit preventing my divine connection, be paralyzed now, in the name of Jesus Christ.
8. O Lord, let Your power be released into this environment now, in the name of Jesus Christ.
9. O Lord, let Your glory overshadow this environment and empower it, now, in the name of Jesus Christ.
10. O Lord, assign legions of angels to minister to me today, in the mighty name of Jesus Christ.
11. O Lord, as I come before You today, touch me with Your powerful hands. Do not let me leave the same way I came in, in the mighty name of Jesus Christ.
12. All spiritual slumber assigned to hinder my spirit man, the Lord rebuke you. Be cut off from me, in the name of Jesus Christ.
13. Holy Spirit, break the power of the slumbering spirit delegated against my spirit man, in the name of Jesus Christ.
14. Holy Spirit break the yoke of spiritual slumber that is upon my life and destiny, in the name of Jesus Christ.
15. Holy Spirit, revive my spirit, in the name of Jesus Christ.
16. O Lord my God, use me this day to expand Your kingdom for Your glory, in the mighty name of Jesus Christ.

17. O Lord my God, establish Your covenant of divine wealth and prosperity upon my life, destiny, finances, and business now, in the mighty name of Jesus Christ.
18. Thank You, Lord, for answering my prayers.

✠ Prayers to Disrupt and Demolish Demonic Activity

Bible Prayer Links

For this purpose the Son of God was manifested, that he might destroy the works of the devil (1 John 3:8b).

For the word of God is quick, and powerful, and sharper than any twoedged sword, piercing even to the dividing asunder of soul and spirit, and of the joints and marrow, and is a discerner of the thoughts and intents of the heart. Neither is there any creature that is not manifest in his sight: but all things are naked and opened unto the eyes of him with whom we have to do (Heb. 4:12-13).

Prayer Focus
- To demolish demonic schemes and rest in the Lord's protection
- To overthrow all forms of demonic oppression and bondage

Prayer Guides
1. O Lord, arise and protect me from the evil one, in the name of Jesus Christ.
2. O Lord, arise and sanctify me by Your Word, in the name of Jesus Christ.
3. All forms of demonic oppression upon my prayer life, disintegrate now, in the name of Jesus Christ.
4. Father Lord, arise and empower my prayer life with Your holy fire, in the name of Jesus Christ.

5. Demonic powers attempting to rule my life, the Lord rebuke you. Loose your hold and depart from me now, in the name of Jesus Christ.

6. O Lord, turn every curse sent against my life and destiny into a blessing and testimony, in the name of Jesus Christ.

7. I thank You, O Lord Jesus Christ, for saving my life, in Your name I pray.

8. Every voice of opposition from the first and second heavens, the Lord rebuke you. Be silenced forever, in the mighty name of Jesus Christ.

9. Every voice of opposition against my life and destiny, career, elevation, and promotion in life, the Lord rebuke you. Be silenced forever, in the name of Jesus Christ.

10. Demonic opposition to my divine liberation, deliverance, establishment, destiny, and restoration, I command you to scatter, in the mighty name of Jesus Christ.

11. O Lord my God, let timetables of failure, affliction, loneliness, backwardness, sickness, lack, and hardship in my life expire now to Your glory, in the name of Jesus Christ.

12. O Lord my God, sanctify me wholly, in the mighty name of Jesus Christ (see 1 Thess. 5:23).

13. O Lord, send down Your Holy Ghost fire to consume everything contrary in my life and destiny, in the name of Jesus Christ.

14. Blood of our Lord and Savior Jesus Christ, deliver my spirit, soul, and body from all demonic bondage, captivity, and affliction, in the mighty name of Jesus Christ.

15. Thank You, Lord, for answering my prayers. Amen.

Endnote

Jessie Penn-Lewis, *War on the Saints,* 9th ed. (New York: Thomas E. Lowe), 279.

5

Overthrowing Demonic Resistance

If you intend to live victoriously, you must also be positioned to destroy the means of the wicked. This means gaining knowledge and understanding of demonic resistance so you are equipped, by the Holy Spirit, to dismantle it.

Fundamentals of Demonic Resistance

Demonic resistance is inherently evil and is experienced by individuals, families, communities, and nations. This evil experience can be felt in the body, observed in the soul, discerned in the spirit, and seen with the physical eyes. Demonic resistance is a wicked and often effective tool of the kingdom of darkness. Although Christians often discuss it, little effort is made to learn how it operates. Without this understanding, there is little chance of countering and overcoming demonic schemes.

The wicked weapon of demonic resistance can be detected in nearly all aspects of life, and is used to discourage and defeat believers' spiritual desires and efforts. It confuses believers of all ages as to the efficacy of their prayers. You can see the potential impact of this evil tool; it must be opposed promptly and destroyed before it destroys.

The Bible is filled with revelations of conflict between the forces of evil and good. These instances are recorded for our instruction and encouragement. Jesus said, "These things I have spoken unto you, that in me ye might have peace. In the world ye shall have tribulation: but be of good cheer; I have overcome the world" (John 16:33). Tribulation can be distress, agony, grief, misery, sorrow, torment, suffering, trouble, or misfortune. Regardless of the type or severity of the struggle, Jesus admonishes us to be of good cheer (comforted and courageous), trusting in the fact that He has overcome all evil. When we understand this, we can experience a joy no tribulation can suppress. Why? Because Jesus Christ has prevailed on our behalf!

When Jesus speaks of "the world" in John 16:33, He means the physical planet and its inhabitants. With that in mind, let's consider what He has overcome:

1. He has conquered all negative uses of our planet by forces of evil.
2. He has conquered all negative schemes that might be generated in the earth by forces of evil.
3. He has conquered all demonic possession of Earth's inhabitants intended to resist or abort the divine plan.

Demonic resistance is a primary source of distress, confusion, and frustration in believers' lives. Knowing this is the first step to defeating the wicked one. As you read and pray, may you be empowered by the Holy Spirit to overthrow all demonic resistance, in the name of Jesus Christ!

The Scope of Demonic Resistance

The Bible uses the word *resist* in several ways. For example, the apostle Paul lamented that his visit with the brethren in Rome had been hindered:

> *Making request, if by any means now at length I might have a prosperous journey by the will of God to come unto you. For I long to see you, that I may impart unto you some spiritual gift, to the end ye may be established; that is, that I may be comforted together with you by the mutual faith both of you and me. Now I would not have you ignorant, brethren, that*

oftentimes I purposed to come unto you, (but was let hitherto,)... (Rom. 1:10-13).

The New American Standard translation says, "I have planned to come to you (and have been prevented so far)" (Rom. 10:13). I believe Paul was hindered, prevented, or resisted by reactionary forces of darkness seeking to undermine God's work through him. The apostle experienced a similar resistance when planning to visit the church in Thessalonica. He specifically named Satan as the culprit:

We, brethren, being taken from you for a short time in presence, not in heart, endeavored the more abundantly to see your face with great desire. Wherefore we would have come unto you, even I Paul, once and again; but Satan hindered us (1 Thess. 2:17-18).

Paul wrote to his spiritual son, Timothy, and described another type of resistance, this time through the actions of a local tradesman. Paul cursed the man because he withstood the gospel:

Alexander the coppersmith did me much evil: the Lord reward him according to his works: of whom be thou ware also; for he hath greatly withstood our words (Tim. 4:14-15).

The word *withstood* here simply means "to resist." Paul used the word again when describing an encounter he and Barnabas had with a sorcerer:

Elymas the sorcerer (for so is his name by interpretation) withstood them, seeking to turn away the deputy from the faith (Acts 13:8).

Elymas had not only resisted an individual's spiritual progress; he resisted God Himself, by distorting the preaching of His gospel!
Demonic resistance sometimes manifests as a hold, interception, or blockage of that which is sought by the believer, leading to

an extended delay with no sign of breakthrough. This was true in Daniel's case, which we discussed earlier. Daniel prayed, but the prince of the kingdom of Persia battled the angel of God who was assigned to deliver the answer to Daniel's prayer (see Dan. 10:13).

Demonic resistance can also be called *demonic opposition.* For example, when someone receives a divine vision of a glorious accomplishment, but finds implementation impossible, he or she is experiencing demonic opposition. Moses, the prophet assigned to lead Israel out of bondage, faced this in Pharaoh's courtyard:

> *Now as Jannes and Jambres withstood Moses, so do these also resist the truth: men of corrupt minds, reprobate concerning the faith* (2 Tim. 3:8).

Demonic resistance can also manifest as demonic projection, an evil diversion by which a human agent of the devil releases demons to possess the soul of one who purposes to do God's will. This was part of the resistance of Elymas the sorcerer. The official named Sergius Paulus summoned Paul and Barnabas because he wanted to hear God's Word. Elymas worked to divert the official's desire and intent (see Acts 13:4-8).

Another aspect of demonic resistance is delegation. In this case, one or more demons are assigned to a person, family, group, or community to frustrate their success. This was the plan of Satan against Joshua the high priest, whom we read about earlier (see Zech. 3:1-2). Until God delivered him, Joshua's ministry was hindered.

Objectives of Demonic Resistance

Since the Fall of Man, Satan and all of his associates have vigorously used resistance to frustrate divine vision and destiny. The main objective is to prevent (or at least delay) the manifestation of God's will. Undertaken by demonic hosts, this resistance is spiritual in nature, being hidden, subtle, and highly coordinated in the realms of the spirit. Its results, however can be seen in the physical realm.

The first physical manifestation of demonic resistance is agitation in the soul. Notice what God's Word says: ""Surely there is an end;

and thine expectation shall not be cut off" (Prov. 23:18). God promises an expected and glorious outcome for those who trust Him. But when expectation is delayed long enough, the believer's spirit and soul are pressed and agitation results.

When expectation appears to be cut off altogether, frustration sets in. The enemy will continue to apply pressure until the believer gives up the fight or is diverted into error. (These objectives are achieved more quickly in believers who are emotion-driven, both spiritually and physically. Impatient people are particularly prone to diversion into error.)

Confusion is one of the wicked one's most powerful means of resistance. When the believer becomes agitated, he or she is more easily driven to strive with others. The apostle James declares in James 3:16 that "where envying and strife is, there is confusion and every evil work." In this way, the attack escalates exponentially.

Job was deeply afflicted by confusion, as his words reveal:

> *If I be wicked, woe unto me; and if I be righteous, yet will I not lift up my head. I am full of confusion; therefore see thou mine affliction* (Job 10:15).

Satan strongly resisted Job's healing and restoration. Confusion set in because Job, who lived righteously, could not understand why such evil had befallen him.

Depression is another tool of demonic resistance, with the final objective being death itself. Depression manifests in many ways, including through lethargy, which keeps a person from undertaking appropriate actions. This was true of Judah's king, Asa:

> *Asa in the thirty and ninth year of his reign was diseased in his feet, until his disease was exceeding great: yet in his disease he sought not to the LORD, but to the physicians. And Asa slept with his fathers, and died in the one and fortieth year of his reign* (2 Chron. 16:12-13).

This subtle resistance masked its ultimate objective. Asa was sick but refused to seek the Lord. In the early years of his reign, Asa experienced the Lord's deliverance from the powerful Ethiopians and Lubims. But when Israel laid siege against Judah, Asa sought protection, not from God, but from Ben-hadad king of Syria.

This, I believe, shows that demonic hosts had possessed Asa's soul, preventing him from seeking the Lord. The resistance was so effective, that when he was taken ill, Asa sought help from his physicians instead of from God. They could not save him, and Asa died.

Demonic resistance is used against people today. Many who have rejected Jesus Christ as their Lord and Savior instead embrace occultic counsel, to their own destruction. Even some believers who are unaware of, or unprepared to resist the enemy, refuse the deliverance God freely offers.

How Evil Forces Carry Out Resistance

Many wicked means have been fashioned against Christian believers. You could say that demonic powers customize their efforts case by case based on the level of a person's spiritual maturity, humility, and surrender to God. It is also tailored to the call of God on a person or organization. Demonic powers carefully match their tactics to the particulars of the individual or entity they are targeting.

Demonic resistance can be carried out by a variety of agents:
1. Satanists (demonized human agents of the devil)
2. Demons
3. Satan himself

Demonic Resistance through Human Agents

Satan works through demonized and other human agents to bring resistance and cause frustration. You have already seen how the wicked one used Elymas the sorcerer (also known as Bar-jesus) to withstand Paul and Barnabas. Remember that an official named Sergius Paulus *asked* to hear Paul and Barnabas speak, but Elymas interfered. Notice Paul's response:

*Then Saul, (who also is called Paul,) filled with the
Holy Ghost, set his eyes on him, and said, O full of all
subtilty and all mischief, thou child of the devil, thou
enemy of all righteousness, wilt thou not cease to pervert the right ways of the Lord? And now, behold, the
hand of the Lord is upon thee, and thou shalt be blind,
not seeing the sun for a season. And immediately
there fell on him a mist and a darkness; and he went
about seeking some to lead him by the hand. Then the
deputy, when he saw what was done, believed, being
astonished at the doctrine of the Lord* (Acts 13:9-12).

Praise the Lord, whose will was done! The official wanted to hear
God's Word; he heard it and believed. Imagine, by the Holy Spirit,
the miracles, signs, and wonders the deputy must have witnessed,
and how they caused him to hunger for the Word.

This is exactly what Satan's emissary, Elymas, opposed. Dear
reader, *every* agent of Satan has specific assignments. Elymas' assignment was to oppose the preaching of the true Word of God. Demonic
possession was supposed to enable him to achieve his mission.

Scripture calls Elymas "a sorcerer, a false prophet, a Jew" (Acts
13:6). All of these facts are meaningful: *Sorcery* is an evil supernat-
ural power involving witchcraft (its power base). It is exerted over
people and their undertakings to achieve Satan's ends. *False prophets*
pretend to have divine power to foretell the future, but instead profess
false "revelations." Being possessed by two demons, one of witchcraft and one of false prophecy, Elymas counterfeited God's ways
and perverted His truth in Paphos—and he was a Jew, one of God's
chosen nation!

There is nothing new under the sun (see Eccles. 1:9); demonized
personalities have carried out their wickedness the same way for
millennia:

*Woe to them that devise iniquity, and work evil upon
their beds! When the morning is light, they practise it,
because it is in the power of their hand. They covet
fields, and take them by violence; and houses, and*

*take them away: so they oppress a man and his house,
even a man and his heritage* (Mic. 2:1-2).

Judgment is pronounced on the likes of Elymas because they devise wickedness (meaning they generate and commit evil) by night and watch the wickedness manifest in the day. But thank God, who by His Spirit reveals the plight of the wicked: they are cursed. Therefore, Paul cursed Elymas!

In Acts 13:9-10 (see above) we see how the apostles knew what to do with Elymas. The Holy Spirit revealed to Paul the demons that Elymas invoked, and Paul addressed them:

1. **The evil spirit of subtlety**

    This spirit is highly deceitful and difficult to detect. Elymas knew how to send the deceiving spirit to customize the deception and confuse Sergius Paulus. The spirit of subtlety is the spirit of unbelief.

2. **The evil spirit of mischief**

    This spirit causes irritation, impatience, and then annoyance, all of which are effective forms of distraction and deception.

If these two demons were allowed to have their way with the official, he would have rejected the gospel. Paul recognized the potential impact and the demonic operation of Elymas, calling Elymas a "child of the devil." The title was appropriate: children are strongly influenced and formed by their parents. Satan formed Elymas in wickedness; Elymas then tried to influence Sergius Paulus, exactly as his father, the devil, wished.

Paul also called Elymas the "enemy of all righteousness" (Acts 13:10). The Bible says Abraham believed the Lord and it was counted for righteousness (see Gen. 15:6). Elymas' mission was to cause the deputy to *disbelieve* the gospel. But the Holy Spirit prompted Paul to pronounce judgment on Elymas. Paul wasted no time doing so. As he told Timothy, "men of corrupt minds, reprobate concerning the faith...shall proceed no further: for their folly shall be manifest unto all men..." (2 Tim. 3:8-9). Once Elymas' folly became evident to Paul, the sorcery proceeded no further!

Two important spiritual lessons are to be learned from this encounter:
1. There is a spirit behind every contrary situation.
2. To ensure liberty and restoration, every source of resistance must be dealt with. (For the deputy to receive the gospel, Elymas the sorcerer had to be eliminated.)

Demonic Resistance through Demons

The scripture below is now familiar: we saw earlier that Daniel's prayer was resisted in the spirit realm. Notice that in this case, it was not a demon-possessed man who enforced the hindrance, but a demonic spiritual being:

> *The prince of the kingdom of Persia withstood me one and twenty days: but, lo, Michael, one of the chief princes, came to help me; and I remained there with the kings of Persia* (Dan. 10:13).

Demonic Resistance through Satan Himself

Let's look again at the oppressed high priest, Joshua. Notice this time that Satan himself was involved in the resistance:[1]

> *He shewed me Joshua the high priest standing before the angel of the LORD, and Satan standing at his right hand to resist him. And the LORD said unto Satan, The LORD rebuke thee, O Satan; even the LORD that hath chosen Jerusalem rebuke thee: is not this a brand plucked out of the fire?* (Zech. 3:1-2).

Now that we have covered multiple aspects of demonic resistance, we can pray effectively using the prayer guides below.

✝ PRAYERS TO BREAK THE POWER OF DEMONIC RESISTANCE AND LIMITATION

BIBLE PRAYER LINKS

Submit yourselves therefore to God. Resist the devil, and he will flee from you (James 4:7).

The LORD is a man of war: the LORD is his name. Pharaoh's chariots and his host hath he cast into the sea: His chosen captains also are drowned in the Red sea. The depths have covered them: They sank into the bottom as a stone. Thy right hand, O LORD, is become glorious in power: Thy right hand, O LORD, hath dashed in pieces the enemy (Exod. 15:3-6).

PRAYER FOCUS
- To demolish all demonic resistance to God's plan
- To break the power of demonic limitations

PRAYER GUIDES
1. Father Lord, arise today and scatter every form of demonic resistance to my divine liberty and fulfillment, in the name of Jesus Christ.
2. Father Lord, arise today and pull down every demonic structure erected in the realm of the spirit to limit my divine purpose, in the name of Jesus Christ.
3. Chain of darkness assigned to bind my destiny (my progress, glory, etc.), be broken into pieces by the thunder of God, in the name of Jesus Christ.
4. Father Lord, I thank You for empowering me by Your holy fire to overthrow demonic resistance, in the name of Jesus Christ.
5. Lord, baptize me continually with Your holy fire to overthrow demonic resistance, in the name of Jesus Christ.
6. I break the power of evil resistance to my spiritual breakthrough by the holy fire of God, in the name of Jesus Christ.

7. Every resistance set up by Satan against my progress (my success, marital destiny, etc.), be overthrown now by the Holy Ghost fire, in the name of Jesus Christ.

8. Prison of darkness assigned to limit my life, be shattered to pieces by the thunder of God, in the name of Jesus Christ.

9. Satanic umbrella covering my glory and limiting my enlargement, catch fire and burn to ashes, in the name of Jesus Christ.

10. Pharaoh of darkness assigned against me, your time is up. I command you to die by the plagues of Almighty God, in the name of Jesus Christ.

11. O Lord, my God, arise and break the power of cruel bondage that is limiting my enlargement and fruitfulness, in the name of Jesus Christ.

12. O Lord, my God, arise and break the power of the demonic oppressors bringing pain and distress to my body, spirit, and soul, in the name of Jesus Christ.

13. O Lord, my God, arise in the power of Your almightiness and scatter the satanic cooperation that is set up to limit my divine purpose in this environment, in the name of Jesus Christ.

14. In the name of Jesus Christ, and by His blood, I overcome every form of demonic resistance and limitation to my destiny fulfillment.

15. Holy Spirit, empower my taking of dominion over the mighty, in the name of Jesus Christ (see Judg. 5:13).

16. Lord Jesus Christ, arise and anoint me now with holy fire for spiritual strength and power.

17. Holy Spirit, arise now and release a divine earthquake to the foundation of my life to dismantle all evil planted therein, in the name of Jesus Christ.

18. O Lord, my God, release Your holy fire into my spirit, soul, and body to incinerate any wickedness, in the name of Jesus Christ.

19. Every demonic power resisting my healing and deliverance, be shaken out of position now by the Holy Ghost earthquake, in the name of Jesus Christ.

20. Power of God, go forth now and scatter the gathering of the wicked who desire my destruction, in the name of Jesus Christ.

21. O Lord, arise today and roll away the reproach of Egypt from my life, in the name of Jesus Christ.

22. Today, in the name of Jesus Christ, I receive the anointing to prosper in my environment. Demonic resistance prospering in my life because of generational sins and iniquities, I hold the blood of Jesus against you. Scatter, in Jesus' name.

23. Demonic resistance prospering in my life as a result of personal sins and iniquities, I hold the blood of Jesus against you. Scatter, in Jesus' name.

24. By the Word of the Lord, I tread upon and crush every demonic serpent and scorpion resisting the fulfillment of my destiny, in Jesus' name (see Ps. 91:13; Luke 10:19).

25. O God whose name alone is Jehovah, arise for my sake and empower me to overthrow all demonic resistances to my breakthroughs, in Jesus' name.

26. O God whose name alone is Jehovah, arise in the power of Your almightiness and neutralize the power of satanic agents resisting my access to my throne of glory, in Jesus' name.

27. Thank You, Lord, for answering my prayers. Amen.

✞ Prayers for Father God to Arise and Rebuke Satan for My Sake

Bible Prayer Links

He shewed me Joshua the high priest standing before the angel of the Lord, and Satan standing at his right hand to resist him. And the Lord said unto Satan, The Lord rebuke thee, O Satan; even the Lord that hath chosen Jerusalem rebuke thee: is not this a brand plucked out of the fire? Now Joshua was clothed with filthy garments, and stood before the angel (Zech. 3:1-3).

Yet Michael the archangel, when contending with the devil he disputed about the body of Moses, durst not

*bring against him a railing accusation, but said, The
Lord rebuke thee* (Jude 1:9).

PRAYER FOCUS
- To be empowered by God's holy fire
- To invoke the Lord's rebuke of Satan

PRAYER GUIDES
1. Thank You, Lord, for rebuking Satan for my sake and destroying his evil works.
2. Satan, the Lord rebuke you. Loose your hold on my life and destiny (my finances, health, etc.), in the name of Jesus Christ.
3. Satan, the Lord rebuke you. Depart from me now! Peace, return to my life (my home, marriage, etc.), in the name of Jesus Christ.
4. Satan, the Lord rebuke you. Depart from me. Healing, return to my spirit, soul, and body now, in the name of Jesus Christ.
5. Every demonic interceptor on assignment to block my spiritual vision, the Lord rebuke you, in the name of Jesus Christ.
6. Every demonic interceptor holding hostage my angels of help, the Lord rebuke you, loosening your power and letting them come to me, in the name of Jesus Christ.
7. Every satanic contention against my life and destiny, the Lord rebuke you. Be overthrown now, in the name of Jesus Christ.
8. Father God, arise now and rebuke Satan for my sake as You did for Joshua the high priest, in the name of Jesus Christ.
9. Father God, arise now and rebuke Satan for the sake of my destiny (health, breakthrough, ministry, finances, etc.), as You did for Joshua the high priest, in the name of Jesus Christ.
10. I lift up the blood of Jesus Christ to counter every demonic attack that may come against me as a result of the prayers I have just prayed, in the name of Jesus Christ.
11. Thank You, Lord, for answering my prayers. Amen.

✞ Prayers to Overthrow Demonic Interceptions, Ambushes, and Diversions by Any Demonic Agents

Bible Prayer Links

Blessed be the LORD my strength, which teacheth my hands to war, and my fingers to fight (Ps. 144:1).

The LORD is my light and my salvation; whom shall I fear? The LORD is the strength of my life; of whom shall I be afraid? (Ps. 27:1).

No weapon that is formed against thee shall prosper; and every tongue that shall rise against thee in judgment thou shalt condemn. This is the heritage of the servants of the LORD, and their righteousness is of me, saith the LORD (Isa. 54:17).

Prayer Focus
- To dislodge and dismantle all forms of interference
- To release all forms of blessing

Prayer Guides
1. Father Lord, I thank You for equipping me with power to overthrow all forms of demonic interference, in Jesus' name.
2. O God who answered Elijah by fire, answer my prayers today by Your grace and mercy, in the name of Jesus Christ.
3. Every agent of the devil assigned to intercept my breakthroughs, be strangulated by the angels of the living God, in the name of Jesus Christ.
4. Every agent of the devil that has laid ambush for my breakthroughs, be consumed in the Holy Ghost fire, in the name of Jesus Christ.
5. Every demonic interceptor standing between me and my breakthroughs, progress, promotion, health, wealth, etc., be dislodged now by Holy Ghost fire, in the name of Jesus Christ.

6. Lord, arise now and scatter any obstacles assigned by the devil to block my angels of help, in the name of Jesus Christ. Every human agent of darkness on assignment to divert my blessings away from me, be exposed and chased from me by Holy Ghost fire, in the name of Jesus Christ.

7. Lord, send Your powerful angel to arrest every demonic interceptor delegated against me by the devil, in the name of Jesus Christ.

8. Any agent of the devil invoking demons to intercept blessings and breakthroughs sent to me by the Lord, be destroyed by the thunder of God, in the name of Jesus Christ.

9. From today forward, all divinely released blessings and breakthroughs shall reach me, in the name of Jesus Christ.

10. Thank You, Lord, for answering my prayers. Amen.

✟ PRAYERS TO OVERCOME DIFFICULTIES

BIBLE PRAYER LINK

Thus saith the LORD to his anointed, to Cyrus, whose right hand I have holden, to subdue nations before him; and I will loose the loins of kings, to open before him the two leaved gates; and the gates shall not be shut; I will go before thee, and make the crooked places straight: I will break in pieces the gates of brass, and cut in sunder the bars of iron: and I will give thee the treasures of darkness, and hidden riches of secret places, that thou mayest know that I, the LORD, which call thee by thy name, am the God of Israel (Isa. 45:1-3).

PRAYER FOCUS
- To give thanks for the Lord's mighty acts and for the excellency of His greatness (see Ps. 150:2)
- To dismantle the roots of difficulty

PRAYER GUIDES

1. O covenant-keeping God, arise. As I appropriate Your Word in my prayers, let it become operational in my life, in the name of Jesus Christ.

2. O Lord, by Your grace, hold my right hand now and subdue all wickedness assigned to embarrass or humiliate me, in the name of the Lord Jesus Christ.

3. O Lord of Hosts, as You did for Cyrus, arise and cut off the strength of demonic powers blocking my way to glory, in the mighty name of Jesus Christ.

4. O Lord, my Father, arise and go before me to make straight the crooked places of my life and destiny (name them specifically), in the name of Jesus Christ (see Isa. 45:1)

5. Gates of brass attached to bars of iron to hinder my blessings and breakthroughs and cause difficulty, I command you by the power of the Holy Spirit, to be broken in pieces and cut asunder, in the name of Jesus Christ (see Ps. 107:16).

6. O Lord, according to Your word, give me the treasures of darkness so that Your praise may be in my mouth forever, in the mighty name of Jesus Christ (see Isa. 45:3).

7. Lord, according to Your Word, give unto me the hidden riches of secret places, that the world may know that I serve a living God, in the mighty name of Jesus Christ.

8. Thank You, Lord Jesus Christ, for answering my prayers. Amen.

✟ PRAYERS TO FIGHT WITH THE ARM OF THE LORD

BIBLE PRAYER LINK

Awake, awake, put on strength, O arm of the LORD; awake, as in the ancient days, in the generations of old. Art thou not it that hath cut Rahab, and wounded the dragon? Art thou not it which hath dried the sea, the waters of the great deep; that hath made the depths of the sea a way for the ransomed to pass over? Therefore the redeemed of the LORD shall return, and come with singing unto Zion; and everlasting joy

*shall be upon their head: they shall obtain gladness
and joy; and sorrow and mourning shall flee away*
(Isa. 51:9-11).

PRAYER FOCUS
- To thwart the works of darkness
- To petition the arm of the Lord to arise in my defense

PRAYER GUIDES
1. O covenant-keeping God, arise and let Your words, which I appropriate in these prayers, become operational instantly, in the name of Jesus Christ.
2. O arm of the Lord, arise for my sake, put on strength, and cut off my oppressors, as in the ancient days, in the name of Jesus Christ.
3. O arm of the Lord, arise for my sake, put on strength, and destroy the demonic powers tormenting my body, (my glory, marriage, etc.) as in the ancient days when you pierced the dragon, in the name of Jesus Christ.
4. O arm of the Lord, arise for my sake, put on strength, and dismantle every obstacle assigned to stagnate my life and destiny, as in the ancient days when You broke up the Red Sea for the Israelites, in the name of Jesus Christ.
5. O arm of the Lord, arise for my sake, put on strength, and remove any demonic objects hindering my physical and spiritual breakthroughs, as You removed the Red Sea waters for the Israelites, in the name of Jesus Christ.
6. O arm of the Lord, arise for my sake, put on strength, and empower my helping angels to break through demonic barriers for me, as in the ancient days when you broke through the Red Sea barrier for the Israelites, in the name of Jesus Christ.
7. O arm of the Lord, arise for my sake, put on strength, and loose me from the hold of demonic captivities (<u>mention them specifically</u>), as in the ancient days, in the name of Jesus Christ.
8. O arm of the Lord, arise for my sake, put on strength, as in the ancient days, and take me out of any demonic pit of

debt, (poverty, bondage, etc.) that has taken me captive, in the name of Jesus Christ.

9. Thank You, Lord Jesus Christ, for answering my prayers. Amen.

✝ PRAYERS ASKING GOD TO ARISE AND COMMAND DELIVERANCE

BIBLE PRAYER LINKS

When the king asked the woman, she told him. So the king appointed unto her a certain officer, saying, Restore all that was hers, and all the fruits of the field since the day that she left the land, even until now (2 Kings 8:6).

Thou art my King, O God: command deliverances for Jacob (Ps. 44:4).

PRAYER FOCUS
- To seek restoration of physical, emotional, material, and spiritual losses
- To seek the Lord's deliverance

PRAYER GUIDES
1. I praise You, O Lord! You command and there can be no resistance.
2. O Lord, remember me for good, and let good things resurrect in my life and destiny today, in the name of Jesus Christ.
3. O Lord, remember me for good and deliver me from all forms of demonic power, in the mighty name of Jesus Christ.
4. O God of grace, arise and forcefully recover everything of mine that is currently held by oppressive powers, in the name of Jesus Christ.
5. Father Lord, command demonic confiscators to restore all that belonged to me now, in the name of Jesus Christ.

6. Father Lord, recover and restore back to me every benefit and blessing that suddenly vanished from me, in the name of Jesus Christ.

7. O Lord, let the creative power of the Holy Spirit come upon my life and destiny and restore its glory, in the name of Jesus Christ.

8. Demonic powers sucking away my virtues, the Lord rebuke you. Be cut off from me now, in the mighty name of Jesus Christ.

9. Thank You, Jesus Christ, for answering my prayers. Amen.

Endnote

1. My book, *Power and Prayers to Prevail over Spiritual Garments of Hindrance*, addresses this issue more fully. It is available at Amazon.com.

6

The Means of the Wicked: Evil Dominion

Those who want to destroy the means of the wicked must know and understand evil dominion. *Dominion* is defined as "control or the exercise of control."[1] It is the ruling by authority over a person, place, or thing by

- taking charge;
- bringing under subjection;
- conquering;
- dominating.

Dominion can be used for evil or for good. The dominion granted by God to Adam and Eve was for His purposes (see Gen. 1:26). The dominion won by Satan in the Garden of Eden produced wickedness. Evil dominion is easily identified; it employs demonic processes or activities that

- replace people's comfort and joy with pain and sorrow;
- bring darkness and chaos to environments;
- turn what is beautiful and glorious into something ugly and useless.

Wicked demonic powers are behind evil dominion. Once it is detected by way of the Holy Spirit, evil dominion can be traced and nullified by the Spirit's power and the blood of Jesus Christ, in His name.

Divine Dominion

Let's look more deeply into divine dominion. As already shown, it is delegated by God, who is its only source. The activation and exercise of divine dominion must always bring Him glory. This was the intent when God created mankind and gave them control over all the earth:

> *God said, Let us make man in our image, after our likeness: and let them have dominion over the fish of the sea, and over the fowl of the air, and over the cattle, and over all the earth, and over every creeping thing that creepeth upon the earth. So God created man in his own image, in the image of God created he him; male and female created he them. And God blessed them, and God said unto them, Be fruitful, and multiply, and replenish the earth, and subdue it: and have dominion over the fish of the sea, and over the fowl of the air, and over every living thing that moveth upon the earth* (Gen. 1:26-28).

The psalmist, by the Holy Spirit, described the divine dominion granted to man at the Creation:

> *What is man, that thou art mindful of him? And the son of man, that thou visitest him? For thou hast made him a little lower than the angels, and hast crowned him with glory and honour. Thou madest him to have dominion over the works of thy hands; thou hast put all things under his feet: all sheep and oxen, yea, and the beasts of the field; the fowl of the air, and the fish of the sea, and whatsoever passeth through the paths of the seas* (Ps. 8:4-8).

Before His resurrection, Jesus declared the following to His disciples:

The Father loveth the Son, and hath given all things into his hand (John 3:35).

Behold, I give unto you power to tread on serpents and scorpions, and over all the power of the enemy: and nothing shall by any means hurt you (Luke 10:19).

The Father delegated to the Son, and the Son delegated to His followers. Satan is aware of this great gift and despises it. Until our Lord Jesus Christ came to recover the power Adam surrendered to Satan, man could not exercise his God-given dominion. Instead, Satan and his agents assumed control. But after the Lord's resurrection, He revealed Himself to the eleven remaining disciples at a mountain in Galilee, where He declared, "All power is given unto me in heaven and in earth" (Matt. 28:18).

This power has been given to us, in His blood and His name. He gave it so that we can tread over all demonic powers—"serpents and scorpions, and over all the power of the enemy" (Luke 10:19). This *treading* is our exercise of control over all demonic powers and activities. An encounter between the apostle Peter and a man named Simon shows what it means to tread over demons:

There was a certain man, called Simon, which before-time in the same city used sorcery, and bewitched the people of Samaria, giving out that himself was some great one: To whom they all gave heed, from the least to the greatest, saying, This man is the great power of God. And to him they had regard, because that of long time he had bewitched them with sorceries. But when they believed Philip preaching the things concerning the kingdom of God, and the name of Jesus Christ, they were baptized, both men and women. Then Simon himself believed also: and when he was baptized, he continued with Philip, and wondered, beholding the miracles and signs which were done (Acts 8:9-13).

Simon, a sorcerer, heard the gospel and believed. Yet he did not understand God's ways where dominion was concerned:

> *And when Simon saw that through laying on of the apostles' hands the Holy Ghost was given, he offered them money, saying, Give me also this power, that on whomsoever I lay hands, he may receive the Holy Ghost. But Peter said unto him, Thy money perish with thee, because thou hast thought that the gift of God may be purchased with money. Thou hast neither part nor lot in this matter: for thy heart is not right in the sight of God. Repent therefore of this thy wickedness, and pray God, if perhaps the thought of thine heart may be forgiven thee. For I perceive that thou art in the gall of bitterness, and in the bond of iniquity. Then answered Simon, and said, Pray ye to the Lord for me, that none of these things which ye have spoken come upon me* (Acts 8:18-24).

By the authentic power of the Holy Spirit, Peter the apostle exercised divine dominion, and stopped Simon's use of evil dominion in oppressing the Samaritans. Peter also exercised divine dominion over the demon of death by raising a woman named Dorcas from the dead:

> *Peter put them all forth, and kneeled down, and prayed; and turning him to the body said, Tabitha, arise. And she opened her eyes: and when she saw Peter, she sat up. And he gave her his hand, and lifted her up, and when he had called the saints and widows, presented her alive* (Acts 9:40-41).

In addition to His blood and His name, our Lord Jesus Christ has also given us the Holy Spirit, the ultimate power behind divine dominion who is in charge of salvation, sanctification, holiness, excellency, and spiritual exploits (including healing, deliverance, casting out of demons, etc.). (God's holy angels are also involved in supporting acts of divine dominion).

Jesus prepared His disciples for the coming of the Spirit:

Ye shall receive power, after that the Holy Ghost is come upon you: and ye shall be witnesses unto me both in Jerusalem, and in all Judaea, and in Samaria, and unto the uttermost part of the earth (Acts 1:8).

The divine dominion given to the disciples was essential during the encounter Elymas the sorcerer had with Paul and Barnabas. Please read this passage and pay close attention to the function of divine dominion:

Then Saul, (who also is called Paul,) filled with the Holy Ghost, set his eyes on him, and said, O full of all subtilty and all mischief, thou child of the devil, thou enemy of all righteousness, wilt thou not cease to pervert the right ways of the Lord? And now, behold, the hand of the Lord is upon thee, and thou shalt be blind, not seeing the sun for a season. And immediately there fell on him a mist and a darkness; and he went about seeking some to lead him by the hand (Acts 13:9-11).

Empowered by the Holy Spirit, Paul confronted Elymas and dislodged the power of evil dominion in which he functioned (this included his use of witchcraft). Paul also exercised his divine dominion to banish the sorcerer to a season of blindness.

Whenever the divine dominion exercised by a Holy Spirit-empowered individual confronts evil dominion exercised by satanic agents, you can rest assured that divine dominion will prevail, bringing physical and spiritual accomplishment and more abundant life.

Evil Dominion and Its Manifestation

Evil dominion can be defined as the exercise of wicked control—the evil ruling by authority over a person, place, or thing. Evil dominion involves

- conquering and ungodly rule;
- spiritual enslavement;
- forceful capture of a person, place, or thing for wicked purposes;
- prevailing over a person, place, or thing for wicked purposes.

If it is not promptly detected, wicked forms of dominion can cause permanent harm and even premature death. Demons can exercise control based on:

- Curses
- Evil covenants
- Sin or iniquity
- Evil inheritances
- Ignorance of spiritual issues

Satan is a counterfeiter and the principal power behind all evil dominion (demons and evil spirits are also involved). Such control can cause physical and spiritual misery, and ultimate death. It can manifest in many ways, including:

1. Addictions (food, sex, drugs, etc.)
2. Sexual promiscuity and perversion
3. Uncontrollable sexual desire
4. Sickness, including common ailments (diabetes, high blood pressure, etc.)
5. Terminal illnesses initiated by the spirit of death and hell
6. Sickness of the spirit caused by intentionally committed sins
7. Sickness of the soul (fragmentation)
8. Sickness of the mind (ungodly imaginations, evil manipulation, etc.)
9. Emotional sickness (anxiety, fear, etc.)
10. Failure (unexplainable failures at the edge of breakthrough)
11. Nonachievement (enduring struggles with no breakthrough or positive results)
12. Poverty (financial problems, lack, etc.)

Access Points for Evil Dominion

Sin is the greatest portal through which evil dominion gains access into a person's life. Yielding to sin (acting contrary to God's will) is an open invitation to evil dominion. Because of sin, the Lord appointed the Philistines to dominate the Israelites:

> *The children of Israel did evil again in the sight of the* *LORD; and the* LORD *delivered them into the hand of* *the Philistines forty years* (Judg. 13:1).

The Word of God confirms this Philistine dominion:

> [Samson's] *father and his mother knew not that it* *was of the* LORD, *that he sought an occasion against* *the Philistines: for at that time the Philistines had* *dominion over Israel* (Judg. 14:4).

Such dominion is exercised in wickedness, which can include brutal enslavement and oppression leading to frustration and depression, as in Israel's case. The children of Israel lamented the wickedness and torment of evil dominion. It was brutal, and they confessed having no power to resist it.

The passage below reveals that evil dominion can afflict humans and animals.

> *Behold, we are servants this day, and for the land* *that thou gavest unto our fathers to eat the fruit* *thereof and the good thereof, behold, we are servants* *in it: and it yieldeth much increase unto the kings* *whom thou hast set over us because of our sins: also* *they have dominion over our bodies, and over our* *cattle, at their pleasure, and we are in great distress* (Neh. 9:36-37).

Sin generated this brutal situation, as the following passage shows:

> *Howbeit thou art just in all that is brought upon us;* *for thou hast done right, but we have done wickedly:* *neither have our kings, our princes, our priests, nor* *our fathers, kept thy law, nor hearkened unto thy*

*commandments and thy testimonies, wherewith thou
didst testify against them. For they have not served
thee in their kingdom, and in thy great goodness that
thou gavest them, and in the large and fat land which
thou gavest before them, neither turned they from
their wicked works* (Neh. 9:33-35).

Israel refused to follow God's divine instructions and instead
served Satan and his demons. No wonder the psalmist prayed
to the Lord:

*Keep back thy servant also from presumptuous sins;
let them not have dominion over me: then shall I be
upright, and I shall be innocent from the great transgression* (Ps. 19:13).

*Order my steps in thy word: and let not any iniquity
have dominion over me* (Ps. 119:133).

Sin is the foundation of all evil dominion.

Domineering Demonic Lords

Isaiah confessed, "O LORD our God, other lords beside thee have
had dominion over us: but by thee only will we make mention of thy
name" (Isa. 26:13).

I believe that the "other lords" mentioned here are heathen gods
the Israelites had previously worshipped and therefore submitted
themselves to. Their strong allegiance to the Queen of Heaven is
an example. This demon spirit caused them to reject the prophet
Jeremiah's call to turn back to God. They heard him, but the domineering Queen of Heaven controlled their souls, as Scripture reveals:

*As for the word that thou hast spoken unto us in the
name of the LORD, we will not hearken unto thee. But
we will certainly do whatsoever thing goeth forth out
of our own mouth, to burn incense unto the queen of*

heaven, and to pour out drink offerings unto her, as we have done, we, and our fathers, our kings, and our princes, in the cities of Judah, and in the streets of Jerusalem: for then had we plenty of victuals, and were well, and saw no evil. But since we left off to burn incense to the queen of heaven, and to pour out drink offerings unto her, we have wanted all things, and have been consumed by the sword and by the famine. And when we burned incense to the queen of heaven, and poured out drink offerings unto her, did we make her cakes to worship her, and pour out drink offerings unto her, without our men? (Jer. 44:16-19).

Evil dominion profoundly affects the lives of those who succumb to it. Before we enter into prayer, remember that curses create legal ground for satanic operation (see Chapter 3). The wicked who exercise evil dominion take advantage of curses, which are essentially assignments that generate evil or harm.

You are now equipped to resist such brutality, because you understand how it operates. The following prayer guides will empower you to pray effectively to dispel all evil dominion, in Jesus Christ's name!

✝ PRAYERS TO SCATTER ANY EVIL DOMINION STAGNATING MY PROGRESS

BIBLE PRAYER LINKS

Keep back thy servant also from presumptuous sins; let them not have dominion over me: then shall I be upright, and I shall be innocent from the great transgression (Ps. 19:13).

Order my steps in thy word: and let not any iniquity have dominion over me (Ps. 119:133).

PRAYER FOCUS

- To break the power of any evil dominion over my life
- To invoke the power and might of the Lord in scattering all evil dominion

PRAYER GUIDES

1. Evil dominion operating over my brain and mind, the Lord rebuke you. Scatter, in the name of Jesus Christ.
2. Holy Spirit anointing that breaks the power of evil dominion, come upon me now, in the name of Jesus Christ.
3. Any dominion assigned by the kingdom of darkness to thwart my divine purpose, life, and destiny, be paralyzed now, in the name of Jesus Christ.
4. By the blood of Jesus Christ, I break the power of any disease or sickness having dominion over my body.
5. By the greatness of the Lord's power, I command all disease and infirmity that has taken dominion over any organ or function of my body (<u>mention them specifically</u>) to wither now, in the name of Jesus Christ.
6. By the greatness of the Lord's power, I command the spirit of insomnia having dominion over my sleep to be cut off from me now, in the name of Jesus Christ.
7. By the authority of the third heaven, I command all evil dominion set over my destiny to come to a perpetual end now, in the name of Jesus Christ.
8. Thank You, Jesus Christ, for answering my prayers. Amen.

✟ PRAYERS TO RECOVER/RESTORE MY DOMINION AUTHORITY

BIBLE PRAYER LINKS

> *God said, Let us make man in our image, after our likeness: and let them have dominion over the fish of the sea, and over the fowl of the air, and over the cattle, and over all the earth, and over every creeping thing that creepeth upon the earth* (Gen. 1:26).

Thou madest him [man] *to have dominion over the works of thy hands; thou hast put all things under his feet* (Ps. 8:6).

PRAYER FOCUS
- To thank the Lord for the dominion He granted His children
- To affirm and actively use the dominion God has woven into my being, as one made in God's image and likeness

PRAYER GUIDES
1. Bless You, Lord, for restoring by Your Spirit my dominion authority over the works of Your hands, in the name of Jesus Christ.
2. By the power of the Holy Spirit, I recover the dominion authority granted by God at my creation, in the name of Jesus Christ.
3. O Lord, arise by Your power to destroy all evil dominion operating around me, in the name of Jesus Christ.
4. By the power of the Holy Spirit, I possess and use my dominion authority to bind and to loose, in the name of Jesus Christ.
5. By the power of the Holy Spirit, I possess and use my dominion authority to cast out every demon oppressing my life, in the name of Jesus Christ.
6. By the power of the Holy Spirit, I possess and use my dominion authority to undo the works of Satan and his agents in my life, in the name of Jesus Christ.
7. By the power of the Holy Spirit, I possess and use my dominion authority to fulfill my divine purpose, in the name of Jesus Christ.
8. By the power of the Holy Spirit, I exercise dominion over my flesh and my time, in the name of Jesus Christ. Therefore, the Lord rebuke now every demonic influence on my body, in the name of Jesus Christ.
9. Thank You, Jesus Christ, for answering my prayers. Amen.

✟ Prayers for Divine Power to Overthrow Evil Dominion

Bible Prayer Links

> *At the name of Jesus every knee should bow, of things in heaven, and things in earth, and things under the earth* (Phil. 2:10).

> *Let them be confounded and put to shame that seek after my soul: let them be turned back and brought to confusion that devise my hurt* (Ps. 35:4).

Prayer Focus
- To praise and worship the Lord
- To trust the all-powerful God in overthrowing evil dominion

Prayer Guides
1. I bless You, Lord, for Your goodness and mercy.
2. I plead the blood of Jesus Christ over myself and my environment.
3. In the name of Jesus Christ, and under the covering of His blood, I confess all personal and ancestral sins and iniquities that have given legal ground to any evil dominion in my life (list them).
4. I declare that the blood of Jesus Christ covers any and all legal ground that has empowered any evil dominion in my life and destiny, in the name of Jesus Christ.
5. By the blood of Jesus Christ, I break the power of sin and iniquity, dissolving its dominion over me, in the name of Jesus Christ.
6. By the blood of Jesus Christ and in His name, I receive my liberty today from the dominion of Satan and his hosts.
7. Spirit of addiction that has taken dominion over my soul, I bind and cast you out, in the name of Jesus Christ.
8. Spirit of sickness and disease that has taken dominion over my body, I bind and cast you out, in the name of Jesus Christ.

9. Spirit of poverty and lack that has taken dominion over my life, I bind and cast you out, in the name of Jesus Christ.

10. Spirit of confusion and disorganization that has taken dominion over my soul, I bind and cast you out, in the name of Jesus Christ.

11. Evil enchantments and assignments having dominion over my destiny, the Lord rebuke you today. Scatter, in the name of Jesus Christ.

12. Demonic powers exercising dominion over my body, soul, and spirit, I overthrow you now by the power of the Holy Spirit, in the mighty name of Jesus Christ.

13. O Lord, arise and baptize me, with the power to overthrow evil dominion now, in the name of Jesus Christ.

14. Thank You, Jesus, for answering my prayers. Amen.

✟ PRAYERS TO DETHRONE SATANIC LORDS, KINGS, AND QUEENS IN CHARGE OF EVIL DOMINION

BIBLE PRAYER LINKS

But if ye shall still do wickedly, ye shall be consumed, both ye and your king (1 Sam. 12:25).

So they hanged Haman on the gallows that he had prepared for Mordecai. Then was the king's wrath pacified (Esther 7:10).

And thou shalt smite the house of Ahab thy master, that I may avenge the blood of my servants the prophets, and the blood of all the servants of the LORD, at the hand of Jezebel. For the whole house of Ahab shall perish: and I will cut off from Ahab him that pisseth against the wall, and him that is shut up and left in Israel: And I will make the house of Ahab like the house of Jeroboam the son of Nebat, and like the house of Baasha the son of Ahijah: And the dogs shall eat Jezebel in the portion of Jezreel, and there shall be none to bury her (2 Kings 9:7-10).

So Jehu slew all that remained of the house of Ahab in Jezreel, and all his great men, and his kinsfolks, and his priests, until he left him none remaining (2 Kings 10:11).

PRAYER FOCUS
- To assert authority over all demonic authorities who exert evil dominion in my life
- To remove them from their seats of power

PRAYER GUIDES
1. I bless You, Lord, for Your right hand that is glorious in power.
2. In the name of Jesus Christ, I plead His blood over myself and my environment.
3. Father God, let the glory of divine liberty be seen on me today and be upon me forever, in the name of Jesus Christ.
4. O Lord, let the greatness of Your power manifest today against every satanic lord, king, or queen that has ever oppressed or enslaved me, in the name of Jesus Christ.
5. O Lord, by Your right hand and outstretched arm, deliver me today from cycles of failure resulting from evil dominion by such powers, in the name of Jesus Christ.
6. O Lord, arise! Stretch forth Your right hand and dash to pieces every satanic lord, king, or queen in charge of any evil dominion in my life, in the name of Jesus Christ.
7. O Lord, arise! Stretch forth Your right hand and tear to pieces all spiritual night raiders making predatory attacks on my blessings and breakthroughs, in the name of Jesus Christ.
8. O Lord arise! Send out Your arrows to scatter and destroy spiritual night caterers on assignment to serve me demonic "food" in my dreams, in the name of Jesus Christ.
9. Any satanic lord, king, or queen manifesting in any form to pollute me sexually, receive the arrows of God and perish, in the name of Jesus Christ.

10. Any marine power or agent having evil dominion over my body, your end has come today. Be destroyed by the right hand of the Lord, in the name of Jesus Christ.

11. Anything from the kingdom of darkness assigned to have dominion over my life, be paralyzed now, in the name of Jesus Christ.

12. By the greatness of the Lord's power, I command every disease or sickness having dominion over any organ of my body (mention them specifically) to wither now, in the name of Jesus Christ.

13. By the authority of the third heaven, I command every evil dominion set over my destiny to come to a perpetual end now, in the name of Jesus Christ.

14. Thank You, Jesus, for answering my prayers. Amen.

✟ Prayers for Divine Power to Shatter the Dominion of Curses

Bible Prayer Links

Come now therefore, I pray thee, curse me this people; for they are too mighty for me: peradventure I shall prevail, that we may smite them, and that I may drive them out of the land: for I wot that he whom thou blessest is blessed, and he whom thou cursest is cursed (Num. 22:6).

Reuben, thou art my firstborn, my might, and the beginning of my strength, the excellency of dignity, and the excellency of power: Unstable as water, thou shalt not excel; because thou wentest up to thy father's bed; then defiledst thou it: he went up to my couch (Gen. 49:3-4).

Prayer Focus
- To discern any evil dominion granted by curses
- To dissolve all evil dominion generated by curses

PRAYER GUIDES

1. Thank You, Lord, for shattering the dominion of curses over my life today, in Your mercy, in Jesus' name.
2. Father God, let the glory of divine liberty be seen on me today. Let it be upon me forever, in the name of Jesus Christ.
3. Father Lord, by the Holy Spirit, empower me today to scatter the dominion of curses over my life, in the name of Jesus Christ.
4. Blood of Jesus Christ, redeem me now and scatter every curse of God that is upon my life, in the name of Jesus Christ.
5. Every curse that suggests, "You shall not excel," and that holds any dominion over my life and destiny, scatter now by the blood of Jesus Christ.
6. Blood of Jesus Christ, redeem me now and scatter every curse of God and of man that has dominion over me, in the name of Jesus Christ.
7. Blood of Jesus Christ, redeem me now and scatter every curse of God and of man that is pursuing me and exerting dominion over me, in the name of Jesus Christ.
8. Foundational curses that have dominion over my life and destiny, scatter now by the blood of Jesus Christ, in His mighty name.
9. Witchcraft curses that have dominion over my life and destiny, scatter now by the blood of Jesus Christ and in His name.
10. Familiar spirit curses that have dominion over my life and destiny, scatter now by the blood of Jesus Christ, in His name.
11. Generational curses that have dominion over my life and destiny, scatter now by the blood of Jesus Christ, in His name.
12. Curses of failure and disfavor that have dominion over my life and destiny, scatter now by the blood of Jesus Christ, in His name.
13. Every blessing and benefit that I have missed as a result of the dominion of curses, be restored unto me now by the blood of Jesus Christ, in His mighty name.
14. From today, O Lord, let the blood of Jesus Christ shield my life and destiny from the dominion of any curse, in the name of Jesus Christ.

15. Any demon assigned to supervise any inherited curse (late marriage, barrenness, poverty, sickness, etc.) in my life, I hold the blood of Jesus against you, and I command you to go away from me now, in the name of Jesus Christ.
16. Any witch or wizard cursing my destiny, in the name of Jesus Christ, I send your curses back to you.
17. I loose myself from all curses, spells, jinxes, and hexes put upon my family line by any satanic agent, in the name of Jesus Christ.
18. Thank You, Jesus, for answering my prayers. Amen.

✟ PRAYERS TO BREAK EVIL CYCLES

BIBLE PRAYER LINKS

But my covenant will I establish with Isaac, which Sarah shall bear unto thee at this set time in the next year. And he left off talking with him, and God went up from Abraham (Gen. 17:21-22).

Then Eli answered and said, Go in peace: and the God of Israel grant thee thy petition that thou hast asked of him. And she said, Let thine handmaid find grace in thy sight. So the woman went her way, and did eat, and her countenance was no more sad. And they rose up in the morning early, and worshipped before the LORD, and returned, and came to their house to Ramah: and Elkanah knew Hannah his wife; and the LORD remembered her. Wherefore it came to pass, when the time was come about after Hannah had conceived, that she bare a son, and called his name Samuel, saying, Because I have asked him of the LORD (1 Sam. 1:17-20).

PRAYER FOCUS
- To praise and worship the Lord
- To break all evil cycles and release cycles of God's goodness

PRAYER GUIDES

1. Father Lord, I praise You as you sit upon the circle of the earth to do wonders (see Isa. 40:22).

2. Lord, as You sit upon the circle of the earth, arise and break evil cycles in my life today, in the name of Jesus Christ.

3. Lord, as You sit upon the circle of the earth, arise and destroy cycles of problems that have been assigned to my life and destiny, in the name of Jesus Christ.

4. O Lord, break any cycles of hardship in my life now, in the name of Jesus Christ.

5. O Lord, break any cycles of failure in my life (my marital destiny, career, etc.), in the name of Jesus Christ.

6. Any demonic programming assigned to impose evil cycles in my life, the Lord rebuke you. Be cut off from me now, in the name of Jesus Christ.

7. Any demonic assignment programmed to impose evil cycles in my life (my productivity, progress, etc.), the Lord rebuke you. Be cut off from me now, in the name of Jesus Christ.

8. Every daily, weekly, monthly, yearly cycle of pain and sorrow in my life, the Lord rebuke you. Break now, in the name of Jesus Christ.

9. O God of time and season, arise and put a perpetual end to any evil cycle in my life, in the name of Jesus Christ.

10. Powers enforcing evil cycles in my life, the Lord rebuke you. Loose your grip now, in the name of Jesus Christ.

11. By the power of the Holy Spirit, I receive the dominion authority to break evil cycles in my life and destiny, in the name of Jesus Christ.

12. Spirit of hard labor that yields no reward, depart from me now, in the name of Jesus Christ.

13. Thank You, Jesus, for answering my prayers. Amen.

Endnote

1. *American Heritage® Dictionary of the English Language, 5th Edition*, 2011, s.v. "dominion," accessed February 12, 2016, http://www.thefreedictionary.com/dominion.

7

The Power of Death

Those who purpose to destroy the means of the wicked must have the knowledge and understanding of death's domineering power and the ways in which it is used.

> *Forasmuch then as the children are partakers of flesh and blood, he also himself likewise took part of the same; **that through death he might destroy him that had the power of death, that is, the devil*** (Heb. 2:14).

Herein lies a great revelation by the Holy Spirit through the writer of Hebrews: Satan has the power of death. It is clear that Satan has the means to kill. Of all the power that Satan possesses, the power of death is one of the foremost methods by which he afflicts and destroys the righteous and comes against all that belongs to them. It is important to point it out here that the devil can use the power of death on things living or non-living, whether visible or invisible.

When the power of death is exerted over lives, possessions, and circumstances, its manifestations vary. *Believers must be able to recognize these manifestations promptly,* in order to counter the power behind the manifestations with the Word of God and prayer, before it is too late.

The psalmist says that the Lord looks down from heaven "to loose those that are appointed to death" (Ps. 102:20). The Word of God reveals here that Satan can prepare some people for death. In

Job chapters 1 and 2, we see how the devil exerted the power of death over Job, his loved ones, and all that belonged to him. Satan delegated that power to one of his generals named Leviathan (see Job 41). Leviathan operates much like a python who has strong teeth to hold his prey, and then kills the prey by squeezing. Notice that the victim is first made weak and unconscious with a blow to the head. The python then coils itself around the prey and applies great pressure, suffocating the victim, but not breaking any bones. Then the python swallows it whole.

The python demon, Leviathan, operates similarly in the realm of the spirit. Leviathan was assigned to administer death to Job. The instruments of death were boils, which tormented him and compromised his skin, the body's largest organ. The power of death was exerted upon Job's children, all of whom were killed. The power of death was also unleashed against Job's properties, wreaking great destruction. (See my book, Power and Prayers to Neutralize Leviathan, available at Amazon.com.)

You can see from Job's trial that the power of death can operate against anything God has blessed you with, including life itself. With this understanding, you can rise up in warfare and destroy the power of death.

Satan's Ways with the Power of Death

Let's lay a foundation for this study with two simple, but realistic statements:
1. Death is an agent of the devil.
2. Because of Jesus' death and resurrection, the power of death that Satan possesses is only to be exerted over the ungodly. A godly person who is assailed by the power of death must use the power and authority delegated by Christ Jesus to break it.

Many people are of the opinion that the devil cannot kill. The Bible, however, makes clear that the devil has the power to kill. Those who refute this truth or claim not to believe it are operating at the highest level of ignorance, and have willfully exposed themselves to added risk.

Some who believe the devil can kill unfortunately have limited knowledge as to the extent of his power and how he uses it. Satan uses the power of death against people, bodily organs, relationships, businesses, finances, possessions, glory, souls, the conscience, the mind, progress, marriages, and so on.

Some years ago, I witnessed Satan's effort to take the life of a brother who was very dear to me. Satan's all-out manner of attack shocked me and other ministers. The first thing I noticed was that Satan told this man to reveal the killer affliction to no one, not even his pastor. Satan told him to fight it alone and he would overcome. This continued until the situation was almost out of control. I did not know how serious it was until the Holy Spirit alerted us to the fact that Satan was exerting his power of death over the man.

My second observation was that Satan was using medical personnel to quicken his agenda. Certain prescriptions worked adversely and came within days of killing him. Thankfully, the problems were discovered and the drugs were stopped. The third observation was that the man's organs were being killed, one by one. The attack was deadly serious.

We began praying around the clock. This promise from the Word of God was fulfilled in our brother's life: "I will ransom them from the power of the grave; I will redeem them from death: O death, I will be thy plagues; O grave, I will be thy destruction: repentance shall be hid from mine eyes" (Hosea 13:14). Praise the Lord!

Without knowledge and understanding such stories tend to end badly. The Bible notes ways in which Satan can use the power of death to attack lives, possessions, and circumstances. We will now explore some of them.

Waves of Death

Waves of death can be thought of as restless feelings of disappointment and insecurity that can lead to death. These feelings create constant fear and allow paralysis to set in.

> *When the waves of death compassed me, the floods of ungodly men made me afraid* (2 Sam. 22:5).

There arose a great storm of wind, and the waves beat into the ship, so that it was now full (Mark 4:37).

He maketh the storm a calm, so that the waves thereof are still (Ps. 107:29).

Satan can generate waves of death against a person. The power and authority of God still them.

How to Nullify Waves of Death

- Get saved, so that you are genuinely born again.
- Invite Jesus into the "boat" of your life (see Matt. 14:31-32).
- Rebuke the waves of death, in the name of Jesus (see Matt. 8:26).
- Stand in the unyielding faith that God is able (see Matt. 14:31).
- Command the waves of death to be still, in the name of Jesus Christ.

Snares of Death

A snare is a trap. Satan is adept at using many types of snares. Ask the Father to open your spiritual eyes to these snares so that you will not be tempted or deceived by any of them. Be aware that certain "attractive" situations are deadly snares by which the devil is able to program you to embrace abominable practices. This is essentially being programmed into the snares of death.

For by means of a whorish woman a man is brought to a piece of bread: and the adulteress will hunt for the precious life (Prov. 6:26).

How to Overcome the Snares of Death

Those who reverently fear the Lord can avoid and/or be released from the snares of death.

The fear of the LORD is a fountain of life, to depart from the snares of death (Prov. 14:27).

The law of the wise is a fountain of life, to depart from the snares of death (Prov. 13:14).

The sorrows of hell compassed me about; the snares of death prevented me; in my distress I called upon the LORD, and cried to my God: and he did hear my voice out of his temple, and my cry did enter into his ears (2 Sam. 22:6-7).

To overcome the enemy's snares:
- Get saved, so that you are genuinely born again.
- Walk in the fear of the Lord.
- Call upon the name of the Lord.

The Shadow of Death

The shadow of death is the shade created by a demon called Death. You could describe it as an evil darkness brought about by Death. When it is cast upon a person, place, or thing, the shadow of death will ultimately cause affliction and/or death. Typically, it brings stagnation before killing its victim through frustration. The shadow of death is the demonic power that seeks to sustain disease and sickness. It must be removed before it kills or destroys.

Let darkness and the shadow of death stain it; let a cloud dwell upon it [the day I was born]; *let the blackness of the day terrify it* (Job 3:5).

When projected by Satan or his associates, the shadow of death stains. By this I mean that it brings shame upon a person's character or reputation._It obscures, casts off authentic identity, and prevents one from shining. The shadow of death brings affliction and bondage:

Such as sit in darkness and in the shadow of death,
being bound in affliction and iron (Ps. 107:10).

There are numerous, diverse physical manifestations of the shadow of death. The following are very common:

- Hard labor
- Rejection
- Abandonment

The shadow of death troubles and tries people. But there are divine solutions!

He [the Lord] *discovereth deep things out of dark-*
ness, and bringeth out to light the shadow of death
(Job 12:22).

He brought them out of darkness and the shadow of
death, and brake their bands in sunder (Ps. 107:14).

Yea, though I walk through the valley of the shadow
of death, I will fear no evil: for thou art with me; thy
rod and thy staff they comfort me (Ps. 23:4).

A cry to the Lord ushers in His visitation, which causes deliverance and the breaking asunder of all bondages. Praise the Lord!

How to Nullify the Shadow of Death

- Command the light of God to shine upon it. The light of God is the divine power that knocks out the shadow of death. The prayer warrior who prays that the light of God will come against the shadow of death will also see deliverance and healing manifested, to the glory of God. The light of God is the light of liberty. It sets the captive free. This was the light that freed the apostle Peter from Herod's prison.

The people that walked in darkness have seen a great light: they that dwell in the land of the shadow of death, upon them hath the light shined (Isa. 9:2).

The people which sat in darkness saw great light; and to them which sat in the region and shadow of death light is sprung up (Matt. 4:16).

To give light to them that sit in darkness and in the shadow of death, to guide our feet into the way of peace (Luke 1:79).

■ Cry out to the Lord. Psalms 107:13-14 reveals that a persistent cry to the Lord will cause Him to bring a person out of the shadow of death. For example, if the shadow of death brings a manifestation of inexplicable sickness over a city, the Lord will make a way of escape for the person who cries out to him.

Then they cried unto the LORD in their trouble, and he saved them out of their distresses. He brought them out of darkness and the shadow of death, and broke their bands in sunder (Psa. 107:13-14).

■ Seek the help of a seasoned deliverance minister.

Gates of Death or Hell

Scripture speaks of the gates of death or hell (see Job 38:17; Ps. 9:13; 107:18). Gates of death give entry to the realm of the dead. Wicked power can draw people to these gates through deception and manipulation. When someone is engaged in spiritual warfare against the powers of darkness, he or she is said to be at the gates of death.

Have the gates of death been opened [revealed] unto thee? or hast thou seen the doors of the shadow of death? (Job 38:17).

140

The writing of Hezekiah king of Judah, when he had been sick, and was recovered of his sickness: I said in the cutting off of my days, I shall go to the gates of the grave: I am deprived of the residue of my years (Isa. 38:9-10).

Have mercy upon me, O LORD; consider my trouble which I suffer of them that hate me, thou that liftest [raised] me up from the gates of death: that I may show forth all thy praise in the gates of the daughter of Zion: I will rejoice in thy salvation (Ps. 9:13-14).

God's power is far greater than the power of the enemy. There is a divine solution for every demonic ploy. Jesus promised victory, and He will deliver according to His words:

I say also unto thee, That thou art Peter, and upon this rock I will build my church; and the gates of hell shall not prevail against it (Matt. 16:18).

How to Nullify the Gates of Death or Hell

- Get saved, so that you are genuinely born again.
- Use the Word of the Lord, saying, "The gates of hell shall not prevail!" (See Matthew 16:18.)
- Pray to be lifted up from the gates of death (see Ps. 9:13, above).
- Use the power of praise (see Ps. 9:14).

Instruments of Death

The devil can program instruments of death to operate in someone's life. They come in various forms, including hypertension, high blood pressure, suicide, and cancer, all of which are instruments of death to the physical body. The devil can also use the power of water, wind, or fire as instruments of death.

He hath also prepared for him the instruments of death; he ordaineth his arrows against the persecutors (Ps. 7:13).

How to Nullify Instruments of Death

- Call out to the Lord for deliverance from death.
- Seek the help of a seasoned deliverance minister.

The most effective way to deal with the instruments of death used by Satan and his associates is to cast the rebuke of the Lord against them.

For he hath looked down from the height of his sanctuary; from heaven did the LORD behold the earth; to hear the groaning of the prisoner; to loose those that are appointed to death (Ps. 102:19-20).

Terrors—The Dread of Death

Dread is a deep, overwhelming sense of foreboding that robs life of all joy. The dread of death weighs heavily, is emotionally incapacitating, and can accelerate physical death.

My heart is sore pained within me: and the terrors of death are fallen upon me (Ps. 55:4).

The terrors of death generate fear.

David said unto all his servants that were with him at Jerusalem, Arise, and let us flee; for we shall not else escape from Absalom: make speed to depart, lest he overtake us suddenly, and bring evil upon us, and smite the city with the edge of the sword (2 Sam. 15:14).

Fearfulness and trembling are come upon me, and horror hath overwhelmed me (Ps. 55:5).

How to Nullify Terrors

- Cast away fear from your mind. Be bold in the Lord.
- Seek the help of a seasoned deliverance minister.

God hath not given us the spirit of fear; but of power, and of love, and of a sound mind (2 Tim. 1:7).

The Ways of Death

The ways of death can be chosen through disobedience. Jonah disobeyed God and chose to go to Tarshish instead of Nineveh. He chose the way of death (see Jon. 1:1-3). The devil can also program a person to follow the way of death by rejecting good and godly counsel. Anyone involved with addiction (drug, sex, alcohol, pornography, etc.) is choosing the way of death.

Unto this people thou shalt say, Thus saith the LORD; Behold, I set before you the way of life, and the way of death (Jer. 21:8).

There is a way which seemeth right unto a man, but the end thereof are the ways of death (Prov. 14:12).

The Lord never leaves us without a way of escape, even from the ways of death:

To give light to them that sit in darkness and in the shadow of death, to guide our feet into the way of peace (Luke 1:79).

The way of life is above to the wise, that he may depart from hell beneath (Prov. 15:24).

In the way of righteousness is life; and in the pathway thereof there is no death (Prov. 12:28).

How to Nullify the Ways of Death

- Obedience—simple, consistent obedience renders the ways of death null and void.
- Those who discover that they are in the way of death can save their lives by seeking help from seasoned deliverance ministers.

"Symptoms" of the Power of Death

As was true in the story of my friend who was nearly destroyed by the power of death, there can be many signs that the power of death is attacking a life, family, or community. The following are some of the most common:

1. **Continual failures**

   When a person's destiny is under the yoke of the power of death, he or she experiences continual failures. It's a "nothing ever works for me" kind of life, full of disappointments and rejection, The person frequently dreams about friends and loved ones who have died.

2. **Ongoing memory loss**

   A person whose soul is under the yoke of the power of death can experience ongoing memory loss. The soul consists of the mind, will, and emotions. When the power of death operates successfully, the person never realizes his or her divine potential.

Behold, the eye of the LORD is upon them that fear him, upon them that hope in his mercy; to deliver their soul from death, and to keep them alive in famine (Ps. 33:18-19).

3. **Difficulty in marriage**
    A marriage affected by the power of death can experience constant arguments, disagreements, threats of divorce, mutual hatred, bad dreams, and other negative effects.

4. **Stifled marital prospects**
    For someone whose marital destiny is under the yoke of the power of death, there can be a delay in marriage, a history of rejection, and other negative effects.

5. **Aborted breakthroughs**
    A person under the yoke of the power of death finds it difficult to make progress and experiences consistent failures when approaching the edge of a breakthrough.

6. **Underachievement**
    A glory (an individual's personal excellency or honor; the divine endowment that is supposed to distinguish a person) that is under the yoke of the power of death will experience dullness in life, is unable to shine no matter the effort. Such a person dreams of greatness that never materializes, and become a non-entity, even though everybody realizes that he or she should be a star.

7. **Aborted ventures**
    A career affected by the power of death will experience the "almost there" syndrome marked by incomplete efforts, diversions, and the abandonment of worthy goals.

8. **Barrenness**
    A womb under the yoke of the power of death experiences barrenness and irregular cycles. Such women dream often of being pregnant and of giving birth.

The power of death is a fierce opponent, but prayer is the believer's "instrument of life."

✝ Prayers to Disable the Power of Death

Bible Prayer Link

I shall not die, but live, and declare the works of the LORD (Ps. 118:17).

Prayer Focus
- To address symptoms of the power of death
- To cancel all assignments and neutralize all functions of the power and instruments of death

Prayer Guides
1. Father Lord, I thank You for undoing the works of the devil in my life.
2. Every messenger of death sent to destroy me and my goods, be routed by confusion, in the name of Jesus Christ.
3. Instruments of death assigned to waste my destiny, be destroyed by Holy Ghost fire, in the name of Jesus Christ.
4. Every instrument of death fashioned against me and my destiny from birth, be roasted by fire, in the name of Jesus Christ.
5. Power of death assigned to wreck my destiny, be neutralized by the blood of Jesus Christ.
6. Lord Jesus, let Your glory overshadow and swallow the shadow of death projected over my glory and life.
7. Gates of death erected to destroy God's plan for my life, burn to ashes in the fire of Almighty God, in the name of Jesus Christ.
8. Lord, break the power of death assigned over my destiny, in the name of Jesus Christ.
9. Holy Spirit, release my destiny from the grip of the power of death, in the name of Jesus Christ (see 1 Pet. 3:18).
10. Waves of death coming against my destiny, be neutralized by the blood of Jesus Christ.
11. The snares of death programmed against my life shall not prosper, in the name of Jesus Christ.

12. Spirit of death sitting on my glory, the Lord rebuke you, in the name of Jesus Christ.
13. Thank You, Jesus Christ, for answering my prayers. Amen.

✝ PRAYERS TO REVOKE THE DOMINION OF THE SPIRIT OF DEATH

BIBLE PRAYER LINK

Knowing that Christ being raised from the dead dieth no more; death hath no more dominion over him (Rom. 6:9).

PRAYER FOCUS
- To come out of subjection to the power of death
- To overthrow the power of death and its dominion

PRAYER GUIDES
1. Father Lord, I thank You for Your faithfulness, in the name of Jesus Christ.
2. I come against and overcome any source or power of evil dominion wielding the power of death against me, in the name of Jesus Christ.
3. My soul, come out of the prison of evil dominion exercising the power of death, in the name of Jesus Christ.
4. Any power assigned by the devil to exert evil dominion over me, or subject me to failure and any form of death, be paralyzed, in the name of Jesus Christ.
5. Any power exerting evil dominion to take over my life (destiny, brain, well-being, etc.), be paralyzed, in the name of Jesus Christ.
6. I refuse to yield dominion to any spirit of addiction, in the name of Jesus Christ.
7. Spirit(s) of evil dominion assigned to exert the power of death by diverting my destiny, be paralyzed, in the name of Jesus Christ.
8. In the name of Jesus Christ and by the power in His blood, I declare that I am an overcomer.

9. Thank You, Jesus, for answering my prayers. Amen.

✠ Prayers for Rescue from the Power of the Grave

Bible Prayer Links

> *Forasmuch then as the children are partakers of flesh and blood, he also himself likewise took part of the same; that through death he might destroy him that had the power of death, that is, the devil* (Heb. 2:14).

> *I will ransom them from the power of the grave; I will redeem them from death: O death, I will be thy plagues; O grave, I will be thy destruction: repentance shall be hid from mine eyes* (Hosea 13:14).

> *But God will redeem my soul from the power of the grave: for he shall receive me. Selah* (Ps. 49:15).

Prayer Focus
- To resist all incursions of death and the power of the grave
- To vanquish the spirit of death and the power of the grave

Prayer Guides
1. Thank You, Jesus Christ, for giving me the victory in this prayer battle.
2. Father God, let the glory of divine liberty be seen on me today and forever, in the name of Jesus Christ.
3. Spirit of the grave sent forth to execute wickedness in my life and family, the Lord rebuke you. Go back and afflict your sender, in the name of Jesus Christ.
4. Graveyard spirit sent to harm me and stagnate my progress, the Lord rebuke you. Go back and afflict your sender, in the name of Jesus Christ.
5. Power of the grave assigned to destroy and kill good things in my life and family, the Lord rebuke you. Depart from me now, in the name of Jesus Christ.

6. Power of the grave assigned to waste my resources and swallow my money, the Lord rebuke you. Be paralyzed now. Devourers, be swallowed up now, in the name of Jesus Christ (see Prov. 1:12).

7. Holy Ghost fire, swallow up the spirit of death that is stealing, killing, and destroying within my life and family, in the name of Jesus Christ.

8. Blood of Jesus Christ, break every yoke established over any organ of my body by the power of the grave, in the name of Jesus Christ.

9. O Lord, by the power of the Holy Spirit, neutralize all activities of the spirit of the grave in my life and family, in the name of Jesus Christ.

10. Holy Spirit, release my life and destiny from the grip of the power of death, in the name of Jesus Christ who died in my place (see 1 Pet. 3:18).

11. Foul spirit of death sitting on my glory and the glory of my family, the Lord rebuke you. Be unseated now, in the name of Jesus Christ.

12. Waves of death blowing against my life and destiny, be diverted from me now, by the blood of the Lord Jesus Christ.

13. Every messenger of death sent to destroy me, my family, and my goods, be blinded, in the name of Jesus Christ.

14. Instruments of death assigned to waste my life or any organ of my body, be destroyed by Holy Ghost fire, in the name of Jesus Christ.

15. Power of death assigned to wreck my life and destiny, be neutralized by the blood of Jesus Christ.

16. Lord Jesus Christ, let Your glory overshadow and swallow the shadow of death projected over my glory and the glory of my family, in the name of Jesus Christ.

17. Gates of death erected to hinder the plan of God for my life and family, burn to ashes in the fire of God, in the name of Jesus Christ.

18. Thank You, Jesus Christ, for answering my prayers. Amen.

✟ PRAYERS FOR THE SWORD OF THE LORD TO ARISE AND KILL THE HINDERING, SUFFOCATING PYTHON

BIBLE PRAYER LINK

In that day the Lord with his sore and great and strong sword shall punish leviathan the piercing serpent, even leviathan that crooked serpent; and he shall slay the dragon that is in the sea (Isa. 27:1).

PRAYER FOCUS
- To arrest the power of the suffocating python in every area of my life

PRAYER GUIDES
1. I bless the Lord who kills every python of hindrance!
2. I plead the blood of Christ over myself and my environment.
3. Father Lord, let the glory of divine liberty be seen on me today and forever, in the name of Jesus Christ.
4. Thank You, Jesus, for by Your sword You will deliver me from the hold of the python demon.
5. O sword of the Lord, arise now and kill every python of hindrance that is operating against my life and destiny, in the name of Jesus Christ.
6. Every python of hindrance hiding in a hole to afflict my life and destiny, be slain now by the sword of the Lord, in the name of Jesus Christ.
7. Every egg laid by the python of hindrance, be crushed to death with the rod of God, in the name of Jesus Christ.
8. Python demon programmed into my body to hinder my spiritual growth, come out of me now and enter no more, in the name of Jesus Christ.
9. Python demon programmed into my hand to afflict my labor, the Lord rebuke you. Come out now and enter no more, in the name of Jesus Christ.

10. Python demon programmed into my legs to afflict my divine positioning, the Lord rebuke you. Come out now and enter no more, in the name of Jesus Christ.

11. Every python demon delegated to attack me at every point of my breakthrough, the Lord rebuke you. Die by the sword of the Lord, in the name of Jesus Christ.

12. Every python demon coiling itself around me to suffocate me, receive the judgment of death by the sword of the Lord, in the name of Jesus Christ.

13. Every python demon that is applying evil pressure upon my life, perish by the sword of the Lord, in the name of Jesus Christ.

14. Every python demon programmed to bite and hold me captive, the Lord rebuke you. Be killed by the sword of the Lord, in the name of Jesus Christ.

15. Every python demon on assignment to choke off my benefits and breakthroughs, the Lord rebuke you. Be killed by the sword of the Lord, in the name of Jesus Christ.

16. Every python-demon-possessed personality warring against my life and glory, the Lord rebuke you. Die now by the sword of the Lord, in the name of Jesus Christ.

17. Every python demon manifesting as a familiar spirit to pollute and hinder my prosperity, the Lord rebuke you. Die by the sword of the Lord, in the name of Jesus Christ.

18. As I drink the blood of Jesus Christ, let the python demon's poison be neutralized, in the name of Jesus Christ (see John 6:53-56).

19. Let the blood of Jesus Christ be transfused into my body now and flush out the eggs of the python demon, in the name of Jesus Christ.

20. Wicked spirit from the water assigned to trouble my life, your time is over. Be slain now by the sword of the Lord, in the name of Jesus Christ.

21. O Lord, let Your sword come against the python demon that is oppressing my life. Slay him, in the name of Jesus Christ.

22. Blood of Jesus Christ, scatter every cycle of attack coming from the python demon, in the name of Jesus Christ.

23. *Lay your hands upon your stomach and pray the following:*
24. Holy Ghost fire, enter into my stomach (womb) and kill every python demon inhabiting it, in the name of Jesus Christ.
25. Anything in my life that is cooperating with the python demon, die, in the name of Jesus Christ.
26. Thank You, Jesus Christ, for defeating the purposes of the python demon in my life. Amen.

✠ PRAYERS TO CRUSH THE HEADS OF TERRITORIAL SERPENTS AND SCORPIONS

Territorial serpents and scorpions are demons operating in localities such as cities, counties, states, or countries. They have spiritual venom that brings affliction (sickness, poverty, and death) when their victims are stung.

BIBLE PRAYER LINKS

Thou, son of man, be not afraid of them, neither be afraid of their words, though briers and thorns be with thee, and thou dost dwell among scorpions: be not afraid of their words, nor be dismayed at their looks, though they be a rebellious house (Ezek. 2:6).

Behold, I give unto you power to tread on serpents and scorpions, and over all the power of the enemy: and nothing shall by any means hurt you (Luke 10:19).

PRAYER FOCUS
- To neutralize the power of all spiritual serpents and scorpions
- To reverse and restore all damages done by their spiritual poison

PRAYER GUIDES
1. Father Lord, I thank and bless You for not giving me as prey to the teeth of the enemy, in the name of Jesus Christ (see Ps. 124:6).

2. Father Lord, let the glory of divine liberty be seen on me today, and be upon me forever, in the name of Jesus Christ.

3. O Lord, release Your thunder now to destroy the stronghold of the serpent and scorpion afflicting me in my current environment, in the name of Jesus Christ.

4. Let the rod of God locate and crush the heads of household serpents and scorpions on evil assignments against me and my household, in the name of Jesus Christ.

5. Let the rod of God locate and crush the heads of the territorial serpents and scorpions on evil assignments against me and my household, in the name of Jesus Christ.

6. O Lord, release Your thunder to destroy the stronghold of the serpent and scorpion afflicting my household, in the name of Jesus Christ.

7. O Lord, bring to desolation the habitation of the serpent and the scorpion in my household, in the name of Jesus Christ.

8. Let the thunder and fire of God come against all the secret places of household serpents and scorpions. Consume them, in the name of Jesus Christ.

9. Let the blood of Jesus Christ nullify all legal grounds from which household serpents and scorpions are afflicting my household, in the name of Jesus Christ.

10. O Lord, in the name of Jesus Christ, arise and crush the powers and spirits who attack me in my dreams, taking the forms of snakes and scorpions.

11. As I drink the blood of Jesus Christ now, I vomit out all poison and venom of the serpent and scorpion now circulating in my body, in the name of Jesus Christ (see John 6:53-56).

12. All serpent and scorpion pollution that is affecting my health, be flushed out of my system now by the blood of Jesus Christ.

13. Let the sting of the serpent and scorpion affecting my finances and prosperity be neutralized now, by the blood of Jesus Christ.

14. Let the good things that have been paralyzed by the poison of the household serpents and scorpions receive the blood of Jesus Christ now and be made whole, in the name of Jesus Christ.

15. Let all activity of any serpents and scorpions operating in any area of my life be stilled, in the name of Jesus Christ.
16. In the name of Jesus Christ, let no serpent or scorpion trouble me, for I bear in my body the blood of Jesus Christ, the Lamb of God.
17. Thank You, Jesus Christ, for answering my prayers. Amen.

✝ PRAYERS TO DEFEAT THE PURPOSES OF WITCHCRAFT

BIBLE PRAYER LINK

Woe to the bloody city! It is all full of lies and robbery; the prey departeth not; the noise of a whip, and the noise of the rattling of the wheels, and of the pransing horses, and of the jumping chariots. The horseman lifteth up both the bright sword and the glittering spear: and there is a multitude of slain, and a great number of carcases; and there is none end of their corpses; they stumble upon their corpses: because of the multitude of the whoredoms of the wellfavoured harlot, the mistress of witchcrafts, that selleth nations through her whoredoms, and families through her witchcrafts. Behold, I am against thee, saith the LORD of hosts; And I will discover thy skirts upon thy face, and I will shew the nations thy nakedness, and the kingdoms thy shame (Nah. 3:1-5).

PRAYER FOCUS
- To expose all witchcraft against me
- To dismantle and disempower all witchcraft against me

PRAYER POINTS
1. Lord, I thank You for the power in the blood of Your Son Jesus Christ that saves me, heals me, and delivers me from the power of witchcraft, in the name of Jesus Christ.
2. All witchcraft power pursing my life, destiny, and well-being, I command you to die, in the name of Jesus Christ.

3. All wickedness and witchcraft power assigned to my life, destiny, finances, family, children, peace of mind, and blessings, be neutralized now by the blood of Jesus Christ.

4. Lord, expose now every form of witchcraft that is operating around me, in the name of Jesus Christ.

5. Witchcraft power on assignment against my life and destiny, the Lord rebuke you. I command you to die, in the name of Jesus Christ.

6. All witchcraft operating from my foundation, the Lord rebuke you, in the name of Jesus Christ.

7. Lord, let all "friendly" powers of witchcraft operating around me be exposed and disgraced, in the name of Jesus Christ.

8. Blood of Jesus Christ, remove every mark of witchcraft upon my life, soul, body, spirit, and destiny, in the name of Jesus Christ.

9. Every enemy disguising itself as a friend to harm me, be exposed now, by Holy Ghost fire, in the name of Jesus Christ.

10. Demonic powers operating in this environment to hinder me, receive the judgment of God, in the name of Jesus Christ.

11. Every witchcraft altar established against me, catch fire and burn to ashes, in the name of Jesus Christ.

12. Every witchcraft power generating demons against me, be visited by the thunder of God and perish, in the name of Jesus Christ.

13. Blood of Jesus Christ, come upon me now and shield me from every attack of witchcraft, in the name of Jesus Christ.

14. Every stubborn obstacle assigned to make me complain about my God, the Lord rebuke you. Give way, now, in the name of Jesus Christ.

15. Anything in my life that is cooperating with financial loss, I command you to vanish, in the name of Jesus Christ.

16. Lord, You are the God of signs and wonders. Let them begin in my life now, in the name of Jesus Christ.

✠ Prayers Pronouncing Judgment on Satanic Manifestations

Bible Prayer Links

How many are the days of thy servant? when wilt thou execute judgment on them that persecute me? (Ps. 119:84).

Happy is he that hath the God of Jacob for his help, whose hope is in the LORD his God: which made heaven, and earth, the sea, and all that therein is: which keepeth truth for ever: which executeth judgment for the oppressed: which giveth food to the hungry. The LORD looseth the prisoners (Ps. 146:5-7).

Prayer Focus
- To loose the hold of satanic power and defeat all attacks
- To call satanic agents to account and pronounce judgment against them

Prayer Guides
1. Lord Jesus, I thank You for making me a king/queen to decree divine sentence on satanic manifestations in my life.
2. O Lord, in Your loving-kindness and mercy, execute the judgment of instant death upon all diseases and infirmities persecuting my body. Make me whole today, in the name of Jesus.
3. O Lord, in Your loving-kindness and mercy, execute Your great judgments on demonic powers holding me (my body, glory, marital destiny, etc.) captive. Set me free today, in the name of Jesus.
4. I pronounce the divine sentence of total destruction on the powers hindering my divine purpose in life, in the name of Jesus.
5. I pronounce the divine sentence of complete disintegration on demonic plantings in my soul and body, in the name of Jesus.

156

6. Let the divine power that set the Israelites free from Egyptian bondage arise now and persecute demonic persecutors of my divine purpose and glory, in the name of Jesus.

7. Any captivity assigned against my glory, loose your hold and scatter, in the name of Jesus.

8. Every spiritual house of bondage holding my life and destiny captive, be consumed now in the fire of God, in the name of Jesus.

9. Father Lord, smite now with blindness and bring to confusion all demonic powers seeking to arrest my destiny and progress, in the name of Jesus.

10. By the Word of God which says that those who demonically strive with me shall perish, I command all wickedness that is striving with my victory, progress, peace, and joy to perish now, in the name of Jesus (see Isa. 41:11).

11. By the Word of God which says that all who are incensed against me shall be confounded, I decree that all demonic powers who are incensed against my glory (my marriage, etc.) be confounded and put to shame, in the name of Jesus (see Isa. 45:24).

12. Satan, by the blood of the Lamb of God, I overthrow your activities in my life and destiny, in the name of Jesus.

13. Thank You, Lord, for answering my prayers. Amen.

8

Evil Assignments and Projections—Part 1

Those who plan to destroy the means of the wicked must have knowledge and understanding of evil assignments and projections. This is part of the effectual working of God's Word in the believer's life.

> *For this cause also thank we God without ceasing, because, when ye received the word of God which ye heard of us, ye received it not as the word of men, but as it is in truth, the word of God, which effectually worketh also in you that believe* (1 Thess. 2:13).

The operation of Satan and other demonic entities (including human agents) against a person is not solely transacted within the body. Much of it occurs outside the physical body, to influence, restrict, divert, or afflict. Although our topic involves satanic operations, we must consider the larger context of the believer's life, as expressed in the following statements:

1. **We serve a God of purpose. His purpose for each of our lives is precisely what the enemy is after.**
   Notice what Jesus told Saul on the road to Damascus:

> *Rise, and stand upon thy feet: for I have appeared unto thee for this purpose, to make thee a minister*

and a witness both of these things which thou hast seen, and of those things in the which I will appear unto thee (Acts 26:16).

Saul's conversion was not random. God made Saul *Paul* for a purpose, just as the Son of God became Jesus the Man for a purpose:

He that committeth sin is of the devil; for the devil sin-neth from the beginning. For this purpose the Son of God was manifested, that he might destroy the works of the devil (1 John 3:8).

Jesus came in the flesh to destroy the works of the devil. His mission was costly, but worthwhile.

We know that all things work together for good to them that love God, to them who are the called according to his purpose (Rom. 8:28).

2. **Certain information about you is available to Satan. Like a spy, he uses it to plan attacks in advance, even years ahead of time. We see this in regard to Jesus' birth.**

When Jesus was born in Bethlehem of Judea in the days of Herod the king, behold, there came wise men from the east to Jerusalem, saying, Where is he that is born King of the Jews? for we have seen his star in the east, and are come to worship him (Matt. 2:1-2).

The so-called wise men recognized Jesus' birth through His star. With this information available, they chose to do good. When Herod laid hold of it, he planned to kill Jesus.

3. **Every believer is under one evil assignment and projection or another. As soon as a person is born again, he or**

she is marked for attack. **The kinds of assignments and projections depend upon the following factors:**

- The person's divine purpose on this earth
- Whether the Lord has called the person to affect the environment in which he or she was born (which means contending against violent opposition)
- The person's personality type, including attitudes the enemy can exploit
- The person's weaknesses (food, sleep, pride, anger, etc.)
- The person's relationship with God
- Whether the person chooses to obey God (including His will for the person's life)

  The obedient believer is divinely shielded; God turns evil assignments and projections to divine accomplishments. Notice what Joseph said to his brothers: "As for you, ye thought evil against me; but God meant it unto good, to bring to pass, as it is this day, to save much people alive" (Gen. 50:20).

- Whether or not the believer yields to Satan's deceptions (this impacts spiritual conflict and its degree)

4. **Assignments and projections are packaged and implemented during certain times and seasons.**

   There is a time to prepare and a time to execute. Job 1:6 speaks of a day; Job 1:13 mentions another day. An evil assignment or projection that is still in the preparation stage can be stopped or neutralized by the prayerful believer who is conscious of and understands the evil agenda behind it.

5. **Not all evil assignments and projections are the result of sin; some exist because of who you are, specifically, who the Lord created you to be on this earth.**

   This is seen in the lives of Moses, Joseph, and others. Because God's plan for their lives was crucial to significant environments, they experienced significant opposition.

The Fundamentals of Assignment and Projection

With our context in mind, what does the word *assign* mean in practical terms?

- To assign means to mark someone or something for a specific purpose. The markings, signs, or symbols are recognized and understood by those called to complete the assignment. Evil assignments mark "targets" for attack.
- To assign is to designate or allocate for a specific purpose. It can also mean to be appointed. Evil assignments appoint the wicked to perform designated tasks.
- To assign can also mean to place a burden upon someone. Evil assignments create heavy loads for those who are targeted, often constricting and restricting them.

Evil markings are spiritual, but easily recognizable by agents of darkness. Familiar spirits, witches, and other agents recognize markings, which include spells, curses, jinxes, and other forms of wickedness (hatred, chronic failure, or disfavor) and evil influence. Curses, spells, and jinxes can be affixed to people and places; hatred, failure, and disfavor are typically affixed to people.

What exactly are projections? Consider the physical parallel of movie projection, by which images are transmitted from one place to another (such as a movie screen). To project can mean

- to throw something forward, the way a hunter throws a spear;
- to send forth, dispatch, or transmit, as with radio waves;
- to influence, in the sense of controlling someone or something remotely, much as a television viewer controls channels, volume, etc. from the comfort of the sofa.

Evil projections are designed to accomplish specific tasks involving specific people in specific places at specific times. Knowing *what* can be projected is important.

- Evil enchantments can be projected.
- Evil words or pronouncements can be projected.
- Evil arrows (confusion, fear, doubt, wrong thoughts, anger, and desire) can be projected.

- Jinxes can be projected.

Evil assignments and projections follow a pattern: First the person or place is marked, by name, for a specific evil purpose. Then the intent is projected through incantations (the oral evoking of evil spirits for specific duties).

Before we proceed, let's stop here and pray this prayer:

> Any demonic personality assigning and projecting evil against me, the Lord rebuke you, in the name of Jesus Christ. No demonic weapon assigned to subdue my mind shall prosper, in the name of Jesus Christ.

Sources of Evil Assignments and Projections

Evil assignments and projections can issue from a variety of personalities:

1. Satan (all evil works serve his purposes)
2. Demons and evil spirits
3. Satanic agents including witches, wizards, marine witches, cults, voodoo priests, those with familiar spirits, black magic practitioners, and demonized prophets and pastors
4. Ordinary people, such as David's former counselor, Ahithophel (see 2 Sam. 15:12)
5. Self, as in the case of Nabal, whose foolishness brought him great destruction (see 1 Sam. 25)

Assignments and Projections from Satan

Satan is a very serious enemy, the chief assigner and projector of evil. Whatever he does, he does with all his might. He takes his time and chooses the best moment to strike. An example of his deadly ways is found in Job 1-5:

> *There was a man in the land of Uz, whose name was Job; and that man was perfect and upright, and one that feared God, and eschewed evil. And there were*

born unto him seven sons and three daughters. His substance also was seven thousand sheep, and three thousand camels, and five hundred yoke of oxen, and five hundred she asses, and a very great household; so that this man was the greatest of all the men of the east. And his sons went and feasted in their houses, every one his day; and sent and called for their three sisters to eat and to drink with them. And it was so, when the days of their feasting were gone about, that Job sent and sanctified them, and rose up early in the morning, and offered burnt offerings according to the number of them all: for Job said, It may be that my sons have sinned, and cursed God in their hearts. Thus did Job continually (Job 1:1-5).

This passage reveals that Job was a great and wealthy man with an excellent destiny. That is exactly what Satan longed to steal, kill, and destroy (see John 10:10). Christian believers must be watchful and prayerful at all times, so as to deny Satan any opportunity to strike.

Consider the details of Satan's attack against Job:

Now there was a day when the sons of God came to present themselves before the LORD, *and Satan came also among them* (Job 1:6).

The Bible reveals that Satan has access to the presence of God, where Satan accuses the brethren:

I heard a loud voice saying in heaven, Now is come salvation, and strength, and the kingdom of our God, and the power of his Christ: for the accuser of our brethren is cast down, which accused them before our God day and night (Rev. 12:10).

Satan accuses day in and day out. When we give him opportunity, he strikes. Timing is a critical factor, and he chooses it carefully.

> *The LORD said unto Satan, Whence comest thou? Then Satan answered the LORD, and said, From going to and fro in the earth, and from walking up and down in it. And the LORD said unto Satan, Hast thou considered my servant Job, that there is none like him in the earth, a perfect and an upright man, one that feareth God, and escheweth evil? (Job 1:7-8).*

Before the Lord asked this question, He knew Satan had tried to attack Job, having marked him and projected evil against him unsuccessfully. How do I know this? Scripture reveals it!

> *Then Satan answered the LORD, and said, Doth Job fear God for naught? Hast not thou made a hedge about him, and about his house, and about all that he hath on every side? thou hast blessed the work of his hands, and his substance is increased in the land (Job 1:9-10).*

Satan was prevented, because God protects the righteous. Satan acknowledged the hedge that was around Job, covering him and his belongings on every side. Satan could not penetrate it. Notice what Satan asked God to do:

> *But put forth thine hand now, and touch all that he hath, and he will curse thee to thy face. And the LORD said unto Satan, Behold, all that he hath is in thy power; only upon himself put not forth thine hand. So Satan went forth from the presence of the LORD. And there was a day when his sons and his daughters were eating and drinking wine in their eldest brother's house (Job 1:11-13).*

Satan can do nothing unless the Lord allows it. Satan had long planned to devastate Job; now he would be successful. He chose a special day for his wickedness—the feast day for Job's children.

There came a messenger unto Job, and said, The oxen were plowing, and the asses feeding beside them: and the Sabeans fell upon them, and took them away; yea, they have slain the servants with the edge of the sword; and I only am escaped alone to tell thee (Job 1:14-15).

The Sabeans were Arabians who lived by robbing and raiding. Because wickedness was set in their foundation, Satan was able to project evil into their minds. Satanically inspired to come against Job, they carried away his livestock and murdered the servants who cared for them.

The story continues:

While he was yet speaking, there came also another, and said, The fire of God is fallen from heaven, and hath burned up the sheep, and the servants, and consumed them; and I only am escaped alone to tell thee. While he was yet speaking, there came also another, and said, The Chaldeans made out three bands, and fell upon the camels, and have carried them away, yea, and slain the servants with the edge of the sword; and I only am escaped alone to tell thee. While he was yet speaking, there came also another, and said, Thy sons and thy daughters were eating and drinking wine in their eldest brother's house: and, behold, there came a great wind from the wilderness, and smote the four corners of the house, and it fell upon the young men, and they are dead; and I only am escaped alone to tell thee (Job 1:16-19).

Satan's attack involved human agents who did his bidding. The assignment's first wave struck Job's economic power. I believe this was an attack against his faith in God and was intended to break him down. Satan's first goal in assigning and projecting evil against a believer is always to destroy the person's faith. Job 1:22 confirms this truth: "In all this Job sinned not, nor charged God foolishly" (Job 1:22).

Job refused to give place to the devil, refraining from any response that would offend God. He certainly did not question God's kindness or goodness. Adam Clarke's Bible commentary speaks eloquently to Job's integrity before God:

> In this, and in this alone, he was a pattern of patience and resignation. In this Satan was utterly disappointed; he found a man who loved his God more than his earthly portion. This was a rare case, even in the experience of the devil. He had seen multitudes who bartered their God for money, and their hopes of blessedness in the world to come for secular possessions in the present. He had been so often successful in this kind of temptation, that he made no doubt he should succeed again. He saw many who, when riches increased, set their hearts on them, and forgot God. He saw many also who, when deprived of earthly comforts, blasphemed their Maker. He therefore inferred that Job, in similar circumstances, would act like the others; he was disappointed. Reader, by riches or poverty, has he succeeded with thee? Art thou pious when affluent, and patient and contented when in poverty?[1]

The Bible records another day when Satan presented himself before the Lord, who asked the same question He asked previously:

> *Again there was a day when the sons of God came to present themselves before the LORD, and Satan came also among them to present himself before the LORD. And the LORD said unto Satan, From whence comest thou? And Satan answered the LORD, and said, From going to and fro in the earth, and from walking up and down in it. And the LORD said unto Satan, Hast thou considered my servant Job, that there is none like him*

166

*in the earth, a perfect and an upright man, one that
feareth God, and escheweth evil? and still he holdeth
fast his integrity,* although thou movedst me against
him, to destroy him without a cause (Job 2:1-3).

Satan gave the same answer he gave the first time. God reiterated
that Job had stood firm despite the attacks, essentially saying, "You
hit My servant Job hard, but he did not surrender his faith in Me."

As stated earlier, not all attacks result from our sin; some things
happen because of whom God created us to be. Satan did not relent;
he asked permission to attack Job with sickness, fully expecting that
an attack like this would crack Job's faith:

*Satan answered the LORD, and said, Skin for skin, yea,
all that a man hath will he give for his life. But put
forth thine hand now, and touch his bone and his flesh,
and he will curse thee to thy face* (Job 2:4-5).

The devil studies and is familiar with our individual weaknesses.
In matters of life and death, human beings are more apt to compro-
mise. The Lord gave permission for a physical attack, knowing it was
designed to further test Job's faith. Job's sickness lingered because
instead of praying, he argued. He looked for pity, and did not go on
the offensive to undo Satan's evil works in his flesh. I believe Job
failed to realize who he was.

Before we continue, please say this simple, but powerful prayer:

Father God, whenever the devil comes into Your presence to accuse me, defend Your interest in me. When
I am assailed, help me to know and remember who I
am in Christ. In the name of Jesus Christ, cause me to
rise up and take back whatever has been stolen. Amen.

Job was not the only strong believer to come under Satan's direct
assignment and projection. King David, was another of Satan's targets for assignment and projection.

"Satan stood up against Israel, and provoked David to number Israel" (1 Chron. 21:1). The king was forbidden by God to count the number of his troops. Satan knew that fact and exploited it. He marked Israel for destruction by projecting error into David's mind. As a result, Israel suffered God's wrath.

In the New Testament, we see the story of Ananias and Sapphira, who also succumbed to satanic provocation:

A certain man named Ananias, with Sapphira his wife, sold a possession, and kept back part of the price, his wife also being privy to it, and brought a certain part, and laid it at the apostles' feet. But Peter said, Ananias, why hath Satan filled thine heart to lie to the Holy Ghost, and to keep back part of the price of the land? (Acts 5:1-3)

Satan projected a wicked lie that "filled" the hearts of Ananias and his wife. *Filled* can be translated here as "instigate" or "impel." Satan instigated their deceitfulness about the sale of their land. It is noteworthy that Ananias and Sapphira were among the early believers who yielded to the power of the gospel. Yet Satan was able to penetrate their hearts and indirectly kill them.

How Satan Assigns and Projects Evil

Satan's methods are simple but effective. He understands human beings well enough to exploit their tendencies. Below are some of the most popular means by which he attacks:

1. Accusation

Satan can assign and or project evil when we grant him the opportunity to accuse us before God.

Satan brings formal charges when we violate spiritual law, and he waits for the perfect timing. His accusations are the source of the evil to be assigned or projected. The assignments and projections are the symptoms.

How to Overcome Accusation

Scripture explains how we overcome Satan's evil assignments and projections:

> *They overcame him by the blood of the Lamb, and by the word of their testimony; and they loved not their lives unto the death* (Rev. 12:11).

- We overcome by the blood of Jesus Christ.
- We overcome by our words of faith.

Now let's return to the most common types of attacks.

2. The flooding of problems
Satan tries to overwhelm Christian believers with problems, hindrances, and diversions to break them down and destroy their faith in God. This manifests as multiple crises and/or hardships in a row or at the same time.

> *The serpent cast out of his mouth water as a flood after the woman, that he might cause her to be carried away of the flood* (Rev. 12:15).

How to Oppose a Flood of Problems

God's Word assures us that, although floods may come, there is a way of escape:

> *The earth helped the woman, and the earth opened her mouth, and swallowed up the flood which the dragon cast out of his mouth* (Rev. 12:16).

- Command the ground to open up and swallow the flood of problems.
- Overwhelm your problems with prayer.

3. Discouraged faithfulness

The enemy longs to drag believers from a walk of faith to a walk of unbelief. He does this in part by discouraging tithing, church attendance, and acts of service. Satan used Job's wife to discourage Job's faithfulness to God. When tragedy befell them, his wife said, "Dost thou still retain thine integrity? curse God, and die" (Job 2:9).

How to Overcome Discouraged Faithfulness

The way to overcome this type of evil assignment and projection is found, as always, in Scripture:

And let us not be weary in well doing: for in due season we shall reap, if we faint not (Gal. 6:9).

Cast not away therefore your confidence, which hath great recompence of reward. For ye have need of patience, that, after ye have done the will of God, ye might receive the promise (Heb. 10:35-36).

One of the best ways to remain *en*couraged is to maintain a long-term vision focused on the promise.

4. Attempts to break your loving spirit

Jesus foretold a time when many hearts would become cold and hard: "Because iniquity shall abound, the love of many shall wax cold" (Matt. 24:12). The love of many has turned to ice because of disappointment, betrayal, and rejection.

The apostle Paul also talked about perilous times in which self-centeredness would permit Satan's evil assignments and projections (see 2 Tim. 3:2-5).

How to Keep Your Heart Tender

Jesus provided the answer: "He that shall endure unto the end, the same shall be saved" (Matt. 24:13).

- We need to press into God and endure.
- He will save us!

Assignments and Projections from Demons or Evil Spirits.

The following Bible passage shows Satan working through demonic entities or evil spirits to project hindrances:

> *When* [Jesus] *was come out of the ship, immediately there met him out of the tombs a man with an unclean spirit, who had his dwelling among the tombs; and no man could bind him, no, not with chains: because that he had been often bound with fetters and chains, and the chains had been plucked asunder by him, and the fetters broken in pieces: neither could any man tame him. And always, night and day, he was in the mountains, and in the tombs, crying, and cutting himself with stones. But when he saw Jesus afar off, he ran and worshipped him, and cried with a loud voice, and said, What have I to do with thee, Jesus, thou Son of the most high God? I adjure thee by God, that thou torment me not. For he said unto him, Come out of the man, thou unclean spirit. And he asked him, What is thy name? And he answered, saying, My name is Legion: for we are many* (Mark 5:2-9).

The man was besieged by darkness and thoroughly incapacitated. But Jesus cast all evil spirits out of him and sent them into a herd of pigs. The pigs perished, but the man was restored!

> *They come to Jesus, and see him that was possessed with the devil, and had the legion, sitting, and clothed,*

171

and in his right mind: and they were afraid. And they that saw it told them how it befell to him that was possessed with the devil, and also concerning the swine (Mark 5:15-16).

Assignments and Projections from Other Satanic Agents

Satan has many accomplices, including witches, wizards, marine witches, occult practitioners, voodoo priests, black magic practitioners, and demonized prophets and pastors, among others. He also works through heavenly bodies and the elements.

The following passage clearly shows Satan and his hosts working through human agents:

There was a certain man, called Simon, which beforetime in the same city used sorcery, and bewitched the people of Samaria, giving out that himself was some great one: To whom they all gave heed, from the least to the greatest, saying, This man is the great power of God. And to him they had regard, because that of long time he had bewitched them with sorceries (Acts 8:9-10).

There is a spiritual lesson here. Simon was converted and believed the gospel of Jesus Christ. After his baptism he continued the work of evangelism with Philip. But because of the level of occultism in his history, Simon needed deeper deliverance. This issue came up when the apostles, Peter and John, arrived in Samaria to impart the Holy Spirit.

Then laid they their hands on them [Samaritans], and they received the Holy Ghost. And when Simon saw that through laying on of the apostles' hands the Holy Ghost was given, he offered them money, saying, Give me also this power, that on whomsoever I lay hands, he may receive the Holy Ghost. But Peter said unto

172

him, Thy money perish with thee, because thou hast thought that the gift of God may be purchased with money. Thou hast neither part nor lot in this matter: for thy heart is not right in the sight of God. Repent therefore of this thy wickedness, and pray God, if perhaps the thought of thine heart may be forgiven thee. For I perceive that thou art in the gall of bitterness, and in the bond of iniquity. Then answered Simon, and said, Pray ye to the Lord for me, that none of these things which ye have spoken come upon me (Acts 8:17-24).

Simon did not seek the power of God to help those in bondage; he was looking for the fame sorcery had previously given him. So he offered to pay for the Spirit's power. Through the Holy Spirit, Peter perceived the workings of the demon of sorcery. Instead of receiving a blessing, Simon received a curse.

Satanic agents can also use heavenly bodies (sun, moon, stars, planets) as mediums through which to assign or project evil. In addition, they can tap into the power of the elements (wind, fire, and water) to assign or project destruction. Satan used the power of both wind and fire to destroy Job's children and animals. Satanic agents can use heavenly bodies and elements to assign and project evils against people, places, and things.

Assignments and Projections from Ordinary People

Ordinary people can be used by the enemy to disrupt or destroy the lives of God's people. King David experienced overwhelming betrayal. In Psalms 41:9, he lamented:

Yea, mine own familiar friend, in whom I trusted, which did eat of my bread, hath lifted up his heel against me.

He was speaking of his chief counselor, Ahithophel who joined forces with David's son, Absalom, to usurp the royal throne in Hebron:

Absalom sent for Ahithophel the Gilonite, David's counseller, from his city, even from Giloh, while he offered sacrifices. And the conspiracy was strong; for the people increased continually with Absalom (2 Sam. 15:12).

Our Lord Jesus Christ also spoke of "an unfriendly friend" who would betray him, namely Judas:

I speak not of you all: I know whom I have chosen: but that the scripture may be fulfilled, He that eateth bread with me hath lifted up his heel against me (John 13:18).

Proverbs 16:29-30, reveals four methods by which Satan assigns and projects, using human agents.

*A violent man **enticeth** his neighbor, and **leadeth** him into the way that is not good. He **shutteth** his eyes to devise froward things: moving his lips he **bringeth** evil to pass* (Prov. 16:29-30).

In this verse a *violent* person is an evil person who brings harm in four basic ways:

- The evil person entices: He or she uses sugarcoated words to deceive the simple-hearted. The Word of God warns us to reject these evil invitations: "My son, if sinners entice thee, consent thou not" (Prov. 1:10).
- The evil person leads others down an ungodly path. He does this by manipulation.
- The evil person closes his or her eyes to devise evil. In this way, the evil person is able to shut out mercy and kindness.
- The evil person speaks words that are designed to bring evil to pass. He conjures evil words and sends them forth to afflict.

Self-Caused Assignments and Projections

Finally, some of the assignments and projections against us are self-inflicted. This happens when we give the enemy legal ground against us.

A biblical example is Nabal, who was deliberately disobedient and brought upon himself the anger of King David. Nabal's wife wisely intervened so that David would not kill her husband. But death came for Nabal soon after (see 1 Sam. 25).

Christian believers who entertain bitterness, anger, jealousy, etc., strongly attract assignments and projections. Those who are disobedient to God's will do the same. Whether the disobedience is deliberate or unwitting, it invites the wicked one to strike. Christian believers involved in abominable practices also attract evil assignments. Scripture lists several practices God hates:

> *These six things doth the LORD hate: yea, seven are an abomination unto him: a proud look, a lying tongue, and hands that shed innocent blood, a heart that deviseth wicked imaginations, feet that be swift in running to mischief, a false witness that speaketh lies, and he that soweth discord among brethren* (Prov. 6:16-19).

Before we enter into prayer, be aware of these additional "triggers" for evil assignments and projections:
- Bondage to sin
- Fearfulness
- Unbelief
- Backsliding
- Spiritual carelessness (bad habits such as overeating; wrong pursuits such as fighting)
- A faulty foundation
- Sexual perversion

✟ PRAYERS FOR DELIVERANCE, BY THE BLOOD OF JESUS CHRIST, FROM EVIL ASSIGNMENTS AND PROJECTIONS

BIBLE PRAYER LINKS

He that eateth my flesh, and drinketh my blood, dwelleth in me, and I in him. As the living Father hath sent me, and I live by the Father: so he that eateth me, even he shall live by me (John 6:56-57).

But those that seek my soul, to destroy it, shall go into the lower parts of the earth (Ps. 63:9).

PRAYER FOCUS
- To apply the blood of Jesus Christ in demolishing all evil assignments and projections
- To disrupt and derail all satanic agents and their assignments against me

PRAYER GUIDES
1. Thank You, Lord, for You will be gracious to me today, in the name of Jesus Christ.
2. Father God, let the glory of divine liberty be seen on me today and forever, in the name of Jesus Christ.
3. Blood of Jesus Christ, loose me now from all curses, spells, and jinxes that are upon my family line, in the name of Jesus Christ.
4. Evil assignments programmed to destroy me, be neutralized now by the blood of Jesus Christ.
5. Evil assignments programmed into the earth to stagnate my progress and make my labor hard and unrewarding, be destroyed by the blood of my Lord and Savior, Jesus Christ.
6. Evil enchantments, assignments, and projections coming from this environment against my life and staff of bread, be neutralized now by the blood of Jesus Christ.

7. All wickedness programmed into the heavenlies to afflict my life and destiny, be pulled down now. Scatter by the blood of Jesus Christ.

8. Father Lord, let the powers that seek my destruction by assigning evils against me go into the lower parts of the earth now, in the name of Jesus Christ.

9. Demonic powers projecting destructive thoughts into my mind, be paralyzed now, by the blood of Jesus Christ.

10. Blood of Jesus Christ, cut off the satanic projection packaged to lead me into error, in the name of Jesus Christ.

11. Blood of Jesus Christ cut off the satanic projection packaged to cause people to disappoint me, in the name of Jesus Christ.

12. Any witch or wizard cursing my life and destiny, I send your curses back to you, in the name of the Lord Jesus Christ.

13. Let the blood of Jesus Christ cover me and my family as a shield keeping us safe from Satan's assignments and projections, in the name of Jesus Christ.

14. Thank You, Jesus Christ, for answering my prayers. Amen.

✝ PRAYERS FOR DIVINE PROTECTION AGAINST EVIL ASSIGNMENTS AND PROJECTIONS

BIBLE PRAYER LINKS

Like a crane or a swallow, so did I chatter: I did mourn as a dove: mine eyes fail with looking upward: O LORD, I am oppressed; undertake for me (Isa. 38:14).

He shall cover thee with his feathers, and under his wings shalt thou trust: His truth shall be thy shield and buckler (Ps. 91:4).

PRAYER FOCUS
- To abide and trust in the Lord's protection
- To cast down all evil assignments and projections

PRAYER GUIDES

1. Father God, as You did for Job, shield my life from Satan's assignments of death, in the name of Jesus Christ.
2. Father God, put a shield of protection round about me and my family. Keep us from Satan's assignments and projections, in the name of Jesus Christ.
3. Father God, put a hedge of protection round about all that belongs to me and my family, in the name of Jesus Christ.
4. I will triumph over the works of the wicked, by the blood of Jesus Christ.
5. Evil assignments projected against my life, I cast you down, in the name of Jesus Christ.
6. Father Lord, defend Your interest in me, in the name of Jesus Christ.
7. Father God, let Your glory defend me from every wicked assignment, just as it defended Caleb and Joshua before the unbelieving Israelites, in the name of Jesus Christ.
8. Father Lord, arise in Your power for my sake. Scatter all evildoers around me and obliterate their works, in the name of Jesus Christ.
9. O God, arise in Your power and scatter evil personalities in my environment, in the name of Jesus Christ.
10. Father Lord, I am oppressed. Undertake for me, in the name of Jesus Christ.
11. Lord of Hosts, deliver me from all forms of oppression, in the name of Jesus Christ.
12. Thank You, Lord Jesus, for answering my prayers. Amen.

✠ PRAYERS TO PREVENT EVIL ASSIGNMENTS FROM TAKING ROOT

BIBLE PRAYER LINKS

The wicked shall be cut off from the earth, and the transgressors shall be rooted out of it (Prov. 2:22).

Let mine adversaries be clothed with shame, and let them cover themselves with their own confusion, as with a mantle (Ps. 109:29).

PRAYER FOCUS
- To invoke God's power to prevent the rooting of evil assignments
- To disrupt and destroy accusations, conspiracies, and other evil works

PRAYER GUIDES
1. Evil assignments and projections coming from my father's house against my life and business, backfire, in the name of Jesus Christ.
2. In the name of Jesus Christ and by His power, I scatter every conspiracy against me.
3. Evil enchantments, assignments, and projections coming from my environment against my life and staff of bread, backfire, in the name of Jesus Christ.
4. Every habitation of evil and wickedness established in my environment to destroy me and my staff of bread, be consumed by the fire of God, as in Elijah's day, in the name of Jesus Christ.
5. I command every conspiracy operating in this environment against me (and my calling) to fail, in the name of Jesus Christ.
6. According to the Word of God, every evil power striving with my life and calling, or coming against my staff of bread, shall perish, in the name of Jesus Christ (see Isa. 41:11).
7. Every mouth opened to destroy or implicate me, anywhere and at anytime, receive an angelic slap and be paralyzed in the name of Jesus Christ.
8. O Lord, forgive and nullify with Your blood every careless word spoken by me that is hindering my spiritual life, in the name of Jesus Christ.
9. All wicked thoughts and assignments projected into my heart to draw me into error, be aborted, in the name of Jesus Christ.

10. Evil assignments programmed into the earth to make me a non-entity, be aborted, in the name of Jesus Christ.
11. Thank You, Lord, for answering my prayers. Amen.

✝ Prayers to Overcome Evil Assignments of Demonic Taskmasters

Taskmasters are demonic and human agents of Satan designated to assign and supervise their captives' hard labor. During their Egyptian captivity, the Israelites had human taskmasters who were assigned by higher-ups to enforce their slavery (see Exod. 1:11). Satan can delegate demons to perform in the spirit realm much as Egyptians did in the physical realm. These are taskmaster demons who assign heavy burdens to oppress and depress their victims.

Taskmasters can be assigned over the lives of individuals, families, tribes, cities, states, or nations, causing the targets of their attacks to lose control over their own lives and destinies. Instead, their lives are dictated, day in and day out, by evil taskmasters.

Bible Prayer Links

Therefore they did set over them taskmasters to afflict them with their burdens. And they built for Pharaoh treasure cities, Pithom and Rameses (Exod. 1:11).

The LORD said, I have surely seen the affliction of my people which are in Egypt, and have heard their cry by reason of their taskmasters; for I know their sorrows; and I am come down to deliver them out of the hand of the Egyptians, and to bring them up out of that land unto a good land and a large, unto a land flowing with milk and honey; unto the place of the Canaanites, and the Hittites, and the Amorites, and the Perizzites, and the Hivites, and the Jebusites (Exod. 3:7-8).

PRAYER FOCUS
- To repent of my sin and give thanks for the finished work of the cross
- To proclaim the Lord's deliverance from the works of evil taskmasters

PRAYER GUIDES
1. Thank You, Jesus Christ, for making provision for my deliverance by Your death on the cross of Calvary.
2. I come to You, Lord, with genuine repentance, and I confess my sins (<u>name them</u>).
3. Thank You, Father, that the blood of Jesus Christ covers all my sins.
4. O Lord, stretch forth Your right hand against the demonic taskmaster assigned to oppress me. Let the ground swallow him, in the name of Jesus Christ.
5. I hold the blood of Jesus Christ against any legal ground occupied by demonic taskmasters to afflict me. I now dissolve that ground, in the name of Jesus Christ.
6. Demonic taskmasters appointed over my life, your assignment is over. Release me and let me go, in the name of Jesus Christ.
7. Demonic taskmasters appointed over my life, hear my word: a divine order of new beginning is in place. Depart from me, in the name of Jesus Christ.
8. Demonic taskmasters appointed over my life to limit me spiritually and financially, the Lord rebuke you, in the name of Jesus Christ.
9. Demonic taskmasters set over my life to afflict me, I dispossess you of your power. Die, in the name of Jesus Christ.
10. Demonic taskmasters set over my career (business) to limit its progress, be paralyzed, in the name of Jesus Christ.
11. Demonic taskmasters set over my marital destiny to cause delay and rejection, die, in the name of Jesus Christ.

12. O Lord, hear my cry! Let the activities of demonic taskmasters be paralyzed today; deliver me from their grip, in the name of Jesus Christ.
13. O Lord, my Father, deliver me from the oppression of demonic taskmasters, in the name of Jesus Christ.
14. O Lord, release me from the bondage of demonic taskmasters and bring me to my promised land, in the name of Jesus Christ.
15. Thank You, Lord, for answering my prayers. Amen.

✝ PRAYERS TO OVERCOME THE EVIL ASSIGNMENTS OF SPOILERS

Spoilers are merciless attackers of that which is precious. They look for glorious things to squander and they spoil with the intention that what they have spoiled can never be repaired again. Because of their ferocity, these spirits sometimes seem to be more wicked than their mentor, the devil.

Spoilers can be assigned against a destiny, life, marriage, career, or relationship, cutting short its life span. The following prayer guides focus on God's deliverance from the spoiler's attack. Notice that Isaiah 21:2 asks the prayer warrior to besiege opponents. In other words, attacking the spoiler in the power of the Holy Spirit brings deliverance.

BIBLE PRAYER LINKS

A grievous vision is declared unto me; the treacherous dealer dealeth treacherously, and the spoiler spoileth. Go up, O Elam: besiege, O Media; all the sighing thereof have I made to cease (Isa. 21:2).

O vine of Sibmah, I will weep for thee with the weeping of Jazer: thy plants are gone over the sea, they reach even to the sea of Jazer: the spoiler is fallen upon thy summer fruits and upon thy vintage (Jer. 48:32).

Woe to thee that spoilest, and thou wast not spoiled; and dealest treacherously, and they dealt not treacherously with thee! when thou shalt cease to spoil, thou shalt be spoiled; and when thou shalt make an end to deal treacherously, they shall deal treacherously with thee (Isa. 33:1).

All my bones shall say, LORD, who is like unto thee, which deliverest the poor from him that is too strong for him, yea, the poor and the needy from him that spoileth him? (Ps. 35:10)

PRAYER FOCUS
- To thank the Lord Jesus Christ for His delivering power
- To spoil the spoiler's works

PRAYER GUIDES
1. I thank You, Jesus Christ, for Your power that delivers.
2. I am grateful, O Lord, for Your divine protection over my life, in the name of Jesus Christ.
3. Let the blood of Jesus Christ shield me from the attack of the spoiler, in the name of Jesus Christ.
4. I declare that my goods shall *not* be spoiled, in the name of Jesus Christ.
5. I forbid the spoiler to come upon my life or destiny, in the name of Jesus Christ.
6. I forbid the spoiler to come upon my staff of bread, in the name of Jesus Christ.
7. The hand of the spoiler shall not fall upon my blessings, in the name of Jesus Christ.
8. The power of the spoiler shall not prevail over my career, in the name of Jesus Christ.
9. My spiritual life shall not succumb to the attack of the spoiler, in the name of Jesus Christ (see Jer. 48:18).
10. In the name of Jesus Christ, let the thunder of God destroy the weapons fashioned against my life and ministry by the spoiler.

11. Every agent of the spoiler around me, I cast you out, in the name of Jesus Christ.
12. I command the power of the spoiler against my staff of bread to perish, in the name of Jesus Christ.
13. I hide my profession, ministry, and/or business behind the cross of Calvary and away from the eyes of the spoiler, in the name of Jesus Christ.
14. I hold the blood of Jesus against the spirit of the spoiler assigned to afflict my marriage, finances, and prosperity, in the name of Jesus Christ.
15. As of today, I render null and void the spoiler's activities in my life, in the name of Jesus Christ.
16. Let the thunder of God scatter the operations of the spoiler against my life and handiwork, in the name of Jesus Christ.
17. By the authority of Calvary, I forbid the spoiler from laying his hands upon my goods to plunder them, in the name of Jesus Christ.
18. Agents of Satan assigning the spoiler against my life and profession, be wasted, in the name of Jesus Christ.
19. Let the tools of the spoiler turn against him, in the name of Jesus Christ.
20. Agents of the spoiler assigned to generate disfavor or disaffection against me in the workplace, loose your hold and be paralyzed, in the name of Jesus Christ.
21. All damage inflicted by the spoiler against my peace and efficiency, be restored now, by the blood of Jesus Christ.
22. Let the warfare prepared against me by the spoiler be neutralized by the power of God.
23. Father God, command Your warring angels to disorganize any evil warfare prepared against my life and profession by the spoiler, in the name of Jesus Christ.
24. Father God, execute judgment upon any powers summoning the spoiler to oppose my life and goods, in the name of Jesus Christ.
25. I thank You, Lord, for answering my prayers. Amen.

✠ Prayers to Defeat Waster Spirits

Waster spirits operate the same way spoilers do. They are wicked and destroy with the intent of wasting, so that whatever was destroyed cannot be recovered or repaired. However, the blood of Jesus Christ recovers and the power of the Holy Ghost can fix anything. Hallelujah!

Bible Prayer Links

Confess Second Timothy 4:18 daily, as often as needed.

The Lord shall deliver me from every evil work, and will preserve me unto his heavenly kingdom: to whom be glory forever and ever. Amen (2 Tim. 4:18).

The king spake, and said, Is not this great Babylon, that I have built for the house of the kingdom by the might of my power, and for the honour of my majesty? While the word was in the king's mouth, there fell a voice from heaven, saying, O king Nebuchadnezzar, to thee it is spoken; The kingdom is departed from thee (Dan. 4:30-31).

By means of a whorish woman a man is brought to a piece of bread: and the adulteress will hunt for the precious life (Prov. 6:26).

Prayer Focus

- To expose, command, and destroy the work of waster spirits
- To cause, by the power of the Holy Spirit, restoration of all damages perpetrated by waster spirits

Prayer Guides

1. Lord Jesus, I thank You for giving me victory in this prayer program.

2. Every waster spirit siphoning off my life and destiny, the Lord rebuke you. Be rendered powerless, in the name of Jesus Christ.

3. Every deception assigned against me by waster spirits, I overcome you now by the blood of Jesus.

4. Every waster spirit that is pursuing my life and career, I rebuke you in the name of Jesus Christ and command you to depart from me, in the name of Jesus.

5. Every waster spirit attacking my time and resources by suggesting error to my mind, the Lord rebuke you.

6. Every waster spirit operating around me, your time is over. Be wasted by Holy Ghost fire, in the name of Jesus.

7. With the rod of God, I break the backbone of every waster spirit pursuing the glory of my career, in the name of Jesus.

8. Dragons of the wilderness assigned to waste my life and destiny, your power shall fail, in the name of Jesus.

9. Demonic connection arranged by waster spirits, scatter by fire, in the name of Jesus.

10. Spiritual adulteress hunting for my glory to waste it, the Lord rebuke you, in the name of Jesus.

11. By the power of the Holy Ghost and in the name of Jesus, I recover my glory from the hold of all waster spirits.

12. Waster spirits assigned to squander my efforts to succeed in life, depart from me, in the name of Jesus.

13. Dragons of the wilderness assigned to waste my defenses and divine inheritance, be destroyed by Holy Ghost fire, in the name of Jesus.

14. Destruction that wastes at noonday, you shall not prosper in my life and destiny, in the name of Jesus (see Ps. 91:6).

15. In the name of Jesus, I recover my glory from the hold of every waster spirit.

16. Holy Spirit, my Comforter, comfort me on all sides, in the name of Jesus.

17. Thank You, Lord Jesus, for answering my prayers. Amen.

✟ PRAYERS TO SPOIL THE SPOILERS AND WASTE THE WASTERS

BIBLE PRAYER LINKS

Thou shalt not be afraid for the terror by night; nor for the arrow that flieth by day; nor for the pestilence that walketh in darkness; nor for the destruction that wasteth at noonday (Ps. 91:5-6).

All my bones shall say, Lord, who is like unto thee, which deliverest the poor from him that is too strong for him, yea, the poor and the needy from him that spoileth him? (Ps. 35:10)

PRAYER FOCUS
- To appeal to the Almighty and apply the blood of Jesus Christ to prevent and reverse all activity of spoilers and wasters
- To declare my authority in Christ over my life, goods, and progress (materially, spiritually, etc.)

PRAYER GUIDES
1. Thank You, Jesus, for releasing Your power and delivering me from the repeated attacks of spoilers and wasters.
2. Father God, let the glory of divine liberty be seen on me today and forever, in the name of Jesus Christ.
3. Let the blood of Jesus Christ shield me (and all that belongs to me) from the repeated attacks of the spoilers, in the name of Jesus Christ.
4. Every waster spirit that is assigned to repeatedly destroy my prosperity, business, or ministry, the Lord rebuke you. Be wasted now by the fire of God, in the name of Jesus Christ.
5. Every waster spirit in charge of recurring waste and destruction in my life, the Lord rebuke you. Be wasted now by the fire of God, in the name of Jesus Christ.
6. Every spoiler spirit assigned to repeatedly spoil my goods, achievements, and spiritual progress, the Lord rebuke you. Be spoiled now by the fire of God, in the name of Jesus Christ.

7. As of today, I forbid the spoilers to come upon my staff of bread, my belongings, and my life, in the name of Jesus Christ.

8. My spiritual life shall not succumb to the spoilers' attacks, in the name of Jesus Christ (see the "spoiler of Moab" in Jer. 48:18).

9. Let the fire of God arise now and destroy the weapons of the spoilers and wasters fashioned against my life, in the mighty name of Jesus Christ.

10. Every agent of spoilers and wasters surrounding me, I cast you out, and render your activities null and void, in the name of Jesus Christ.

11. I hide my life, ministry, marriage, business, etc., behind the cross of Calvary, away from the monitoring eyes of spoilers and wasters, in the name of Jesus Christ.

12. I hold the blood of Jesus Christ against all spoiler and waster spirits assigned to afflict my finances and prosperity, in the name of Jesus Christ.

13. Thunder of God, scatter the operations of spoilers and wasters against the works of my hands, in the name of Jesus Christ.

14. By the authority of Calvary, I forbid spoilers and wasters to touch or plunder any aspect of my life, in the name of Jesus Christ.

15. Thank You, Jesus Christ, for answering my prayers. Amen.

Endnote

1. *The Holy Bible, Containing the Old and New Testaments, vol. 2* (New York: N. Bangs and J. Emory, 1828), notes at Job 1:22.

9

Evil Assignments and Projections—Part 2

Areas Affected by Assignments and Projections

The topic of satanic assignments and projections is vital, so we continue to study them. They can be sent through any accessible means—the eyes, mind, sleep, and spoken words—to produce a variety of effects in the areas discussed below.

Effects on the Mind

These wicked means can be sent into the mind to cause confusion and weariness, making it difficult to obey God. The assailed mind is subtly programmed not to desire holy fellowship with God or other believers. This wickedness also leads to error, as it did with Balaam, who was hired by the Moabite king, Balak, to curse Israel. God gave Balaam clear instructions:

> *Thou shalt not go with them; thou shalt not curse the people: for they are blessed* (Num. 22:12).

But Balaam disobeyed God and fell into error. Through the spoken word and evil persistency, a wicked assignment helped him yield to evil demands.

> *Balaam rose up in the morning, and saddled his ass,*
> *and went with the princes of Moab. And God's anger*
> *was kindled because he went: and the angel of the*
> *LORD stood in the way for an adversary against him.*
> *Now he was riding upon his ass, and his two servants*
> *were with him* (Num. 22: 21-22).

Error is costly, as Balaam learned. But assignments and projections must first impact the target. Then the following effects are realized:

Effects on the Soul

The following passage describes Jesus' travail the night before He was crucified:

> *Then cometh Jesus with them unto a place called*
> *Gethsemane, and saith unto the disciples, Sit ye here,*
> *while I go and pray yonder. And he took with him*
> *Peter and the two sons of Zebedee, and began to be*
> *sorrowful and very heavy. Then saith he unto them,*
> *My soul is exceeding sorrowful, even unto death:*
> *tarry ye here, and watch with me* (Matt. 26:36-38).

Jesus' soul was under satanic pressure, which produced inner conflict. This was not bodily pain; it came from within. Satan bombarded Jesus' soul with terrible visions of what He would suffer. The wicked one's voice delivered anguish, evil, and reproach. Hence, Jesus' lament: "My soul is exceeding sorrowful, even unto death."

Even today, Satan uses this method of assigning and projecting evil to affect the human soul. Jesus overcame this wicked method of attack by praying. You and I must do the same!

The Bible reveals how such curses can be assigned to the soul:

> *Neither have I suffered my mouth to sin by wishing a*
> *curse to his soul* (Job 31:30).

Through Job, the Holy Spirit reveals that a curse can be assigned to a person's soul by wishing it. This is an important revelation for us to grasp!

A person targeted in this way can lose control of his or her mind, will, and emotions, resulting in chronic failures.

The Soul of Man Is Also the Target of Evil Spirits

The mind, will, and emotions can be attacked by demons and other evil spirits to incite the following calamities:

1. Suicide
2. Marital breakdown
3. Disobedient children
4. Godlessness
5. Child abuse
6. Drug addiction
7. Emotional distress
8. Discouragement

Effects on the Body

Evil projections can attack a person physically to incite ungodly desires, including inappropriate sexual desires. In the same way, evil assignments can be sent to cause physical cravings and sickness.

Effects on Marriage and Family

Constant disagreement and suspicion can signal evil assignments and projections against a marriage. For the family, a lack of understanding and an atmosphere of strife can also result.

✞ PRAYERS TO SEND EVIL ARROWS BACK TO THEIR SENDERS

Evil arrows of confusion, fear, doubt, wrong thoughts, anger, and desire were briefly mentioned earlier. The best definition of the term was one I found many years ago when a man of

God called it an invasion sent by envious opponents who seek our harm and even our death.

If an evil arrow is an invasion, it must have a route, a medium by which it reaches its destination. There are several: the air and waters, and the heavenly bodies, such as the sun, moon, and stars. Satanic agents know that programming evil into the heavenly bodies can wreak havoc in the physical realm. The table below lists six types of evil arrows that travel these "routes."

Curses	Spells	Evil words and pronouncements
Evil enchantments	Hexes	Jinxes

Demons do not originate assignments, but they carry evil arrows to their destinations. Evil arrows can be originated by witches and wizards, occult operators, voodoo priests, practitioners of black magic, those having familiar spirits, marine witches, and demonized prophets and pastors.

Evil arrows are sent to kill, steal, and destroy by wreaking physical, emotional, and spiritual havoc. Our response is to pray!

BIBLE PRAYER LINKS

For, lo, the wicked bend their bow, they make ready their arrow upon the string, that they may privily shoot at the upright in heart (Ps. 11:2).

Hide me from the secret counsel of the wicked; from the insurrection of the workers of iniquity: who whet their tongue like a sword, and bend their bows to shoot their arrows, even bitter words: that they may shoot in secret at the perfect: Suddenly do they shoot at him, and fear not. They encourage themselves in an evil matter: they commune of laying snares privily; they say, Who shall see them? They search out iniquities; they accomplish a diligent search: Both the inward thought *of every one* of them, *and the heart, is deep. But God shall shoot at them* with *an arrow; suddenly shall they be wounded* (Ps. 64:2-7).

PRAYER FOCUS
- To divert and reassign all evil arrows to affect their senders

PRAYER GUIDES
1. Any evil arrow coming against me from the heavenlies, I post God's angels across your path. Return to your sender, in the name of Jesus Christ.
2. All evil arrows programmed into the heavenlies against my glory and destiny, I withdraw you now and command you to return to your sender, in the name of Jesus Christ.
3. In the name of Jesus Christ, I command that all hosts of darkness assigned to destroy me with evil arrows must instead destroy one another, as in King Jehoshaphat's day (see 2 Chron. 20:20-25).
4. Any demon assigned to abort my blessings, I return you to your sender, in the name of Jesus Christ.

✞ PRAYERS TO CRUSH ALL EVIL NIGHT PLOTTERS AND NIGHTTIME PLOTS—PART 1

Night plotters are human and spirit agents of Satan that plan evils by night in order to achieve the destruction of lives and properties. Psalms 37:12 says, "The wicked plotteth against the just, and gnasheth upon him with his teeth." In Jesus' name their agendas will be crushed.

Timing is essential to the means of the wicked. The psalmist shares important information about the timing and kinds of evil assignments and projections:

Thou shalt not be afraid for the terror by night; nor for the arrow that flieth by day; nor for the pestilence that walketh in darkness; nor for the destruction that wasteth at noonday (Ps. 91:5-6).

Certain evil assignment and projections are meant only for night, or day, or noonday, or the dark hours. Satanic agents, including night plotters, understand these timing details and cooperate with them. But through prayer, holy living, and complete obedience to the will of God, these evil assignments and projections can be cut off!

BIBLE PRAYER LINKS

Woe to them that devise iniquity, and work evil upon their beds! When the morning is light, they practise it, because it is in the power of their hand. They covet fields, and take them by violence; and houses, and take them away: so they oppress a man and his house, even a man and his heritage (Mic. 2:1-2).

No weapon that is formed against thee shall prosper; and every tongue that shall rise against thee in judgment thou shalt condemn. This is the heritage of the servants of the Lord, and their righteousness is of me, saith the LORD (Isa. 54:17).

PRAYER FOCUS
- To expose and arrest all night plotters and plots, in the name of Jesus Christ
- To assert my authority in the name of Jesus and obliterate their works

PRAYER GUIDES
1. Thank You, Jesus Christ, for being my strong tower and my shelter from all night plotters (see Ps. 61:3).

2. Father Lord, I thank You for not giving me as a prey to the teeth of the enemy (see Ps. 124:6).

3. Father Lord, I thank You for giving me victory over all oppressive forces, through Jesus Christ (see 1 Cor. 15:57).

4. I declare that the Lord is perfecting that which concerns me, in the name of Jesus Christ (see Ps. 138:8).

5. In the name of Jesus Christ, I receive the Holy Spirit anointing to destroy the works of evil night plotters.

6. O Lord, arise now and destroy the works of the evil night plotters against my life and destiny, in the mighty name of Jesus Christ.

7. O Lord, arise now and scatter the evil agreement of the night plotters concerning my life and destiny. Their agendas shall not stand, in the name of Jesus Christ.

8. O Lord, arise now and let the evil night plotters working against my divine purpose perish with their plots, in the name of Jesus Christ.

9. O Lord, expose the plans and activities of those opposing my blessings and breakthroughs. Let them be disgraced, in the name of Jesus Christ.

10. O Lord, frustrate the means and methods of the night plotters attacking my blessings and breakthroughs, and let these evils boomerang against them, in the name of Jesus.

11. O Lord, send forth Your judgment of fire against every evil night plotter working for my destruction, in the name of Jesus Christ.

12. Let the chanting of the wicked against my success backfire against them, in the name of Jesus Christ.

13. Every satanic agent in my environment using the hours of the night to oppress me, the Lord rebuke you. Be frustrated, in the mighty name of Jesus Christ.

14. Powers of the night assigned to steal my miracles, the Lord rebuke you. Be frustrated, in the mighty name of Jesus Christ.

15. According to the Word of the Lord, no weapon that is formed against me shall prosper. Therefore, all wickedness set against me by night plotters is now null and void, in the name of the Lord Jesus Christ.

16. Every mind devising evil against me (my business, marriage, finances, etc.) in the hours of the night, be confused, in the mighty name of Jesus Christ.
17. Thank You, Lord, for by Your favor You have made my mountain stand strong (see Ps. 30:7).
18. Thank You, Jesus Christ, for answering my prayers. Amen.

✝ PRAYERS TO CRUSH ALL EVIL NIGHT PLOTTERS AND NIGHTTIME PLOTS—PART 2

BIBLE PRAYER LINK

The Lord is with me as a mighty terrible one: therefore my persecutors shall stumble, and they shall not prevail: they shall be greatly ashamed; for they shall not prosper: their everlasting confusion shall never be forgotten (Jer. 20:11).

PRAYER FOCUS
- To destroy the means and plots of night plotters
- To invoke prayers of imprecation against the wicked

PRAYER GUIDES
1. Father Lord, I thank You for being with me as the mighty, terrible One, in the name of Jesus Christ.
2. Evil plotters of the night summoning me (my glory, promotion, finances, etc.) at the gate of the grave, be paralyzed, in the name of Jesus Christ.
3. Father Lord, laugh at the plot of the wicked against me and let me see the day of their destruction, in the name of Jesus Christ.
4. Lord, let the swords drawn against me by night plotters be cast down to pierce their own hearts, in the mighty name of Jesus Christ.
5. Father Lord, let the bow raised toward me by my enemies be broken into pieces, in the name of Jesus Christ.
6. Father God, mobilize Your angels to neutralize any attacks by oppressors of the night, in the mighty name of Jesus Christ.

7. God, arise and scatter my gathering persecutors with a confusion they shall never forgot, in the name of Jesus Christ.

8. God of true justice, let me see Your vengeance upon my oppressors, in the name of Jesus Christ.

9. Agents of wickedness pursuing me from any coven or other location, receive the judgment of God and be cut off forever, in the name of Jesus Christ.

10. In the name of Jesus Christ and by His blood, I declare that the yoke of the destroyer shall not prosper in my life, household, or family.

11. Thank You, Lord, for answering my prayers. Amen.

✞ PRAYERS TO BRING THE JUDGMENT OF GOD ON SATANIC MANIFESTATIONS

Satanic manifestations are Satan's works against a person or a person's possessions. These works include sudden illness, depression, equipment malfunctions, continuous disagreement over irrelevant issues, and other disruptions. God's judgments must be brought to bear against these satanically worked physical manifestations.

BIBLE PRAYER LINKS

The LORD your God is God of gods, and Lord of lords, a great God, a mighty, and a terrible, which regardeth not persons, nor taketh reward: he doth execute the judgment of the fatherless and widow, and loveth the stranger, in giving him food and raiment (Deut. 10:17-18).

The Lord is known by the judgment which he executeth: the wicked is snared in the work of his own hands (Ps. 9:16).

Thou didst cause judgment to be heard from heaven;
the earth feared, and was still, when God arose to
judgment, to save all the meek of the earth. Selah
(Ps. 76:8-9).

PRAYER FOCUS

- To bring the judgment of God to bear against wicked means
- To destroy the hindrances and barriers erected against me by the wicked

PRAYER GUIDES

1. Thank You, Lord Jesus, for You are my God as I pray.
2. Authority of darkness assigned to oppress or depress me, lose your power, in the name of Jesus Christ.
3. O Lord, in the name of Jesus Christ, arise in the power of Your anger and destroy the powers sponsoring wickedness against my life and destiny.
4. O Lord, in the mighty name of Jesus Christ, arise in the power of Your anger and destroy the evil powers that intend to decide how far I will go in life.
5. O Lord, in the mighty name of Jesus, arise in the power of Your anger and destroy the powers that have entered into secret covenant to end my life prematurely (to afflict me with strange sickness, hardship, etc.).
6. O Lord, in the name of Jesus Christ, arise in the power of Your anger and destroy the powers that say I am not qualified to occupy my throne of glory.
7. Every long-standing problem that has caused people to ask "Where is your God?"—your end has come. Vanish and be no more, in the name of Jesus Christ.
8. By the authority of the third heaven, I reverse every evil decree (of sickness, poverty, loneliness, rejection, addiction, failure, and backwardness, etc.) that has prospered against my life and destiny, in the name of Jesus Christ.
9. My Father and my God, release violent earthquakes to destroy satanic barriers hindering my purpose in life, in the name of Jesus Christ.

10. By the power of the Holy Spirit, I command every cycle of hardship in my life and destiny to break now, in the mighty name of Jesus Christ.

11. O Lord, by the Holy Spirit let every area of my life needing divine restoration and replacement receive it now, to Your glory, in the mighty name of the Lord Jesus Christ.

12. Thank You, Jesus Christ, for answering my prayers. Amen.

✟ PRAYERS TO RESCUE THE SOUL FROM SATANIC ASSIGNMENTS AND PROJECTIONS

As already shown, the soul can come under evil influences leading to a slide into error and unholy living. However, the soul can be rescued from the wicked control that is manifesting in wrong beliefs and behaviors (including error, drug use, illicit sex, anger, bitterness, etc.), and restored.

BIBLE PRAYER LINKS

He restoreth my soul: he leadeth me in the paths of righteousness for his name's sake (Ps. 23:3).

The LORD redeemeth the soul of his servants: and none of them that trust in him shall be desolate (Ps. 34:22).

To deliver their soul from death, and to keep them alive in famine (Ps. 33:19).

PRAYER FOCUS
- To cast down wicked powers, means, and results aimed against my soul
- To restore my soul to wholeness and soundness

PRAYER GUIDES
1. Father God, arise in Your creative power and call out my soul from the shadow of death, in the name of Jesus Christ.

2. Father God, let Your creative Word go forth and reintegrate my fragmented soul, in the name of Jesus.

3. Bad attitudes, habits, and decisions generated from the pit of hell and programmed into my soul, I cast you out now, in the name of Jesus Christ.

4. Any area of my soul that is under bondage, receive freedom now, in the name of Jesus Christ.

5. My mind, receive freedom now, in the name of Jesus Christ.

6. My will, receive freedom now, in the name of Jesus Christ.

7. My emotions, receive freedom now, in the name of Jesus Christ.

8. Every evil assignment or restriction working in my soul to destroy my divine destiny, give way now, in the name of Jesus Christ.

9. Every stone of darkness in my soul, melt away, in the name of Jesus Christ.

10. Arrows that fly by day and are prospering in my soul, die, in the name of Jesus Christ.

11. Father Lord, let the powers seeking to destroy my soul go into the lower parts of the earth, in the name of Jesus Christ (see Ps. 63:9).

12. Father Lord, let the powers seeking to arrest my soul fall by Your sword, in the name of Jesus Christ (see Ps. 63:10).

13. Every magic mirror conjuring my face, break to pieces, in the name of Jesus Christ.

14. Thank You, Lord Jesus, for answering my prayers. Amen.

✝ PRAYERS TO RESCUE HEART AND MIND FROM EVIL ASSIGNMENTS AND PROJECTIONS

The prime access point of the devil and his agents is the human mind. The forces of evil can render a once spiritually-powerful person powerless through evil projections into the mind.

BIBLE PRAYER LINK

God hath not given us the spirit of fear; but of power, and of love, and of a sound mind (2 Tim. 1:7).

PRAYER FOCUS
- To uproot and negate all evil assignments against my mind
- To appeal to the Holy Spirit and the blood of Jesus to defend and restore my mind

PRAYER GUIDES
1. Every power assigned to darken my mind, the Lord rebuke you, in the name of Jesus Christ.
2. In the name of Jesus Christ, every satanic projection or assignment against my heart to waste my destiny, be blotted out by the blood of Jesus.
3. Demons assigned to manipulate my mind toward idleness and prayerlessness, the Lord rebuke you, in the name of Jesus Christ.
4. Every satanic projection aimed at programming me for error, be cut off with the blood of Jesus Christ.
5. I command my thought life to refuse cooperation with any assignment and projection coming from environmental powers seeking to destroy me, in the name of Jesus Christ.
6. Holy Spirit, empower my thought life to resist evil assignments and projections of failure, in the name of Jesus.
7. Every satanic projection into the mind of people to disappoint me, I cut you off with the blood of Jesus.
8. Holy Spirit, overhaul my thought life with your fire, in the name of Jesus.
9. Satanic assignment of weariness against my mind, be cut off with the blood of Jesus.
10. Every assignment sent from the second heaven to make my love cold, I rebuke you, in the name of Jesus.
11. Every power projecting destructive thoughts into my mind, be paralyzed, in the name of Jesus.
12. Thank You, Lord, for answering my prayers. Amen.

✟ PRAYERS TO NEUTRALIZE SICKNESS AND TO APPROPRIATE GOD'S CREATIVE POWER TO HEAL

Every sickness and disease derives its strength from the evil spirit behind it. That spirit is the life-giver—the one animating the ailment. Once the life-giver is conquered and destroyed, healing and wholeness are instantaneous.

Sins, sicknesses, and diseases can be rooted in family lines going back many generations. That is why we need to pray to cut off every evil ancestral river flowing down to our generation. This must be done in the name of Jesus Christ.

BIBLE PRAYER LINKS

Asa in the thirty and ninth year of his reign was diseased in his feet, until his disease was exceeding great: yet in his disease he sought not to the LORD, but to the physicians (2 Chron. 16:12).

There sat a certain man at Lystra, impotent in his feet, being a cripple from his mother's womb, who never had walked: The same heard Paul speak: who steadfastly beholding him, and perceiving that he had faith to be healed, said with a loud voice, Stand upright on thy feet. And he leaped and walked (Acts 14:8-10).

*It came to pass on a certain day, as he was teaching, that there were Pharisees and doctors of the law sitting by, which were come out of every town of Galilee, and Judea, and Jerusalem: **and the power of the Lord was present to heal them*** (Luke 5:17).

I will restore health unto thee, and I will heal thee of thy wounds, saith the LORD; because they called thee an Outcast, saying, This is Zion, whom no man seeketh after (Jer. 30:17).

PRAYER FOCUS
- To resist and destroy evil assignments against my health
- To appropriate God's creative power to heal

PRAYER GUIDES
1. Thank You, Lord, for bearing my sickness and setting me free. By Your stripes I was healed! (See Isaiah 53:4-5; First Peter 2:24.)
2. Thank You, Lord, for redeeming me from sin, sickness, and disease.
3. Thank You, Lord, for my deliverance in both soul and body.
4. Father God, arise in Your creative power and replace any of my bodily organs that are diseased, in the name of Jesus.
5. Father God, let Your creative words penetrate any deep places (strongholds) where disease is hiding in my body, and destroy it, in the name of Jesus.
6. Father God, arise in Your creative power and command every unwelcome foreign cell in my body to disappear, in the name of Jesus.
7. Father God, breathe on me and let every dead or dying organ in my body receive life, in the name of Jesus.
8. I destroy with the fire of the Holy Ghost anything that gives life to any cancer or other disease in my body, in the name of Jesus.
9. Lord Jesus, by the power and the authority of Your Word that dried up the useless fig tree, let every sickness or disease in my body die now from its roots, in the name of Jesus Christ.
10. Lord Jesus, by the power and the authority of Your Word that dried up the useless fig tree, let all roots and tentacles of cancer die now, in the name of Jesus Christ.
11. Father God, speak Your creative Word into the diseased part of my body and render it "very good," as it was in the beginning, in the name of Jesus Christ.
12. Thank You, Lord, for answering my prayers. Amen.

✟ Prayers to Negate Evil Assignments Delegated to Cause Poverty

There are many routes by which poverty can enter a person's life. These include evil assignments that cause a person to reject good financial counsel. Such assignments can also program a person to repeat the same mistakes over and over again until poverty results. The following prayers will remove or negate such evil assignments so lasting prosperity can come.

Bible Prayer Links

Jesus sat over against the treasury, and beheld how the people cast money into the treasury: and many that were rich cast in much. And there came a certain poor widow, and she threw in two mites, which make a farthing. And he called unto him his disciples, and saith unto them, Verily I say unto you, That this poor widow hath cast more in, than all they which have cast into the treasury: for all they did cast in of their abundance; but she of her want did cast in all that she had, even all her living (Mark 12:41-44).

Bring ye all the tithes into the storehouse, that there may be meat in mine house, and prove me now herewith, saith the Lord *of hosts, if I will not open you the windows of heaven, and pour you out a blessing, that there shall not be room enough to receive it* (Mal. 3:10).

Prayer Focus
- To negate all assignments against my financial well-being

Prayer Guides
1. Every satanic assignment to destroy me financially, be neutralized by the blood of Jesus Christ.

2. Any demon delegated to attract poverty into my life, be paralyzed, in the name of Jesus Christ.
3. Demonic hindrance assigned against my progress, be dismantled by the fire of God, in the name of Jesus Christ.
4. Every demon assigned to attract me to useless ventures, the Lord rebuke you, in the name of Jesus Christ.

✝ Prayers to Negate Evil Assignments Delegated to Cause Depression

How can evil assignments cause depression? The answer is simple: depression manifests wherever frustration, limitation, or stagnation exist. Some evil assignments are designed to neutralize a person's most diligent efforts and hard work.

The most important weapon against depression is singing to the Lord "praises with understanding" (Ps. 47:7). By this I mean first using spiritual songs, worship songs, and hymns to attack the problem causing depression, and then to follow your praises with prayer.

The following prayers will help you to negate such assignments and will inspire other prayers that address your needs.

Bible Prayer Links

We are troubled on every side, yet not distressed; we are perplexed, but not in despair (2 Cor. 4:8).

I had fainted, unless I had believed to see the goodness of the LORD in the land of the living (Ps. 27:13).

Be of good courage, and he shall strengthen your heart, all ye that hope in the LORD (Ps. 31:24).

Why art thou cast down, O my soul? and why art thou disquieted within me? Hope thou in God: for I shall

205

*yet praise him, who is the health of my countenance,
and my God* (Ps. 42:11).

PRAYER FOCUS
- To negate all attempts of the enemy to afflict me with depression

PRAYER GUIDES
1. Lord Jesus, I thank You for breaking the power of depression off my life during this prayer program.
2. By the blood of Jesus Christ, I command any evil assignment delegated to cause depression to be destroyed now, in the name of Jesus Christ.
3. Evil assignment of discouragement and hopelessness, die now, in the name of Jesus Christ.
4. Every problem generated to depress me, I overcome you now by the blood of Jesus Christ and the words of my testimony, in the name of Jesus Christ.
5. Father Lord, by the Holy Spirit, empower me now to overcome any depression in my life, in the name of Jesus Christ.
6. Let the praise of the Lord fill my mouth and defeat any wicked agendas to cause depression in my life, in the name of Jesus Christ.
7. O Lord, arise and render the power of depression null and void in my life, in the name of Jesus Christ.
8. By the power of the Holy Spirit, I bind and cast out the evil assignment(s) sent to generate confusion, in the name of Jesus Christ.
9. Thank You, Lord, for answering my prayers. Amen.

✠ PRAYERS TO NEGATE EVIL ASSIGNMENTS DELEGATED TO CAUSE UNTIMELY DEATH

Evil assignments can be sent to kill. Usually, they are undertaken by night, such as when a person sleeps and dreams of being wounded by gunfire or by an arrow that pierces the body. If the harm that occurred in the dream is not addressed spiritually, it can translate into an actual physical illness that leads to an untimely death. Prayers such as those below can negate these deadly assignments.

BIBLE PRAYER LINKS

I shall not die, but live, and declare the works of the LORD (Ps. 118:17).

Art thou not from everlasting, O LORD my God, mine Holy One? **we shall not die.** *O LORD, thou hast ordained them for judgment; and, O mighty God, thou hast established them for correction* (Hab. 1:12).

PRAYER FOCUS
- To identify and uproot all assignments of untimely death
- To invoke the blood of Jesus and the power of His name to preserve life

PRAYER GUIDES
1. By the blood of Jesus Christ, I renounce and revoke any conscious or unconscious covenant of sudden or untimely death in my family, in the name of Jesus Christ.
2. By the power of the Holy Spirit, I declare that the spirit of death and hell has no power over me or any member of my family, in the name of Jesus Christ.
3. You evil covenant of death, loose your attachment to my life, in the name of Jesus Christ.
4. With the blood of Jesus Christ, and in His name, I delete my name and the names of my family members from the register of early death.
5. I break every curse of death upon my life, in the name of Jesus Christ.
6. O Lord, remove from my life any garment of death as you did for the three Hebrew men, in the name of Jesus Christ (see Dan. 3:27).

7. I break the hold of the spirit of death upon my life and receive divine deliverance from its attack, in the mighty name of Jesus Christ.

8. Any demonic power that is ready to deliver me to death, be swallowed up suddenly in the wrath of God, in the name of Jesus Christ.

9. I command every instrument of death in my body to be destroyed now, in the name of Jesus Christ.

10. In the name of Jesus Christ, every form of poison transferred into my body by the spirit of death, be neutralized by the blood of Jesus Christ.

11. Lion of the Tribe of Judah, arise now and devour every demonic lion roaring against my life, in the name of Jesus Christ.

12. I break any yoke of stagnancy assigned to me by the spirit of death, in the name of Jesus Christ.

13. I reject, revoke, and nullify any spiritual transaction or covenant with the dead or the spirit of the dead, in the name of Jesus Christ.

14. Every spirit of the grave assigned against my life, the Lord rebuke you, in the name of Jesus Christ.

15. I terminate every terminator of life that is pursuing me, in the name of Jesus Christ.

16. Any satanic carpenter constructing a coffin for me, I command you to enter into your coffin, in the name of Jesus Christ.

17. Demon of death, I command you to leave my body now, in the name of Jesus Christ.

18. No arrow of death and hell shall locate me, in the name of Jesus Christ.

19. Every form of poison injected into my spirit, soul, and body in my dreams, be neutralized with the blood of Jesus Christ, in the name of Jesus Christ.

20. Thank You, Lord, for answering my prayers. Amen.

✟PRAYERS TO NULLIFY EVIL ASSIGNMENTS OF MINISTRY FAILURE

As already mentioned, some evil assignments are meant to frustrate, stagnate, and limit. When these assignments are sent against ministers of the gospel, their efforts do not yield the meaningful results they should. Prayer is powerful to negate these hindrances.

BIBLE PRAYER LINKS

In stripes, in imprisonments, in tumults, in labours, in watchings, in fastings; by pureness, by knowledge, by longsuffering, by kindness, by the Holy Ghost, by love unfeigned, by the word of truth, by the power of God, by the armour of righteousness on the right hand and on the left, by honour and dishonour, by evil report and good report: as deceivers, and yet true; as unknown, and yet well known; as dying, and, behold, we live; as chastened, and not killed; as sorrowful, yet alway rejoicing; as poor, yet making many rich; as having nothing, and yet possessing all things (2 Cor. 6:5-10).

PRAYER FOCUS
- To disrupt and destroy all evil assignments against my ministry and calling
- To revoke and neutralize all legal grounds of attack

PRAYER GUIDES
1. Father Lord, I thank You for Your call upon my life. Holy Spirit, redirect my spirit, soul, and body to focus on God and His Word, in the name of Jesus Christ.
2. Evil assignments and projections from my environment that are against my ministry and calling, backfire, in the name of Jesus.

3. Habitation of evil and wickedness established in my environment to destroy my ministry and calling, be consumed in the fire of God witnessed by Elijah, in the name of Jesus Christ.

4. I command every conspiracy in my environment that has assembled against my ministry and calling to fail, in the name of Jesus Christ.

5. Because I have made the Lord my refuge, no witchcraft projection against my ministry shall succeed, in the name of Jesus Christ.

6. Lord, let the projections of all household enemies against my destiny boomerang to them, in the name of Jesus Christ.

7. Every astral projection against my life, I frustrate and dismantle you, in the name of Jesus Christ.

8. I hold the blood of Jesus against the demon assigned to afflict my destiny with rejection, in the name of Jesus Christ.

9. By the authority of Calvary, I withdraw all evil pronouncements registered by the sun, moon, and stars against my advancement, in the name of Jesus Christ.

10. By the blood of Jesus, I cancel every witchcraft curse projected into the heavens against my divine destiny, in the name of Jesus Christ.

11. Every evil projection coming against my ministry from within the river or the sea, be blown away by the thunder of God, in the name of Jesus Christ.

12. In the authority of Calvary, I command every affliction and hindrance assigned against my ministry from any coven and registered in the cycle of the moon to be destroyed now, in the name of Jesus Christ.

13. I revoke with the blood of Jesus, the ancestral covenant that has given legal ground to the working of evil assignments against my ministry, in the name of Jesus Christ.

14. Glory of God, overshadow my ministry and release me from the yoke of evil assignments and projections, in the name of Jesus Christ.

15. Thank You, Lord, for answering my prayers. Amen.

✝ Prayers to Disrupt and Destroy Evil Assignments Sent to Destroy My Child(ren)

Children are often targeted by wicked assignments, but parents don't always perceive the attacks. Examples include children who exhibit strange behaviors or claim that strange powers are urging them to do evil. When a young man raped an eighty-year-old woman, he said, "Something asked me to do it." This is very unusual. But the following prayers will help destroy evil assignments sent against children.

Bible Prayer Links

All thy children shall be taught of the LORD; and great shall be the peace of thy children (Isa. 54:13).

Thus saith the LORD, Even the captives of the mighty shall be taken away, and the prey of the terrible shall be delivered: for I will contend with him that contendeth with thee, and I will save thy children (Isa. 49:25).

Prayer Focus
- To invoke the name, Word, and blood of Jesus on behalf of my child(ren) in every area of life
- To cancel all assignments against my parent-child relationship(s)

Prayer Guides
1. Father God, You said that even the captives of the mighty shall be taken away. Now by Your Word, I command the release of my child(ren) from any demonic assignments (and their effects), in the name of Jesus Christ.
2. Father God, You said that the prey of the terrible shall be delivered. Now by Your Word, I command the deliverance of my child(ren) from every demonic hold, in the name of Jesus Christ.

3. Father God, You said You would contend with those that contend with me. Now arise in Your anger and discomfit any demonic powers contending with the destiny of my child(ren), in the name of Jesus Christ.

4. Satan, hear the Word of the Lord: Even the captives of the mighty shall be taken away. Now I wrest the spirit and soul of my child(ren) from your hold, in the name of Jesus Christ.

5. Hiding place of darkness in the life of my child(ren), be exposed and become desolate, in the name of Jesus Christ.

6. O Lord my Father, deliver my child(ren) from the hold of last days' satanic assignments, in the name of Jesus Christ.

7. O Lord, my Father, remove my child(ren) from any hard dominion of wicked spirits, in the name of Jesus Christ.

8. Any demonic power that wastes away life, release my child(ren) now, in the name of Jesus Christ.

9. Foundation of darkness in the life of my child(ren), be dismantled, in the name of Jesus Christ.

10. Any aspect of life for my child(ren) that is connected to any dark power, receive the light of God. Be exposed and cut off now, in the name of Jesus Christ.

11. Father God, lead my child(ren) in paths of righteousness for Your name's sake, in the name of Jesus Christ (see Ps. 23:3).

12. Father God, if the enemy has tampered with my child's soul, restore it now, in the name of Jesus Christ (see Ps. 23:3).

13. By the Word of God, which says that the seed of the righteous shall be delivered, I release my child(ren) from the hold of any spirits of disobedience and rebellion, in the name of Jesus Christ (see Prov. 11:21).

14. Father God, open the ears of my children to receive correction, so they will not be rebellious, in the name of Jesus Christ (see Isa. 50:5).

15. Voice of God, speak and neutralize every evil pronouncement that is affecting the destiny of my child(ren), in the name of Jesus Christ.

16. Evil ministrations into the mind of my child(ren), (<u>insert names</u>), be cut off by the blood of Jesus Christ.

17. Every habitation of demonic powers in the life of my child(ren), (insert names), become desolate, in the name of Jesus Christ.
18. I soak the mind and life of (insert name) in the blood of Jesus Christ.
19. Evil assignments delegated to create problems between me and my child(ren), be cut off by the blood of Jesus Christ.
20. Any legal ground occupied by evil powers to confuse my child(ren) about accepting Jesus as Savior and Lord, be revoked by the blood of Jesus Christ.
21. Any stronghold setting my child(ren) against me, be dismantled by the thunder of God, in the name of Jesus Christ.
22. Any demonic power aspiring to break the bond I share with my child(ren), your wicked means shall turn against you, in the name of Jesus Christ.
23. O Lord, create a new heart in my child so he/she can serve You forever, in the name of Jesus Christ.
24. Any demonic power projecting disobedience and rebellion into the heart of my child(ren), be exposed and put to shame, in the name of Jesus Christ.
25. Lord Jesus, fill the heart of my child(ren) with Your love and truth, that they might reign with You now and in the world to come, in the name of Jesus Christ.
26. Father God, by the power and authority with which You commanded light to swallow darkness in the beginning, decree obedience to swallow rebellion in the life of my child(ren), in the name of Jesus Christ.
27. Thank You, Lord, for answering my prayers. Amen.

✟ PRAYERS FOR REDEMPTION THROUGH GOD'S GREAT JUDGMENTS

Having covered in prayer many wicked assignments and projections, it is now time to thank Father God for His resolute and redemptive justice.

BIBLE PRAYER LINKS

Wherefore say unto the children of Israel, I am the LORD, and I will bring you out from under the burdens of the Egyptians, and I will rid you out of their bondage, and I will redeem you with a stretched out arm, and with great judgments (Exod. 6:6).

Zion shall be redeemed with judgment, and her converts with righteousness (Isa. 1:27).

Therefore the ungodly shall not stand in the judgment, nor sinners in the congregation of the righteous (Ps. 1:5).

PRAYER FOCUS
- To appeal to the Father's just and right ways
- To acknowledge the working of His power on my behalf

PRAYER GUIDES
1. Lord, I thank You for the favor I receive from You every day, in the name of Jesus Christ.
2. Any demonic power resisting my healing (breakthroughs, blessings, elevation, and deliverance), receive God's great judgments and perish as Pharaoh did, in the name of Jesus Christ.
3. Any demonic power vowing to keep me in bondage (sickness, poverty, lack, etc.) when the Lord has ordered my freedom and blessing, be destroyed as Pharaoh was, in the name of Jesus Christ.
4. Father God, arise now, and with Your great judgments redeem my life (my destiny, calling, breakthroughs, and blessings) from any satanic hold, in the name of Jesus Christ.
5. O Lord, assign Your great judgments against the "Pharaoh" that is holding my life (my destiny, progress, breakthroughs, and blessings) captive. Set me free, in the name of Jesus Christ.

6. O Lord, arise now and bring great judgments upon whatever holds me in bondage. Set me free and release me to Your glory, in the name of Jesus Christ.

7. O Lord, arise now and bring great judgments upon any satanic embargoes (wicked restrictions or restraints designed to stifle destiny and the testimony of God's goodness) that have kept me stagnant. Move me forward now, in the name of Jesus Christ.

8. O Lord, assign Your great judgment against anything that is oppressing my life, destiny, brain, calling, or career, and deliver me now, in the name of Jesus Christ.

9. Father Lord, arise now and pronounce great judgment of destruction upon any wickedness sown into my body or life to limit my divine purpose, in the name of Jesus Christ.

10. By the power of the Holy Spirit, I bring the written judgment of fire upon the demonic powers on assignment to hinder my breakthroughs and blessings, in the name of Jesus Christ.

11. Every longtime problem defying resolution in my life, receive the great judgment of destruction and vanish now, in the name of Jesus Christ.

12. Let the written judgment of failure be assigned against any demonic power that is attacking my prosperity, health, glory, or progress, in the name of Jesus Christ.

13. Thank You, Jesus, for answering my prayers. Amen.

10

The Wicked Means of Bewitchment

Those who plan to destroy the means of the wicked must have knowledge and understanding of bewitchment—a kind of captivity that causes a person to yield entirely to the will of another. Bewitchment is a type of spell that can involve the use and influence of charms and incantations.

Bewitchment is entirely demonic. It drives even the exalted into downward spirals and eventual worthlessness, preventing and diverting goodness so that only bad outcomes are possible. When Israel's King Saul enquired of a familiar spirit, for example, disaster was the result (see 1 Sam. 28).

Bewitchment can oppress the human soul and produce bondages such as drug, alcohol, and other addictions; talkativeness; and other spiritual maladies. Bewitchment enforces these bondages so powerfully that steps are not taken to deal with the problem's source.

Bewitchment is mentioned in Scripture: "O foolish Galatians, who hath bewitched you, that ye should not obey the truth…" (Gal. 3:1). Bewitchment works to strip away that which the Lord God lovingly deposits in the lives of His children, so that they stray from Him and His ways.

In Acts 8:9-11, we read about

> *a certain man, called Simon, which beforetime in the same city used sorcery, and bewitched the people of Samaria, giving out that himself was some great*

*one: to whom they all gave heed, from the least to the
greatest, saying, This man is the great power of God.
And to him they had regard, because that of long time
he had bewitched them with sorceries.*

Satan used Simon shrewdly. The entire city believed he was God-
sent with divine power. But the Bible says he used evil powers. I
believe he would have used them to bewitch Philip. But Simon and
his powers failed. I also believe this experience led Simon to accept
the gospel preached by Philip, so that he believed in Christ Jesus.

Nevertheless, Simon still craved the recognition he was accus-
tomed to receiving. When the apostles Peter and John baptized
Samaritans with the Holy Spirit, Simon asked to buy the Holy Spirit
with money. For this evil request, he was banished.

Who bewitched Simon? The chief bewitcher is Satan. His ranks
include demons, territorial spirits (spirits attached to particular ter-
ritories, districts, or localities), witches and wizards, satanic priests,
and those with familiar spirits who carry out his assignments.

Bewitchment can be used against young and old. A person whose
body is under bewitchment can experience sicknesses for which
no sources are found. Properties and material things can also be
bewitched. For example, if a person's car is bewitched, it can be
used to drain the person's finances. Even structures and workplaces
can be bewitched, so that occupants need the spiritual cleansing of
deliverance. We can cleanse ourselves from the adverse effects of
being in these places by saying the following prayer:

> O Lord, arise and make void the adverse effects
> of bewitchments that came upon me while living/
> working in (name the place/structure), in the mighty
> name of Jesus Christ.

The following can also be bewitched:
1. A life
2. A destiny
3. A person's understanding
4. A person's soul

5. A person's memory
6. Relationships

The enemy uses a variety of items in the process of bewitchment, including the following:
1. The four elements: fire, water, earth (including the sand, dust, and ground), and air
2. The astral elements: sun, moon, and stars
3. Photographs of people
4. Any product of the human body, such as hair

Another method of bewitchment is astral projection. The children of darkness are able to project out of their bodies and travel through spirit realms to bewitch others.

Many believe this information is fantasy; but it could not be more real. Bewitchment is a wicked tool used by Satan to keep believers from the glory of God. Unfortunately, because many believers are unaware of it, they do not seek freedom. Many lives and destinies have been derailed, truncated, stunted, and stopped, due to this lack of knowledge and understanding.

Bewitchment is designed to bring misery and destruction to individuals, couples, families, and other groups being targeted. In marital relationships, for example, it creates an atmosphere perpetually under attack and without peace.

As believers in the Lord Jesus Christ, we must stand against this, in prayer!

✝ PRAYERS TO BANISH THE POWER OF BEWITCHMENT IN MY LIFE

BIBLE PRAYER LINK

The soul that turneth after such as have familiar spirits, and after wizards, to go a whoring after them, I will even set my face against that soul, and will cut him off from among his people. Sanctify yourselves therefore, and be ye holy: for I am the LORD your God (Lev. 20:6-7).

PRAYER FOCUS

- To counter, cancel, and reverse all forms and effects of bewitchment in my life

PRAYER GUIDES

1. Father Lord, let the blood of Jesus Christ neutralize every form of bewitchment cast upon my labor, in the mighty name of Jesus Christ.
2. Father Lord, let the blood of Jesus Christ come against and destroy every bewitching spirit assigned to destroy me and my staff of bread, in the mighty name of Jesus Christ.
3. O Lord, arise today and destroy every agent of bewitchment operating around me, in the name of Jesus Christ.
4. Power of bewitchment operating in my life and destiny, be paralyzed now by the redeeming blood of Jesus Christ.
5. Wickedness of bewitchment, die in my life and destiny today, in the name of Jesus Christ.
6. Every mouth anointed by Satan to bewitch me, I command you to be silenced forever, in name of Jesus Christ.
7. The joy of the Lord will strengthen me today to subvert and demolish all forms of bewitchment aimed at my life and destiny, in the mighty name of Jesus Christ.
8. O Lord, if any bewitchment prevents my being Your true disciple, remove it from me, in the mighty name of Jesus Christ.
9. In the mighty name of Jesus Christ, I plead the power of the blood of Jesus Christ to cleanse any bewitchment of my spirit, soul, or body
10. Any demonic power chanting bewitchment over my photograph, receive an angelic slap and be paralyzed, in the mighty name of Jesus Christ.
11. Any demonic power or agent using my photograph to project evil against me or my life, destiny, marital destiny, finances, and business enterprises, the Lord rebuke you. Be paralyzed now, in the mighty name of Jesus Christ.

12. Any demonic power or agent using evil means against me, the Lord rebuke you. Be paralyzed now, in the mighty name of Jesus Christ.

13. Any power or demonized agent using the night hours to project bewitchment against me, the Lord rebuke you. Be paralyzed now, in the mighty name of Jesus Christ.

14. Every evil transmission from the dark world against my life, destiny, home, family, finances, business enterprises, promotion and elevation, or health and wealth, be cut off now, by the redeeming blood and the name of Jesus Christ.

15. Any occult personality or other satanic agent using witchcraft devices to attack my life, destiny, home, family, finances, business enterprises, promotion and elevation, or health and wealth, I command your tools to turn back against you, in the mighty name of Jesus Christ.

16. Demonic wind from any evil domain that is stirred up against my life, destiny, home, family, finances, business enterprises, promotion and elevation, or health and wealth, I command you to stop now and return to your source, in the mighty name of Jesus Christ.

17. O Lord, by a strong east wind, drive away the darkness that is surrounding my life, destiny, home, family, finances, business enterprise, promotion and elevation, health and wealth, excellency and glory, marital destiny, calling and ministry, and well-being, by the redeeming blood and the name of Jesus Christ.

18. O Lord my God, arise on the day of satanic siege or temptation and be my God, in the mighty name of Jesus Christ.

19. O Lord my God, arise on the day of satanic overwhelming and be my God, in the mighty name of Jesus Christ.

20. O Lord my God, let every satanic accord against my life and destiny be broken and shattered to pieces, in the mighty name of my Lord and Savior, Jesus Christ.

21. Thank You, Lord, for answering my prayers. Amen.

✝ Prayers to Cast Off Agents and Works of Bewitchment

Bible Prayer Links

> *He* [Manasseh] *caused his children to pass through the fire in the valley of the son of Hinnom: also he observed times, and used enchantments, and used witchcraft, and dealt with a familiar spirit, and with wizards: he wrought much evil in the sight of the Lord, to provoke him to anger* (2 Chron. 33:6).

> *I will cut off witchcrafts out of thine hand; and thou shalt have no more soothsayers* (Mic. 5:12).

Prayer Focus
- To arrest all agents of bewitchment sent against me
- To cancel, root out, and destroy all bewitchment in my life

Prayer Guides
1. Every bewitching power assigned to turn me away from the gospel of Jesus Christ, the Lord rebuke you. Be paralyzed, in the name of Jesus Christ.
2. Every bewitching power operating around me, the hand of the Lord is upon you now. Be exposed and disgraced, in the mighty name of Jesus Christ.
3. Every child of the devil who vowed to bewitch me into error and failure, the hand of the Lord is upon you. Expire now, in the mighty name of Jesus Christ.
4. Every child of the devil troubling my life and destiny through sorcery, the hand of the Lord is upon you now. Lose your peace forever, in the mighty name of Jesus Christ (see Isa. 48:22).
5. In the mighty name of Jesus, woe be unto every child of the devil pursuing my life, destiny, finances, health, and wealth through bewitchment.

6. Wickedness of bewitchment, die in my life, destiny, marital destiny, home, finances, business, health, and wealth, in the name of Jesus Christ.

7. Every familiar spirit attacking and attempting to bewitch and rule my life and destiny, I command you to die, by the redeeming blood, and in the name of Jesus Christ.

8. By the blood of Jesus, I command every bewitchment and bewitching power programmed into my life and destiny to die by Holy Ghost fire, in the name of Jesus Christ.

9. All forms of bewitchment assigned to my head, I shake you off now, in the mighty name of Jesus Christ.

10. Every form of bewitchment assigned to my hands, I shake you off now, in the mighty name of Jesus Christ.

11. Every form of bewitchment assigned to my legs, I shake you off now, in the mighty name of Jesus Christ.

12. Every form of bewitchment assigned to my bodily organs, functions, and activity, I shake you off now, in the mighty name of Jesus Christ.

13. Thank You, Lord, for answering my prayers. Amen.

✝ Prayers to Destroy Generational Bewitchment

Bible Prayer Link

> *Blotting out the handwriting of ordinances that was against us, which was contrary to us, and took it out of the way, nailing it to his cross; and having spoiled principalities and powers, he made a shew of them openly, triumphing over them in it* (Col. 2:14-15).

Prayer Focus

- To cleanse my ancestral roots of all bewitchment
- To uproot and demolish all bewitchments affecting me and my generations

PRAYER GUIDES

1. Thank You, Almighty God, that as I pray You are disappointing the devices of my enemies, in the name of Jesus Christ.

2. Thank You, Lord, for blotting out the handwriting of the evil ordinances that are against me, in the name of Jesus Christ.

3. O Lord, by the greatness of Your power, nullify all generational bewitchment that brings hardship to my labor. Give me the anointing of ease today, in the mighty name of Jesus Christ.

4. O Lord, by the greatness of Your power nullify every generational bewitchment of nonachievement and backwardness in my life and destiny. Now, O Lord, advance every course of mine to glory, in the name of Jesus Christ.

5. O Lord, by the greatness of Your power nullify every generational bewitchment of sickness, disease, and untimely death in my life. Bless me with good health and long life, in the name of Jesus Christ.

6. Ancestral powers sitting on my progress, be unseated now by the power of the Holy Ghost, in the name of Jesus Christ.

7. Every evil transmission from my roots sent to bewitch my life and destiny, be cut off now by the blood of Jesus Christ, in His name.

8. O God, arise and shake all foundations of ancestral witchcraft and bewitchment. Remove them from my life, in the name of Jesus Christ.

9. O God, arise and shake all foundations of ancestral sickness and disease. Remove them from my body and life, in the mighty name of Jesus Christ.

10. O God, arise and shake all foundations of ancestral failure affecting my life and destiny. Remove them, in the name of the Lord Jesus Christ.

11. O God, arise and shake all foundations of ancestral poverty and backwardness out of my life and destiny, in the name of Jesus Christ.

12. Lord, by a strong east wind, drive away all darkness surrounding and bewitching my life and destiny, in the name of Jesus Christ.

13. O Lord, deliver me from the terror of the night and the arrows by day that are generated in my environment, in the name of Jesus Christ (see Ps. 91:5).
14. Demonic wind stirred up against me from any evil domain of my roots, I command you to stop and return to your source, in the name of Jesus Christ, my Lord and Savior.
15. Thank You, Lord, for answering my prayers. Amen.

✟ PRAYERS TO DESTROY BEWITCHMENT

BIBLE PRAYER LINK

He disappointeth the devices of the crafty, so that their hands cannot perform their enterprise (Job 5:12).

PRAYER FOCUS
- To oppose, rescind, and reverse all forms of bewitchment

PRAYER GUIDES
1. Thank You, Almighty God, for disappointing the bewitchments of my enemies during this prayer program.
2. Thank You, Lord, for blotting out the handwriting of the evil ordinances that are against me, in the name of Jesus Christ.
3. Any agent of darkness using bewitchment to sit on and stifle my progress, be unseated by the power of the Holy Ghost, in the name of Jesus Christ.
4. Every evil transmission of bewitchment from the dark world against my life and destiny, be cut off, in the name of Jesus Christ.
5. Lord, by a strong east wind, drive away all darkness surrounding my life and destiny, in the name of Jesus Christ.
6. O Lord, deliver me from the terror of the night and the arrows by day that are generated in my environment, in the name of Jesus Christ (see Ps. 91:5).
7. Any agent of bewitchment chanting my name, receive angelic attack and be destroyed, in the name of Jesus Christ.

8. Any occult personality using witchcraft to attack me, the Lord rebuke you. I command your tools to turn against you now, in the mighty name of Jesus Christ.

9. In the name of Jesus Christ, any occult personality generating a demon of death against me, the Lord rebuke you, and may your tools work against you.

10. O Lord, to the glory of Your name, let me hear of the death of the personality seeking my death, in the name of Jesus Christ.

11. Thank You, Lord, for answering my prayers. Amen.

✞ PRAYERS TO NEUTRALIZE BEWITCHMENT

BIBLE PRAYER LINKS

But there was a certain man, called Simon, which beforetime in the same city used sorcery, and bewitched the people of Samaria, giving out that himself was some great one: to whom they all gave heed, from the least to the greatest, saying, This man is the great power of God (Acts 8:9-10).

O foolish Galatians, who hath bewitched you, that ye should not obey the truth, before whose eyes Jesus Christ hath been evidently set forth, crucified among you? (Gal. 3:1).

PRAYER FOCUS
■ To render all works and strategies of bewitchment null and void

PRAYER GUIDES
1. Thank You, Lord, for Your faithfulness to those who trust in Your name for their deliverance from all bewitchment, in the name of Jesus Christ.

2. I plead the blood of Jesus Christ that nullifies all bewitchment over my spirit, soul, body, and environment now, in the name of Jesus Christ.

3. Every power that has bewitched my life (marital destiny, finances, etc.) with failure, the hand of the Lord is upon you to destroy your works now, in the name of Jesus Christ.

4. Woe unto every child of the devil that is pursuing my life and destiny with evil. Your bewitchment schemes are neutralized now, in the name of Jesus Christ.

5. Every demon assigned to sustain bewitchment in my life and destiny, your time is over. Come out now and go back to your assigner, in the name of Jesus Christ.

6. By the word of the Lord, I, (name), run into the name of the Lord and I am safe from all bewitchment; His name is my strong tower, in the name of Jesus Christ (see Ps. 61:3).

7. Thank You, Lord for answering my prayers. Amen.

✝ PRAYERS FOR DIVINE PURGING

BIBLE PRAYER LINKS

Wash you, make you clean; put away the evil of your doings from before mine eyes; cease to do evil; learn to do well; seek judgment, relieve the oppressed, judge the fatherless, plead for the widow. Come now, and let us reason together, saith the LORD: Though your sins be as scarlet, they shall be as white as snow; though they be red like crimson, they shall be as wool (Isa. 1:16-18).

If the blood of bulls and of goats, and the ashes of an heifer sprinkling the unclean, sanctifieth to the purifying of the flesh: how much more shall the blood of Christ, who through the eternal Spirit offered himself without spot to God, purge your conscience from dead works to serve the living God? (Heb. 9:13-14)

He shall sit as a refiner and purifier of silver: and he shall purify the sons of Levi, and purge them as gold and silver, that they may offer unto the Lord *an offering in righteousness* (Mal. 3:3).

Prayer Focus

- To be cleansed, restored, and refreshed by God's holy fire

Prayer Guides

1. Thank You, Jesus Christ, for Your manifested destruction of the devil's works in my life.
2. All evil dirt in my spirit, soul, and body, receive the cleansing fire of the Holy Spirit and be made whole, in the name of Jesus Christ.
3. Purge me, O Lord, with Your fire, in the name of Jesus Christ.
4. Holy fire of God, possess me now and sanctify me, in the mighty name of Jesus Christ.
5. Holy fire of God, flow into my body. Challenge and destroy every stranger therein, in the name of Jesus Christ.
6. By faith, I drink the blood of Jesus Christ to destroy every demonic deposit in my body, in the name of Jesus Christ.
7. Inherited strangers (such as demonic poisons or demonic arrows) in my body, be melted and flushed out of my body by the holy fire of God, in the name of Jesus Christ.
8. O Lord, cleanse my waste places today. Make my wilderness a garden of joy and gladness, in the name of Jesus Christ (see Isa. 51:3).
9. Thank You, Jesus, for answering my prayers. Amen.

✟ Prayers to Purge Demonic Powers

Bible Prayer Link

As soon as they hear of me, they shall obey me: the strangers shall submit themselves unto me. The strangers shall fade away, and be afraid out of their close places (Ps. 18:44-45).

PRAYER FOCUS
- To cast out all unholy agents and revoke their wicked works

PRAYER GUIDES
1. Thank You, Lord, for my salvation. You decreed it, and no power can reverse it.
2. In the name of Jesus Christ, I cancel with the blood of Jesus Christ every evil spiritual promise or covenant made on my behalf by my parents or by any of my ancestors, whether consciously or unconsciously.
3. In the name of Jesus Christ, I decree that all evil spiritual strangers programmed into my body, spirit, and soul shall now receive from the Lord the arrow of fire, and die.
4. *Lay your hands on multiple parts of your body and pray:* I decree, in the mighty name of Jesus Christ, that all spiritual serpents programmed into my body during my sleep now receive from the Lord the arrow of fire. Die, in the name of Jesus Christ.
5. In the name of Jesus Christ, I command all agents of darkness that are energizing demonic elements in my body (such as sickness and disease) to depart from me now.
6. I challenge all demonic elements in my body with Holy Ghost fire, and I command them to die and be flushed out of me with the blood of Jesus Christ.
7. Holy Ghost fire, pass through my body and kill every demonic power programmed there to serve as informant to any household enemy, in the name of Jesus Christ.
8. By the Word of God that says strangers will obey me as soon as they hear of me, I command all the serpents and demonic creatures inside of me to come out now and die, in the name of Jesus Christ. *Now continue to demand that they come out. Spend quality prayer time on this.*
9. By the Word of the Lord which says that strangers shall fade away, I command all strangers of the water, trees, and rocks to fade away right now. Leave my body and never return, in the name of Jesus Christ.

10. Holy Ghost fire, break the powers of the serpentine demons programmed into my body during my sleep and consume them, in the name of Jesus Christ.
11. Evil workers sent to bring poverty, I bind you and cast you out, in the name of Jesus Christ.
12. Evil workers sent to bring sickness, I bind you and cast you out, in the name of Jesus Christ.
13. Evil workers sent to bring famine, I bind you and cast you out, in the name of Jesus Christ.
14. Evil workers sent to hinder, I bind you and cast you out, in the name of Jesus Christ.
15. O Lord, glorify Your name in my life and destiny. Put all the enemies of my destiny to shame, in the name of Jesus Christ.
16. Thank You, Lord, for answering my prayers. Amen.

11

The Means of the Wicked: Dryness

Those who plan to destroy the means of the wicked must know and understand the state of dryness. The following passage describes the condition:

> *The hand of the LORD was upon me, and carried me out in the spirit of the LORD, and set me down in the midst of the valley which was full of bones, and caused me to pass by them round about: and, behold, there were very many in the open valley; and, lo, they were very dry* (Ezek. 37:1-2).

Notice that the valley is a place of shadows. Those who experience dryness are in darkness. The Lord told Ezekiel what the children of Israel were saying: "Our bones are dried, and our hope is lost: we are cut off for our parts" (Ezek. 37:11). The attack of dryness convinced Israel that all hope was lost. Dryness has the same effect in our lives.

Manifestations of Dryness

Obviously, dryness is a lack of moisture, typically a lack of water, as in a drought. When drought comes, barrenness follows. Dry ground cannot support growth. Spiritually speaking, dryness indicates a lack of spiritual nourishment. We were created to thirst for God. The Spirit of God is the life-giver who satisfies our thirst and conquers death.

Dry things wither. Famine, poverty, and failure are dry states in which prospects seem to wither. When we speak of dryness in a person's life, we often refer to deep-seated poverty, or prolonged failure, or affliction.

Dryness is the opposite of the divine fruitfulness and multiplication God decreed for man in the beginning (see Gen. 1:28). It is a demonic oppressor that must be neutralized. When dryness is invoked against a person, a corresponding physical manifestation is experienced. This can be a drying up of finances, health, or goods. There can be physical, spiritual, and material dryness. Dryness can affect prayer, as it did when Jesus asked His disciples to pray and they kept falling asleep (see Matt. 26:36-46).

The Disciples' Dryness

There are many biblical examples of dryness, and many examples of people who overcame it. Jesus' disciples experienced dryness in ministry when faced with a deaf and dumb spirit (see Mark 9:14-29). While Jesus, Peter, James, and John were on the Mount of Transfiguration, a man asked the remaining disciples to cast a spirit out of his son. But they could not, because they were spiritually dry.

When Jesus heard what had happened, He cast out the demon, and the man's son was made whole. Privately, the disciples asked Jesus why He succeeded where they had failed.

> *When he was come into the house, his disciples asked*
> *him privately, Why could not we cast him out? And he*
> *said unto them, This kind can come forth by nothing,*
> *but by prayer and fasting* (Mark 9:28-29).

After being with the Lord for many months, the disciples lacked the power to cast out the demon. The anointing was absent; they experienced dryness in their calling. But that dryness was eventually overcome by the descent of the Holy Spirit, who watered their callings and brought His fire upon them. "Fear came upon every soul: and many wonders and signs were done by the apostles" (Acts 2:43).

Hannah's Dryness

A godly woman named Hannah faced an extended period of dryness. She longed to conceive a child, but could not. Her husband Elkanah's other wife, Peninnah, had born him children, making the situation even more painful for Hannah (see 1 Sam. 1:1-2).

The Bible explains that the Lord closed Hannah's womb. Nevertheless, Hannah rose up in faith. She decided to do more than average, everyday praying. When she and her husband went to the temple, she added vows to her prayer, and wept profusely.

> *Now Eli the priest sat upon a seat by a post of the temple of the LORD. And she* was *in bitterness of soul, and prayed unto the LORD, and wept sore. And she vowed a vow, and said, O LORD of hosts, if thou wilt indeed look on the affliction of thine handmaid, and remember me, and not forget thine handmaid, but wilt give unto thine handmaid a man child, then I will give him unto the LORD all the days of his life, and there shall no razor come upon his head* (1 Sam. 1:9-11).

Eli the priest watched as Hannah agonized in prayer, and blessed her.

> *Wherefore it came to pass, when the time was come about after Hannah had conceived, that she bare a son, and called his name Samuel,* saying, *Because I have asked him of the LORD* (1 Sam. 1:20).

Hannah cried out to the Lord; He responded by opening her womb and conquering her barrenness!

The Dryness of Jabez

The biblical account of Jabez is short but powerful. In just a few words, we see a man who overcame a very bad start in life:

> *Jabez was more honourable than his brethren: and his mother called his name Jabez, saying, Because I bare him with sorrow. And Jabez called on the God of Israel, saying, Oh that thou wouldest bless me indeed, and enlarge my coast, and that thine hand might be with me, and that thou wouldest keep* me *from evil, that it may not grieve me! And God granted him that which he requested* (1 Chron. 4:9-10).

Jabez was born into difficult circumstances and great need. But, just as Hannah rose up and petitioned the Lord, so did Jabez. All dryness in his life disappeared. In its place, God's hand and glory were seen.

The Dryness of Lazarus the Beggar

There are also stories of those whose dryness followed them to the grave.

> *There was a certain beggar named Lazarus, which was laid at his gate, full of sores, and desiring to be fed with the crumbs which fell from the rich man's table: moreover the dogs came and licked his sores. And it came to pass, that the beggar died, and was carried by the angels into Abraham's bosom* (Luke 16:20-22).

Although Lazarus suffered degradation in this life, he was comforted in death.

Asa, the king of Judah, experienced prominence in life, but dryness in his body. Yet, he failed to seek the Lord, and his ailment killed him.

Asa in the thirty and ninth year of his reign was diseased in his feet, until his disease was exceeding great: yet in his disease he sought not to the Lord, but to the physicians. And Asa slept with his fathers, and died in the one and fortieth year of his reign (2 Chron. 16:12-13).

These manifestations exemplify a diminished, dehydrated condition, the absence of God's glory. But dryness—no matter how dry—is never beyond the reach of His love, power, and might. Nor is God's glory beyond our reach. Therefore, we pray for dryness to go and His glory to be seen!

✝ Prayers to Conquer Dryness in Jesus Christ's Name

Bible Prayer Links

Ephraim is smitten, their root is dried up, they shall bear no fruit: yea, though they bring forth, yet will I slay even the beloved fruit of their womb (Hosea 9:16).

It came to pass in the mean while, that the heaven was black with clouds and wind, and there was a great rain. And Ahab rode, and went to Jezreel (1 Kings 18:45).

Prayer Focus
- To condemn all assignments of dryness and prophesy "rehydration"
- To be revived by God's heavenly river

Prayer Guides
1. Thank You, Lord, for reviving me during this prayer program, in the name of Jesus Christ.
2. O Lord, let Your resurrection power possess me now and revive me physically and spiritually, in the name of Jesus Christ.

3. O Lord, let the dryness of my foundation that brings hardship into my life receive divine water now. Release comfort into my life and destiny, in the name of Jesus Christ.

4. My dry bones (of marital destiny, finances, business, etc.), receive the resurrection power of Jesus Christ and be revived, in His name.

5. By the Holy Spirit's divine empowerment, I prophesy revival to my dry bones, in the name of Jesus.

6. Father Lord, let Your heavenly river be channeled to my life and destiny, to water them. Let me be comforted and nourished, in the name of Jesus Christ.

7. Father Lord, arise now and revive my dry and grieving soul (my sick/diseased body, broken marital destiny, sick finances, etc.) by Your Holy Spirit, in the name of Jesus Christ.

8. Power of the grave holding my life and destiny captive, hear the Word of the Lord; loose your hold and let go now, in the name of Jesus Christ.

9. Blood of Jesus, disconnect my life today from any demonic power arrayed against me to drain and dry up my life, in the name of Jesus Christ.

10. Father Lord, arise now and overrule every evil decree spoken to dominate and dry up my life and destiny, in the name of Jesus Christ.

11. Holy Ghost anointing, come upon me now and neutralize the spiritual dryness that has been assigned to make me powerless, in the name of Jesus Christ.

12. Holy Ghost anointing, come upon me now and neutralize the spiritual dryness that has been assigned to make me prayerless, in the name of Jesus Christ.

13. O Lord arise. Breathe into me now and give me life more abundantly, in the name of Jesus Christ (see John 10:10).

14. My revived life, hear the Word of the Lord. Receive the Spirit of God and thrive, in the name of Jesus Christ.

15. My revived destiny, hear the Word of the Lord. Receive the Spirit of God and thrive, in the name of Jesus Christ.

16. Thank You, Jesus, for answering my prayers. Amen.

✠ Prayers for God's Glory to Be Seen upon Me

Bible Prayer Links

Arise, shine; for thy light is come, and the glory of the LORD is risen upon thee. For, behold, the darkness shall cover the earth, and gross darkness the people: but the LORD shall arise upon thee, and his glory shall be seen upon thee (Isa. 60:1-2).

Lift up your heads, O ye gates; and be ye lift up, ye everlasting doors; and the King of glory shall come in. Who is this King of glory? The LORD strong and mighty, the LORD mighty in battle (Ps. 24:7-8).

Prayer Focus
- To invoke the name and power of the King of glory on my behalf
- To arise in His strength and glory

Prayer Guides
1. Father Lord, thank You for Your goodness and faithfulness to me, in the name of Jesus Christ.
2. God of glory, arise. Overshadow my glory so that it might be revealed, in the name of Jesus Christ.
3. O King of glory, arise now and clothe me in Your glory, in the name of Jesus Christ.
4. O King of glory who is mighty in battle, arise now and fight against the forces that are oppressing my glory, in the name of Jesus Christ.
5. O King of glory, arise now and put on me Your crown of glory, in the name of Jesus Christ (see Prov. 4:9).
6. Father Lord, give me divine direction that will change my dryness to a life of glory, in the name of Jesus Christ.
7. Father Lord, by the Holy Spirit, transform my spiritual weakness to strength, in the name of Jesus Christ.
8. Holy Spirit, activate the will of God in my life and destiny, in the name of Jesus Christ.

9. Holy Spirit, arise and promote me (spiritually, financially, etc.), in the name of Jesus Christ.

10. By the Word of the Lord, I, (insert your name), arise and shine, for my time has come, in the name of Jesus Christ (see Ps. 102:13).

11. Thank You, Lord, for answering my prayers. Amen.

✝ Prayers Declaring That God's Glory Will Be Seen upon Me

Bible Prayer Links

Thou shalt also decree a thing, and it shall be established unto thee: and the light shall shine upon thy ways (Job 22:28).

Then said the LORD unto me, Thou hast well seen: for I will hasten my word to perform it (Jer. 1:12).

Prayer Focus
- To speak in the authority of the Word and the name of Jesus Christ to declare His will for my life
- To confess Isaiah chapter 60

Prayer Guides
1. By the Word of the Lord, I declare that His glory is seen upon me, in the name of Jesus Christ.

2. By the Word of the Lord, I declare that multitudes shall come to my light to take refuge, in the name of Jesus Christ.

3. By the Word of the Lord, I declare that kings shall be attracted to the brightness of my rising, in the name of Jesus Christ.

4. By the Word of the Lord, I declare that I shall see and be radiant and my heart shall tremble with joy at the glorious deliverance that shall come my way, in the name of Jesus Christ.

5. By the Word of the Lord, I declare that the abundance of the sea, ground, and air shall be converted unto me, in the name of Jesus Christ (see Isa. 60:5).

6. By the Word of the Lord, I declare that people shall give their treasures to me, in the name of Jesus Christ.

7. By the Word of the Lord, I declare that the sons of strangers shall build up my walls, and their kings (chiefs) shall minister to me, in the name of Jesus Christ (see Isa. 60:10).

8. By the Word of the Lord, my gates shall be opened day and night for men to bring to me the wealth of the nations, in the name of Jesus Christ.

9. By the Word of the Lord, I declare that the sons of those who despised and afflicted me shall bow down at my feet, in the name of Jesus Christ.

10. By the Word of the Lord, I declare that God shall make me an eternal excellency and a joy of many generations, in the name of Jesus Christ (see Isa. 60:15).

11. By the Word of the Lord, I declare that the power of the oppressor shall be broken and oppression (wickedness) shall cease in my life, in the name of Jesus Christ.

12. By the Word of the Lord, I declare that my dwelling place shall experience no evil wasting, in the name of Jesus Christ.

13. By the Word of the Lord, I declare that the destruction that wastes at noonday and at nighttime shall not locate my home, in the name of Jesus Christ (see Ps. 91:5-6).

14. By the Word of the Lord, I declare that affliction shall not rise up against any member of my household, in the name of Jesus Christ.

15. By the Word of the Lord, I declare that my walls (my body, spirit, and soul) shall be delivered and I will be in good health and enjoy prosperity, in the name of Jesus Christ.

16. By the Word of the Lord, I declare that my mouth shall bring forth praises to the Lord, in the name of Jesus Christ.

17. By the Word of the Lord, I declare that the Lord shall be to me an everlasting light, in the name of Jesus Christ (see Isa. 60:19).

18. By the Word of the Lord, I declare that the Lord shall be my glory, in the name of Jesus Christ (see Isa. 60:19).

19. By the Word of the Lord, I declare that He has become my everlasting light. Therefore, my sun shall no longer go down and my moon shall not withdraw itself, in the name of Jesus Christ.

20. By the Word of the Lord, I declare that my days shall be fulfilled, in the name of Jesus Christ.

21. Father Lord, hasten to fulfill Your words in my life, that Your name might be glorified. Amen.

✟ Prayers for My Glory to Flourish

Bible Prayer Links

What is man, that thou art mindful of him? and the son of man, that thou visitest him? For thou hast made him a little lower than the angels, and hast crowned him with glory and honour (Ps. 8:4-5).

The Word was made flesh, and dwelt among us, (and we beheld his glory, the glory as of the only begotten of the Father,) full of grace and truth (John 1:14).

This beginning of miracles did Jesus in Cana of Galilee, and manifested forth his glory; and his disciples believed on him (John 2:11).

Awake up, my glory; awake, psaltery and harp: I myself *will awake early* (Ps. 57:8).

Prayer Focus

- To oppress every oppressor of the glory within me
- To awaken the glory within me

PRAYER GUIDES

1. I praise You, O Lord, for You have awesomely and wonderfully made me (see Ps. 139:14).
2. O Lord, arise and let my glory manifest, in the name of Jesus Christ.
3. O Lord, arise and anoint my glory with Your glory, in the name of Jesus Christ.
4. My glory, my glory, my glory—awake and be revealed, by the power of the Holy Ghost, in the name of Jesus Christ.
5. O Lord, by the Holy Spirit, reveal and disgrace every glory suppressor that is assigned against me, in the name of Jesus Christ.
6. By the power of the Holy Ghost, my glory shall not be suppressed but revealed, in the name of Jesus Christ.
7. Demonic powers afflicting my glory, the Lord rebuke you. Be paralyzed, in the name of Jesus Christ.
8. Every evil assigned to suppress my glory, fail, in the name of Jesus Christ.
9. Power of the grave assigned against my glory, the Lord rebuke you. Depart, in the name of Jesus.
10. Shadow of death assigned to cover my glory, receive the light of Jesus Christ and vanish, in the name of Jesus Christ.
11. Every evil cloud assigned to suppress my glory, scatter by the thunder of God, in the name of Jesus Christ.
12. O Lord, arise and pronounce judgment upon the sons of men who have purposed to turn my glory to shame, in the name of Jesus Christ.
13. Any agent of darkness working against my glory, your wickedness shall turn against you, in the name of Jesus.
14. Blood of Jesus, come against and neutralize every curse pronounced upon my glory, in the name of Jesus Christ.
15. Thank You, Lord, for answering my prayers. Amen.

I encourage you to return often to the prayer topics in this and preceding chapters. In addition, use the prayer guides in the Appendix that follows. Persistency in prayer will pay off in a changed life—the life the Lord Jesus Christ died for you to live!

Appendix

Additional Prayers for Overcoming Wicked Means

W e have studied the means of the wicked and prayed specifically for God's help in overcoming them. This Appendix contains many more prayers on a variety of topics related to our study and to spiritual warfare in general. I pray that this additional resource will undergird you as you dismantle every attempt by the enemy to keep you from the fullness of your destiny in God, in Jesus' mighty name!

Aligning with Divine Rule

✟ PRAYERS OF ALIGNMENT WITH DIVINE RULE, POWER, AND AUTHORITY AGAINST THE WORKS OF DARKNESS—PART 1

BIBLE PRAYER LINKS

> *Jesus said unto them, Verily I say unto you, That ye which have followed me, in the regeneration when the Son of man shall sit in the throne of his glory, ye also shall sit upon twelve thrones, judging the twelve tribes of Israel* (Matt. 19:28).

> *Rise ye up, take your journey, and pass over the river Arnon: behold, I have given into thine hand Sihon the*

Amorite, king of Heshbon, and his land: begin to pos-
sess it, and contend with him in battle (Deut. 2:24).

Upon mount Zion shall be deliverance, and there
shall be holiness; and the house of Jacob shall pos-
sess their possessions (Obad. 1:17).

Prayer Focus

- To honor and align myself with the authority of the Most High God
- To stand against the enemy's works

Prayer Guides

1. By faith I align myself with the unfailing rule, power, and authority of the Lord Jesus Christ.
2. Father Lord, I thank You for fulfilling Your promise of power to tread on serpents and scorpions, and over all the enemy's power, in the name of Jesus Christ (see Luke 10:19).
3. According to the Word, my position in Christ, and the unfailing promise of the Lord, I arise and sit upon the twelve thrones of heaven to terminate the power of afflictions (non-achievement, poverty, lack, sickness, limitations, etc.) in my life and destiny, in the name of Jesus Christ.
4. According to the Word, my position in Christ, and the unfailing promise of the Lord, I arise and sit upon the twelve thrones of heaven to overthrow the demonic powers occupying my throne of glory, grace, promotion, elevation, and prosperity, in the name of Jesus Christ.
5. Father Lord, by Your grace and mercy, I have come to mount Zion. Grant me success as I contend against the enemy to repossess all that he has stolen since my conception (my prosperity, peace of mind, glory, marital destiny, honor, life, destiny, promotion, health, elevation, progress, advancement, and wealth), in the name of Jesus Christ.
6. I, (insert name), arise now by the Word of God to contend for my life, destiny, health, kingdom service, peace of mind,

wealth, progress, prosperity, promotion, and well-being. I repossess it now, in the name of Jesus Christ.

7. Thank You, Lord, for answering my prayers. Amen.

✞ Prayers of Alignment with Divine Rule, Power, and Authority against the Works of Darkness — Part 2

Bible Prayer Links

All this came upon the king Nebuchadnezzar. At the end of twelve months he walked in the palace of the kingdom of Babylon. The king spake, and said, Is not this great Babylon, that I have built for the house of the kingdom by the might of my power, and for the honour of my majesty? While the word was in the king's mouth, there fell a voice from heaven, saying, O king Nebuchadnezzar, to thee it is spoken; The kingdom is departed from thee. And they shall drive thee from men, and thy dwelling shall be with the beasts of the field: they shall make thee to eat grass as oxen, and seven times shall pass over thee, until thou know that the most High ruleth in the kingdom of men, and giveth it to whomsoever he will (Dan. 4:28-32).

Pride goeth before destruction, and an haughty spirit before a fall (Prov. 16:18).

Again the word of the Lord came unto Haggai in the four and twentieth day of the month, saying, Speak to Zerubbabel, governor of Judah, saying, I will shake the heavens and the earth; and I will overthrow the throne of kingdoms, and I will destroy the strength of the kingdoms of the heathen; and I will overthrow the chariots, and those that ride in them; and the horses and their riders shall come down, every one by the sword of his brother (Haggai 2:20-22).

PRAYER FOCUS

- To ask God's shaking of both heavens and earth to overcome demonic rule
- To bring the rule of the King to bear on my life and destiny

PRAYER GUIDES

1. Every demonic power (territorial, environmental, ancestral, foundational, marine/water, or evil strongman) that boasts against my liberty, healing, progress, deliverance, advancement, freedom, and destiny fulfillment, lose your power now, as Nebuchadnezzar did, in the name of Jesus Christ.

2. Every situation of poverty, lack, failure, hardship, restlessness, nonachievement, backwardness, sickness, unfulfilled life and destiny, limitation to financial success and prosperity, and every problem that resists solution in my life and destiny, receive the judgment of God and vanish, in the name of Jesus Christ.

3. Lord, arise for my sake. Shake both heavens and earth to overthrow any demonic powers (territorial, environmental, ancestral, foundational, marine/water, or evil strongman) controlling my life, destiny, finances, progress, deliverance, destiny fulfillment, and prosperity, in the name of Jesus Christ.

4. Lord, arise for my sake. Shake both heavens and earth to destroy the strength of any demonic powers aborting my blessings and breakthroughs and troubling my life and destiny, in the mighty name of Jesus Christ.

5. Lord, arise for my sake. Shake both heavens and earth to destroy the strength of any demonic powers programming sickness, illness, failure, hardship, delay, limitations, nonachievement, and any other evil into my life and destiny, in the name of Jesus Christ.

6. O Lord my God, arise now and be my Shepherd. Make me to lie down in green pastures so that I and the members of my household lack nothing (spiritually, physically, financially, or materially), in the mighty name of Jesus Christ (see Ps. 23:1-2).

7. O Lord my God, arise now and lead me beside still waters so that my thirst (all that I need, seek, and desire spiritually, physically, financially, or materially) may be quenched, in the name of the Lord Jesus Christ (see Ps. 23:2).
8. Father Lord, grant me the fullness of Your abundant blessings, in the mighty name of Jesus Christ.
9. Thank You, Jesus Christ, for answering my prayers. Amen.

✞ PRAYERS OF ALIGNMENT WITH DIVINE RULE, POWER, AND AUTHORITY AGAINST THE WORKS OF DARKNESS—PART 3

BIBLE PRAYER LINKS

Return, O Lord, how long? and let it repent thee concerning thy servants. O satisfy us early with thy mercy; that we may rejoice and be glad all our days. Make us glad according to the days wherein thou hast afflicted us, and the years wherein we have seen evil. Let thy work appear unto thy servants, and thy glory unto their children. And let the beauty of the Lord our God be upon us: and establish thou the work of our hands upon us; yea, the work of our hands establish thou it (Ps. 90:13-17).

Ye shall be named the Priests of the Lord: men shall call you the Ministers of our God: ye shall eat the riches of the Gentiles, and in their glory shall ye boast yourselves (Isa. 61:6).

Thou shalt also suck the milk of the Gentiles, and shalt suck the breast of kings: and thou shalt know that I the Lord am thy Saviour and thy Redeemer, the mighty One of Jacob (Isa. 60:16).

PRAYER FOCUS
- To see the rule of the King of kings established in my life
- To seek reversal and restitution all evil "rulings" against me

PRAYER GUIDES

1. Thank You, Jesus, for hearing my prayers and bringing Your kingdom rule to bear in my life.

2. O fire of God, arise. Come down and consume every seed of poverty, lack, limitations, hardship, and backwardness that has reigned in my life and destiny, in the name of Jesus Christ.

3. O fire of God, arise. Come down and consume every serpent of poverty, hardship, lack, failure, limitation, and backwardness that has ruled my life and destiny, in the name of Jesus Christ.

4. O fire of God, arise. Come down and consume every spirit of the snail governing my life and destiny, finances, health, progress, promotion, and elevation, in the mighty name of Jesus Christ.

5. O fire of God, arise from the throne of Almighty God. Consume every cobweb of poverty, hardship, hindrance, lack, and limitation that has restrained any area of my life, in the name of Jesus Christ.

6. O fire of God, arise from the altar of God and consume every witchcraft spider that seeks to lord over my prosperity, wealth, health, finances, blessings, and breakthroughs, in the name of Jesus Christ.

7. O fire of God, arise and consume every demonic serpent swallowing my kingdom blessings, including my prosperity, breakthroughs, success, and prayer life, in the name of Jesus Christ.

8. Demonic serpent caught swallowing my prosperity, success, blessings, breakthroughs, progress, and prayer life, your end has come today. Die in the fire of the one true God who rules and reigns, in the name of the Lord Jesus Christ.

9. O Lord my God, restore Your kingdom rule in my life! Arise and make me glad according to the years and days that the enemy has afflicted my life and destiny with evil. Turn around my situation for Your glory, in the mighty name of Jesus Christ.

10. O Lord, arise and manifest Your glory and Your kingdom in my, my children's, and my household members' lives and destinies, and also in my body, circumstances, calling, and ministry, in the name of Jesus Christ.

11. O Lord my God, according to Your Word, establish my business, career, calling, and ministry. Bring Your kingdom to bear wherever You lead me, in the mighty name of Jesus Christ.
12. O Lord my God, arise and let me drink the milk and eat the riches of the Gentiles, in the name of Jesus Christ.
13. Thank You, Lord God, for answering my prayers. Amen.

Annihilating Satanic Means

✠ PRAYERS TO CONQUER SATAN'S INFLUENCE IN AND AGAINST MY LIFE

Satan and his hosts are expert at influencing people. Their influence can be detected when a pressing sense of urgency—a "do it quick or else" approach—arises in relation to an issue or problem.

BIBLE PRAYER LINKS

Peter said, Ananias, why hath Satan filled thine heart to lie to the Holy Ghost, and to keep back part of the price of the land? (Acts 5:3).

Satan stood up against Israel, and provoked David to number Israel (1 Chron. 21:1).

Then entered Satan into Judas surnamed Iscariot, being of the number of the twelve (Luke 22:3).

PRAYER FOCUS
- To arrest all satanic "arresters" of my life and destiny
- To resist all satanically-inspired thoughts and actions; to overcome all satanic influence

PRAYER GUIDES

1. Father Lord, by Your Spirit and Your Word, empower me to conquer the influences of Satan in and against my life, in the name of Jesus Christ.

2. Demonic powers on assignment to arrest me physically and spiritually, the Lord rebuke you. Depart now, in the name of Jesus Christ.

3. Every strongman of the kingdom of darkness delegated to influence and afflict my life with fear and failure, the Lord rebuke you. Depart now, in the name of Jesus Christ.

4. Every strongman of the kingdom of darkness delegated to influence my mind, the Lord rebuke you. Be cut off from me now, in the name of Jesus Christ.

5. Demonic arresters delegated to arrest my blessings and break-through, the Lord rebuke you. Be arrested and destroyed, in the name of Jesus Christ.

6. O God who set the apostle Peter free from Herod's prison, arise today and set me free from demonic influence and detention, in the name of Jesus Christ.

7. In the name of Jesus Christ, I break down the walls of every demonic prison holding my spirit and soul captive.

8. Every demonic "arrest warrant" issued and/or enforced against my spirit, soul, and body, expire now by the blood of Jesus Christ.

9. O LORD, arise now and empower me by Your holy fire to conquer all influences of Satan in and against my life, in the name of Jesus Christ.

10. Thank You, Lord, for answering my prayers. Amen.

✟ PRAYERS TO ANNIHILATE THE EVILS OF SATAN AND HIS AGENTS

In speaking of Satan's evils, we speak of his works, which our Lord Jesus Christ was manifested to destroy. The works of Satan and his agents occur at a variety of levels, some being more apparent than others. With the help of the Holy Spirit, Satan's work at every level can be discerned.

BIBLE PRAYER LINKS

The evil bow before the good; and the wicked at the gates of the righteous (Prov. 14:19).

The eyes of the LORD *are in every place, beholding the evil and the good* (Prov. 15:3).

The Lord shall deliver me from every evil work, and will preserve me unto his heavenly kingdom: to whom be glory for ever and ever. Amen (2 Tim. 4:18).

Where envying and strife is, there is confusion and every evil work (James 3:16).

I heard a loud voice saying in heaven, Now is come salvation, and strength, and the kingdom of our God, and the power of his Christ: for the accuser of our brethren is cast down, which accused them before our God day and night. And they overcame him by the blood of the Lamb, and by the word of their testimony; and they loved not their lives unto the death (Rev. 12:10-11).

PRAYER FOCUS
- To thwart the work of Satan and his agents against me
- To invoke God's power on my behalf

PRAYER GUIDES
1. Blood of Jesus Christ, arise and cover me now, in the name of Jesus Christ.
2. I thank You, Lord, for You shall deliver me from every evil work today, in the name of Jesus Christ.
3. By the spirit of prophecy, I declare today that the satanic agents that have fought my destiny for (<u>insert number</u>) years, are crushed and shall never arise again, in the name of Jesus Christ.

4. By the blood of the Lamb of God, I overthrow every satanic plan that is set for my destruction, and I command it to backfire against its planners, in the name of Jesus Christ.

5. By the power of the Holy Spirit, I decree woe to any satanists who are devising evil against my life and destiny, in the name of Jesus Christ.

6. My Lord whose eyes are in every place, arise now and behold the evils being plotted against me and scatter them, in the name of Jesus Christ.

7. My Lord whose eyes are in every place, arise now and behold the evil plotters gathered against me. Discomfit them with Your thunder, in the name of Jesus Christ.

8. By the spirit of prophecy, I declare that the wicked shall bow at my gates, in the name of Jesus Christ.

9. Every success, glory, and breakthrough that the Lord has woven into my life and destiny when He created me, begin to manifest now, in the name of Jesus Christ.

10. From today forward, by the power of the Holy Spirit, I become invisible to the demonic pursuers of my life and destiny, in the name of Jesus Christ.

11. Thank You, Lord, for answering my prayers. Amen.

✟ PRAYERS OF WARFARE TO BREAK THE POWER OF EVIL BONDAGES

Bondage is a spiritual or physical condition and/or state of being bound. Spiritual bondage is a very wicked form of subjection to an evil force or influence.

BIBLE PRAYER LINK

The Lord shall deliver me from every evil work, and will preserve me unto his heavenly kingdom: to whom be glory for ever and ever. Amen (2 Tim. 4:18).

PRAYER FOCUS
- To discern areas of spiritual vulnerability

- To confront and confound all attempts and schemes to hold me in bondage

PRAYER GUIDES

1. Lord Jesus, I thank You for the work of redemption by which You have given me authority over all evil bondages, in Your mighty name.
2. Every bondage assigned to limit my spiritual growth and power, be broken now and release me, in the name of Jesus Christ.
3. Father Lord, by the Holy Spirit, thank You for giving me dominion over my bad habits, including (name them), in the name of the Lord Jesus Christ.
4. Every habit, including (name them), that diminishes my beneficial communion with the Holy Spirit, be destroyed now, in the mighty name of Jesus Christ.
5. Holy Spirit, help me to see the weaknesses in my spiritual walk that open me to bondages, in the name of Jesus Christ.
6. Every power assigned to distract my prayer life and Bible studies, the Lord rebuke you. Depart from me now, in the name of Jesus Christ.
7. Holy Spirit, order my life according to the Lord's righteous ways and let not any iniquity have dominion over me anymore, in the name of Jesus Christ (see Ps. 119:133).
8. Holy Spirit, release me from every bondage and make me ready for the spiritual tasks ahead of me, in the name of Jesus Christ.
9. Satan, I resist you and bind your activities in my life now, in the name of Jesus Christ.
10. Satanic assignments deposited into my life to limit my spiritual and physical breakthroughs, be evacuated now, in the mighty name of Jesus Christ.
11. Holy Spirit, release now the power and anointing to conquer any generational bondage confronting my life, in the name of Jesus Christ.
12. Thank You, Jesus, for answering my prayers. Amen.

✟ Prayers for Deliverance from the Grip of the Mighty

Bible Prayer Link

> *Shall the prey be taken from the mighty, or the lawful captive delivered? But thus saith the Lord, Even the captives of the mighty shall be taken away, and the prey of the terrible shall be delivered: for I will contend with him that contendeth with thee, and I will save thy children. And I will feed them that oppress thee with their own flesh; and they shall be drunken with their own blood, as with sweet wine: and all flesh shall know that I the Lord am thy Saviour and thy Redeemer, the mighty One of Jacob* (Isa. 49:24-26).

Prayer Focus
- To invoke the deliverance of the Most High God

Prayer Guides
1. Thank You, Lord, that Your promises never fail, in the name of Jesus Christ.
2. Thank You, Lord, that the grip of the wicked one cannot prevail over the power of Your great love for me, in Jesus' name.
3. Holy Ghost fire, attack and destroy every source of evil power from my birthplace that is afflicting my life and destiny with failure and sickness, in the name of Jesus Christ.
4. Father Lord, let every enemy like Haman that has purposed to terminate my life or any good in my life, hang now in the noose he prepared for me, in the mighty name of Jesus Christ.
5. Father Lord, according to Your Word, feed the powers that are oppressing me with their own flesh. Let them become drunk with their own blood, in the name of Jesus Christ.
6. Thank You, Jesus, for answering my prayers. Amen.

Appropriating God's Grace

✝ PRAYERS FOR GRACE TO DEFEAT THE AGENDAS OF EVIL PURSUERS

BIBLE PRAYER LINKS

He said unto me, My grace is sufficient for thee: for my strength is made perfect in weakness. Most gladly therefore will I rather glory in my infirmities, that the power of Christ may rest upon me (2 Cor. 12:9).

The prophet Gad said unto David, Abide not in the hold; depart, and get thee into the land of Judah. Then David departed, and came into the forest of Hareth (1 Sam. 22:5).

The LORD said unto him, Go, return on thy way to the wilderness of Damascus: and when thou comest, anoint Hazael to be king over Syria (1 Kings 19:15).

PRAYER FOCUS
- To appropriate God's grace for spiritual battle
- To be released from the fear of evil pursuers; to cut off their works

PRAYER GUIDES
1. Thank You, Lord, that as you counseled Your kings and prophets, You also grant me the grace to confront and defeat all wicked pursuers of my life. You are doing this even as I pray, in the name of Jesus Christ.
2. I receive the anointing of the Holy Ghost and the grace to confront and defeat the agendas of those who pursue my life and destiny for evil, in the name of Jesus Christ.
3. O Lord, arise in the power of Your thunder. As You pour out Your grace to me, cut off anything that is pursuing my life and destiny for evil, in the name of Jesus Christ (Ps. 54:5).

4. Every demonic power on assignment to block the fulfillment of my destiny, the Lord rebuke you. Be diverted away from me, in the name of Jesus Christ.

5. Blood of Jesus, wipe away my secrets from the hands of those who pursue my life and destiny for evil, in the name of Jesus Christ.

6. Demonic informants collaborating with the evil pursuers of my life and destiny, the Lord rebuke you. Expire now, in the name of Jesus Christ

7. Demonic pursuers working to hold me captive, the Lord rebuke you. Perish now, in Jesus Christ's name.

✟ PRAYERS FOR GRACE TO FULFILL DESTINY

Destiny is the divine program and purpose established for a person's life in the earth. When Jesus was brought before Pilate, the prefect asked, "Art thou a king then? Jesus answered Thou sayest that I am a king. To this end was I born, and for this cause came I into the world, that I should bear witness unto the truth. Every one that is of the truth heareth my voice" (John 18:37). Jesus spoke of the reason for His earthly incarnation; this was His destiny, already anticipated by the Trinity.

BIBLE PRAYER LINKS

Thine eyes did see my substance, yet being unperfect; and in thy book all my members were written, which in continuance were fashioned, when as yet there was none of them (Ps. 139:16).

Knowing this, that the trying of your faith worketh patience. But let patience have her perfect work, that ye may be perfect and entire, wanting nothing (James 1:3-4).

PRAYER FOCUS
- To consecrate my journey of destiny fulfillment to Jesus' Lordship
- To cast off all evil restraints and wicked means assigned to interfere with my life and destiny

PRAYER GUIDES
1. Father Lord, thank You! You are faithful to Your promises. Your grace is sufficient in this journey, in the name of Jesus Christ.
2. Demonic powers on assignment to divert me from my destiny, the Lord rebuke you. According to God's authority and grace to me, I command you to be cut off from me, in the name of Jesus Christ.
3. Every agent of darkness programmed to hinder me from embarking on and fulfilling my destiny, the Lord rebuke you. Depart from me, in the name of Jesus Christ.
4. Ancestral curses and covenants hindering me from embarking on and fulfilling my destiny, be neutralized now by the blood of Jesus, in the name of Jesus.
5. Wickedness assigned to abort my spiritual efforts, scatter, in the name of Jesus Christ.
6. I bind and cast out every spirit of tiredness and weariness assigned to disrupt my journey of destiny fulfillment, in the name of Jesus Christ.
7. By the grace of God, I arise and confidently embark on my journey of destiny fulfillment, in the name of Jesus Christ.
8. By the grace of God, I rise up now and progress on my journey of destiny fulfillment, in the name of Jesus Christ.
9. By Your grace, O God, I shall reach my promised land, in the name of Jesus Christ.
10. Thank You, Lord, for answering my prayers. Amen.

✟ Prayers to Appropriate God's Grace for Divine Connections

Bible Prayer Links

God is able to make all grace abound toward you; that ye, always having all sufficiency in all things, may abound to every good work (2 Cor. 9:8).

Thine ears shall hear a word behind thee, saying, This is the way, walk ye in it, when ye turn to the right hand, and when ye turn to the left (Isa. 30:21).

Shew me thy ways, O LORD; teach me thy paths (Ps. 25:4).

Thou crownest the year with thy goodness; and thy paths drop fatness (Ps. 65:11).

Prayer Focus
- To thank God for His boundless grace
- To invoke His grace to discern all God-ordained paths, ensure all God-appointed connections, and disrupt all evil diversions

Prayer Guides
1. Thank You, Lord, for opening the door of Your grace to me and releasing divine connections, in the name of Jesus Christ.
2. O God of grace and mercy, visit me now and glorify Your name in my life, in the name of Jesus Christ.
3. By the grace of God, I shall not miss my God-ordained paths or divine connections, in the name of Jesus Christ.
4. By the grace of God, all satanic connections assigned to pull me down shall be cut off from me and scattered, in the name of Jesus Christ.
5. Father Lord, if I have missed any divine connection, arise now in the power of Your grace and mercy and reconnect me, in the name of Jesus Christ.

6. Father Lord, if I have missed any portion of my divine path, empower me to access it now, by Your grace and the power of the Holy Spirit, in the name of Jesus Christ.

7. Every blocker spirit sent to divert me from my divine connections and path, be paralyzed, in the name of Jesus Christ.

8. Father Lord, arise and connect me to those whom you assigned to bring positive change to my life and destiny, in the name of Jesus Christ.

9. Today, Father Lord, grant me the grace to be connected to Your power and wisdom in the time of distress, in the name of Jesus Christ.

10. Thank You, Jesus, for answering my prayers. Amen.

✟ PRAYERS TO CUT OFF SATANIC INFLUENCES, BY THE GRACE OF GOD

BIBLE PRAYER LINKS

The following Scriptures provide examples of satanic influences. Previously listed passages speak of God's grace.

Satan stood up against Israel, and provoked David to number Israel (1 Chron. 21:1).

Peter said, Ananias, why hath Satan filled thine heart to lie to the Holy Ghost, and to keep back part of the price of the land? (Acts 5:3).

Then entered Satan into Judas surnamed Iscariot, being of the number of the twelve (Luke 22:3).

Supper being ended, the devil having now put into the heart of Judas Iscariot, Simon's son, to betray him (John 13:2).

The sower soweth the word. And these are they by the way side, where the word is sown; but when they have heard, Satan cometh immediately, and taketh away the word that was sown in their hearts (Mark 4:14-15).

PRAYER FOCUS

- To invoke and appropriate God's grace for battle against satanic influences
- To cut off the wicked works of satanic influence in my life, family, church, and destiny

PRAYER GUIDES

1. Thank You, Lord, for by Your grace satanic influences shall be cut off from me today.
2. Today, by the grace of God, I shall trample upon demonic serpents and scorpions, in the name of Jesus Christ.
3. By the grace of God, I receive Holy Spirit empowerment to cut off satanic influences in my life and destiny, in the name of Jesus Christ.
4. Satan, the Lord rebuke you and your influences in my life, family, and destiny, in the name of Jesus Christ.
5. Satan, the Lord rebuke you and your influences in this church, in the name of Jesus Christ.
6. Satanic influence that has kept me in the wilderness of life, be cut off now by the grace of God, in the name of Jesus Christ.
7. Lord, arise today in the power of Your grace and nullify all evils being projected by Satan against my success and break-through, in the name of Jesus Christ.
8. Lord, arise today in the power of Your grace and nullify every satanic agenda for my life and destiny, in the name of Jesus Christ.
9. Thank You, Lord, for answering my prayers. Amen.

Binding Wicked Spirits

✝ PRAYERS TO DEFEAT THE PURPOSES OF MONITORING POWERS

Monitoring powers are spirit and human associates of Satan assigned to keep track of individuals' lives and destinies using evil spiritual devices. These powers include ancestral spirits, witches, wizards, local demons, etc., that collect information about an individual's activities, progress, and pursuit of divine purpose. They report this information back to the dark world with the intent to kill, steal, and destroy.

BIBLE PRAYER LINK

Therefore I will be unto them as a lion: as a leopard by the way will I observe them (Hosea 13:7).

PRAYER FOCUS
- To intercept, confuse, and prevent all functions of monitoring spirits
- To bring to blindness all evil spirits assigned to observe and diminish my life

PRAYER GUIDES
1. Thank You, O Lord, for defeating the purposes of all monitoring powers during this prayer program.
2. Let the voice of the monitoring spirits be silenced permanently in my life and household, in the name of Jesus Christ.
3. O Lord my God, destroy the weapons of any monitoring spirit assigned against my life and destiny, in the name of Jesus Christ.
4. Every monitoring eye observing and/or recording my daily activities, be blinded, in the name of Jesus Christ.
5. Any power beneath the water that is monitoring my life and destiny, the Lord rebuke you, in the name of Jesus Christ.
6. All monitoring powers and authorities gathered for my destruction, receive the thunder of God and scatter, in the mighty name of Jesus Christ.
7. Any power assigned to monitor my life and destiny, receive the sword of Holy Ghost fire, in the name of Jesus Christ.
8. Every wicked authority observing and challenging the move of God in my life and destiny, be paralyzed, in the name of Jesus Christ.

9. I command all demonic mirrors and monitoring gadgets rigged against my spiritual life, destiny, and sound health to shatter in pieces, in the name of Jesus Christ.

10. O Lord, shield my life from all evil observers and monitors, in the mighty name of my Lord Jesus Christ.

11. Marine powers monitoring my life and destiny, I bring the hook and rebuke of the Lord upon you, and I anchor your heads to divine judgment, in the name of Jesus Christ.

12. Every strange/evil eye transmitting and reporting on my progress to the demonic world, be permanently blinded, in the name of Jesus Christ.

13. In the name of Jesus Christ, I command spiritual confusion to come upon every evil monitoring device set up against my life and destiny, in the name of Jesus Christ.

14. Every magic mirror conjuring my face, break to pieces, in the mighty name of the Lord Jesus Christ.

15. Every witchcraft altar established to monitor my life and destiny, be roasted by the fire of God, in the name of Jesus Christ.

16. Thank You, Lord, for answering my prayers. Amen.

✟ Prayers to Bind All Blockers, Exchangers, and Killers of Divine Blessings

Blocker powers are evil spiritual powers that intercept and hold back the delivery of good things. As spirits of hindrance, they work to frustrate their target victims. A biblical example is the prince of Persia, the demon that detained the angel of God who was responding to Daniel's prayer request (see Dan. 10:13).

Exchanger powers are the evil spiritual powers that use wicked means to forcefully replace good with bad and living with dead. A biblical example in the physical realm is the surreptitious exchange of one harlot's living baby for the dead child of another (see 1 Kings 3:20).

BIBLE PRAYER LINK

Finally, my brethren, be strong in the Lord, and in the power of his might. Put on the whole armour of God, that ye may be able to stand against the wiles of the devil. For we wrestle not against flesh and blood, but against principalities, against powers, against the rulers of the darkness of this world, against spiritual wickedness in high places (Eph. 6:10-12).

PRAYER FOCUS
- To disrupt and defeat all satanic personalities countering my progress and destiny

PRAYER GUIDES
1. O Lord, I bless and worship You with all my soul, in the name of Jesus Christ.
2. Thank You, O Lord, for Your blessings that shall be revived in my life today, in the name of Jesus Christ.
3. O Lord, arise. Expose and cast away every crafty and dangerous personality in our midst, in the name of Jesus Christ.
4. Every blocker of divine blessing operating around and against me, be exposed and destroyed, in the name of Jesus Christ.
5. Every exchanger of divine blessing operating around and against me, be exposed and destroyed, in the name of Jesus Christ.
6. Every killer of divine blessing operating around and against me, be exposed and destroyed, in the name of Jesus Christ.
7. O Lord, by Holy Ghost fire, arise and unseat demonic powers sitting on my divine blessings, in the name of Jesus Christ.
8. Demonic terminator opposing my divine blessing, your time is up. Be consumed in the fire of God, in the name of Jesus Christ.
9. Glory of God, overshadow me now and revive my divine blessings, in the name of Jesus Christ.
10. Thank You, Lord, for answering my prayers. Amen.

✟ PRAYERS TO DEFEAT THE VAGABOND SPIRIT

Vagabond spirits are wandering spirits. When programmed into lives, they keep their targets moving from place to place without genuine cause or purpose. Vagabond spirits also influence thoughtless snap decisions that lead to regret.

BIBLE PRAYER LINK

When thou tillest the ground, it shall not henceforth yield unto thee her strength; a fugitive and a vaga-bond shalt thou be in the earth (Gen. 4:12).

PRAYER FOCUS
- To uproot from my life any vagabond spirit
- To bring order and focus to my life, and completion to my assignments

PRAYER GUIDES
1. Every vagabond spirit operating in my life and destiny, depart from me now, in the name of Jesus Christ.
2. All demons assigned to disorganize my life, leave me now, in the name of Jesus Christ.
3. I declare that I will concentrate on all I do and finish each task, in the mighty name of Jesus Christ.
4. I command the spirit of excellence to come upon me now, in the name of Jesus Christ.
5. O Lord arise and dismantle the stronghold of vagabond power in my life and my children's lives, in the name of Jesus Christ.
6. O Lord, my Father, rearrange my life and my children's lives to suit your purposes and confound the vagabond spirit, in the name of Jesus Christ.
7. Lord, let your kingdom be established in every department of my life and my children's lives, in the name of Jesus Christ.
8. I refuse to be wasted by the wasters. My life shall have meaning, in the name of Jesus Christ.

9. My children shall not be wasted by the wasters. Their lives shall have meaning, in the mighty name of Jesus Christ.

10. I break any yoke of evil family patterns that is affecting my children's lives, in the mighty name of Jesus Christ.

11. I break the hold of familiar spirits over the lives of all members of my household, in the mighty name of Jesus Christ.

12. Thank You, Jesus Christ, for answering my prayers. Amen.

Bringing Judgment against Wicked Troublers

✝ PRAYERS FOR THE LORD TO ARISE AND JUDGE ALL THAT OPPOSES ME—PART 1

BIBLE PRAYER LINKS

The LORD executeth righteousness and judgment for all that are oppressed (Ps. 103:6).

Which executeth judgment for the oppressed: which giveth food to the hungry. The LORD looseth the prisoners (Ps. 146:7).

Arise, O God, judge the earth: for thou shalt inherit all nations (Ps. 82:8).

Lift up thyself, thou judge of the earth: render a reward to the proud (Ps. 94:2).

PRAYER FOCUS
- To bring God's judgment to bear on all that opposes His goodness in my life

PRAYER GUIDES
1. Father Lord, I thank You for the changes that will occur during this prayer program, in the name of Jesus Christ.

2. O Lord, arise and make the impossible possible in my life, in the name of Jesus Christ.

3. O Lord, arise and let the impossibilities in my life and destiny vanish today, in Jesus' name.

4. Father Lord, arise now and pronounce great judgment upon the wickedness sown into my body to oppress me, in the name of Jesus Christ.

5. Father Lord, arise now and pronounce great judgment upon the wickedness sown into my life to limit my divine purpose, in Jesus' name.

6. By the power of the Holy Spirit, I bring the divine judgment of destruction upon that which was assigned to humiliate me. Be banished, in Jesus' name.

7. By the power of the Holy Spirit, I bring the written judgment of fire upon the demonic powers assigned to hinder my breakthroughs, in Jesus' name.

8. O Lord, let Your great judgment of paralysis come upon the demonic powers that have vowed to destroy me, in Jesus' name.

9. Every longtime problem that has defied solution in my life, receive the judgment of destruction now. Vanish, in Jesus' name.

10. Let the judgment of frustration and failure be assigned against any wicked power that pursues my prosperity, in Jesus' name.

11. Thank You, Jesus, for answering my prayers. Amen.

✟ PRAYERS FOR THE LORD TO ARISE AND JUDGE ALL THAT OPPOSES ME — PART 2

BIBLE PRAYER LINKS

Now is the judgment of this world: now shall the prince of this world be cast out (John 12:31).

Arise, O Lord; let not man prevail: let the heathen be judged in thy sight. Put them in fear, O Lord: that the nations may know themselves to be but men. Selah (Ps. 9:19-20).

Thou didst cause judgment to be heard from heaven; the earth feared, and was still, when God arose to judgment, to save all the meek of the earth. Selah (Ps. 76:8-9).

Zion shall be redeemed with judgment, and her converts with righteousness (Isa. 1:27).

PRAYER FOCUS

- To bring God's judgment to bear on satanic troublers in my life

PRAYER GUIDES

1. Father Lord, I thank You for judging my troublers and setting me free, in the name of Jesus Christ.
2. Arise, O Lord. With Your judgment, redeem my life and destiny from evil oppression, in the name of Jesus Christ.
3. Arise, O Lord. Judge my problems and cast out the evil forces responsible for them, in the name of Jesus Christ.
4. Arise, O Lord. Judge my sicknesses (<u>list any known ailments</u>) and heal me today, in the name of Jesus Christ.
5. Arise, O Lord. Judge my bondage and set me free today, in the name of Jesus Christ.
6. Demonic powers limiting my enlargement and fruitfulness, receive the judgment of the Lord today and perish, in the name of Jesus Christ.
7. Arise now, O Lord, and bring the judgment of destruction upon anything that is blocking my progress, in the name of Jesus Christ.
8. Thank You, Lord, for answering my prayers. Amen.

Casting Off Satanic Burdens

✞ Prayers to Cast Off Satanic Burdens — Part 1

Satanic burdens are heavy spiritual loads assigned to oppress. This is the opposite of the divine burden, which is light (see Matt. 11:30). Satanic burdens are assigned by agents of darkness to weigh down the human spirit and soul. When warfare prayers are raised against these burdens, there is release and freedom!

Bible Prayer Links

It shall come to pass in that day, that his burden shall be taken away from off thy shoulder, and his yoke from off thy neck, and the yoke shall be destroyed because of the anointing (Isa. 10:27).

They shall hang upon him all the glory of his father's house, the offspring and the issue, all vessels of small quantity, from the vessels of cups, even to all the vessels of flagons. In that day, saith the Lord of hosts, shall the nail that is fastened in the sure place be removed, and be cut down, and fall; and the burden that was upon it shall be cut off: for the Lord hath spoken it (Isa. 22:24-25).

Come unto me, all ye that labour and are heavy laden, and I will give you rest. Take my yoke upon you, and learn of me; for I am meek and lowly in heart: and ye shall find rest unto your souls. For my yoke is easy, and my burden is light (Matt. 11:28-30).

Prayer Focus

- To refuse to carry illegitimate, evil burdens, and to cast them off

PRAYER GUIDES

1. Let the blood of Jesus Christ manifest now and empower me to overcome as I pray, in the name of Jesus Christ.
2. Thank You, O Lord, for Your promise of rest to those who are heavy laden, in the name of Jesus Christ.
3. O Lord, assign powerful angels to come around me now to dismantle, cast off, and cut down all evils during this prayer session, in the name of Jesus Christ.
4. Lord Jesus, arise and relieve me of every ancient, satanic, spiritual load that weighs upon me and hinders my advancement, in the name of Jesus Christ.
5. Demonic powers inflicting upon me evil loads that are not mine to carry, the Lord rebuke you. Perish in the fire of Almighty God, in the name of Jesus Christ.
6. All rightful owners of the satanic loads laid upon me, I command you in the name of Jesus Christ, to come and carry your own burden.
7. Demonic installers of evil loads in my birthplace and environment, the Lord rebuke you. Carry your own burdens, in the name of Jesus Christ.
8. Satanic burden of sickness, die now and leave my body, in the name of Jesus Christ.
9. Satanic burdens of failure and backwardness, be cut down, in the name of Jesus Christ.
10. Satanic burdens assigned to make me restless and disorganized, die now, in the name of Jesus Christ.
11. Thank You, Jesus Christ, for answering my prayers. Amen.

✞ PRAYERS TO CAST OFF SATANIC BURDENS — PART 2

BIBLE PRAYER LINKS

Wherefore say unto the children of Israel, I am the LORD, and I will bring you out from under the burdens of the Egyptians, and I will rid you out of their bondage, and I will redeem you with a stretched out arm, and with great judgments (Exod. 6:6).

He turned the sea into dry land: they went through the flood on foot: there did we rejoice in him. He ruleth by his power for ever; his eyes behold the nations: let not the rebellious exalt themselves. Selah (Ps. 66:6-7).

PRAYER FOCUS

- To receive all power and understanding to cast off all evil burdens

PRAYER GUIDES

1. Father Lord, I thank You for making Your power available to me through the Holy Spirit.
2. In the name of Jesus Christ, the Word of God shall comfort me on every side during this prayer program.
3. O God to whom all power belongs, arise and break the power that is oppressing me with evil burdens, in the name of Jesus Christ.
4. O Lord, arise and banish all activity of the oppressor designed to weigh down my life and destiny, in the name of Jesus Christ.
5. By the anointing of the Holy Ghost and fire, I receive the power of spiritual understanding and wisdom to cast off evil burdens, in the name of Jesus Christ.
6. By the anointing of Holy Ghost and fire, I receive the power to be healed and prosper, free of satanic burdens, in the name of Jesus Christ.
7. By the anointing of the Holy Ghost and fire, I receive the power to overthrow every demonic king and queen ruling my life, in the name of Jesus Christ.
8. By the anointing of the Holy Ghost and fire, I receive the anointing to confront and conquer any wickedness and cast off any burden that is assigned to destroy me, in the name of Jesus Christ.
9. By the anointing of the Holy Ghost and fire, I receive the anointing to dismantle all satanic programming that is working against my life and destiny, in the name of Jesus Christ.

10. By the anointing of the Holy Ghost and fire, I receive the power to arise, shine, and be fulfilled, in the name of Jesus Christ.
11. Thank You, Lord, for answering my prayers. Amen.

✞ PRAYERS TO CAST OFF SATANIC BURDENS — PART 3

BIBLE PRAYER LINKS

For thou hast broken the yoke of his burden, and the staff of his shoulder, the rod of his oppressor, as in the day of Midian (Isa. 9:4).

That I will break the Assyrian in my land, and upon my mountains tread him under foot: then shall his yoke depart from off them, and his burden depart from off their shoulders (Isa. 14:25).

Cast thy burden upon the LORD, and he shall sustain thee: he shall never suffer the righteous to be moved (Ps. 55:22).

PRAYER FOCUS
- To break off yokes, loads, and limitations from my life and destiny

PRAYER GUIDES
1. Thank You, O Lord, for Your burden that is light, in the name of Jesus Christ (see Matt. 11:30).
2. O Lord, assign ministering angels to come around me now as I enter this prayer session, in the name of Jesus Christ.
3. Let the blood of Jesus Christ manifest now and empower me to overcome as I pray.
4. Yokes of hardship and limitation set against my life and destiny, break by the power of the Holy Spirit, in the name of Jesus Christ.

5. Father Lord, I cast my burden upon You today. Arise, sustain me, and give me rest, in the name of Jesus Christ.
6. Let the rod of God arrest all satanic powers afflicting me with evil burdens, and destroy them, in the name of Jesus Christ.
7. O Lord, let Your rod come upon and destroy the yoke that fastens evil burdens to my life and destiny, in the name of Jesus Christ.
8. Satanic burdens blocking my advancement, be undone now, in the name of Jesus Christ.
9. Any burden that constricts my potential, shatter now. All God-given potential, be fulfilled, in the name of Jesus Christ.
10. Holy Ghost anointing for accelerated progress, come upon me now and dislodge all evil burdens, in the name of Jesus Christ.
11. Demonic powers resisting advancement toward my glory, be electrocuted by the fire of the Holy Ghost, in the name of Jesus Christ.
12. Every burden levied to restrict the physical and spiritual enlargement of my family, be destroyed by Holy Ghost fire, in the name of Jesus Christ.
13. Thank You, Jesus Christ, for answering my prayers. Amen.

Defeating Hopelessness

✠ Prayers for the Courage That Overcomes Hopelessness — Part 1

Hopelessness is a demonic state of being that depresses its victims, promotes self-destructive behaviors, and typically causes mental and emotional passivity. Depression is conquered by spiritual warring in prayer, in the name of Jesus Christ.

Bible Prayer Links

Behold, the eye of the Lord is upon them that fear him, upon them that hope in his mercy; to deliver their soul from death, and to keep them alive in famine (Ps. 33:18-19).

Awake, awake, put on strength, O arm of the LORD; *awake, as in the ancient days, in the generations of old. Art thou not it that hath cut Rahab, and wounded the dragon?* (Isa. 51:9).

PRAYER FOCUS
- To trust and find courage in the Lord's watchful care and boundless strength
- To declare death to every death sentence that feeds hopelessness

PRAYER GUIDES
1. Father Lord, thank You for keeping Your eye on me to deliver my soul from death and keep me alive in famine, in the name of Jesus Christ.
2. By the blood of the Lamb of God and the word of my testimony, I possess the courage that overcomes hopelessness, in the name of Jesus Christ.
3. By the blood of the Lamb of God and the word of my testimony, let good courage incubate within me to defeat all hopelessness sent against me by the wicked one and his cohorts, in the name of Jesus Christ.
4. Anything labeled *hopeless* in my life, be divinely comforted and cheered, in the name of Jesus Christ.
5. O arm of the Lord, awake, put on strength, and deliver me from any hopelessness that has been programmed into my life and destiny, in the name of Jesus Christ.
6. O arm of the Lord, awake, put on strength, and deliver me from the power of hopelessness that wars against Your intended blessings for my life and destiny, in the name of Jesus Christ.
7. O arm of the Lord, awake, put on strength, and deliver me into gladness and joy, in the name of Jesus Christ.

8. O arm of the Lord, awake, put on strength, and deliver me so that sorrow and mourning flee, in the name of Jesus Christ.

9. Let the blood of Jesus Christ arise now and revoke every death sentence sent against my life and divine destiny, in the name of Jesus Christ.

10. Let the blood of Jesus Christ arise now and revoke every death sentence sent against the work of my hands and my divine purpose, in the name of Jesus Christ.

11. Let the blood of Jesus Christ arise now and revoke every death sentence sent against my body, spirit, and soul, in the name of Jesus Christ.

12. Let the blood of Jesus Christ arise now and revoke every death sentence sent against the Lord's Creation blessings of fruitfulness and multiplication for my life and destiny, in the name of Jesus Christ (see Gen. 1:22).

13. Let the blood of Jesus Christ arise now and revoke every death sentence sent against the dominion the Lord gave me when He formed me, in the name of Jesus Christ.

14. Lord Jesus, baptize me now with fresh holy fire to activate divine courage in me, in the name of Jesus Christ.

15. Thank You, Lord, for answering my prayers. Amen.

✟ PRAYERS FOR THE COURAGE THAT OVERCOMES HOPELESSNESS — PART 2

BIBLE PRAYER LINKS

Be strong and of a good courage: for unto this people shalt thou divide for an inheritance the land, which I sware unto their fathers to give them. Only be thou strong and very courageous, that thou mayest observe to do according to all the law, which Moses my servant commanded thee: turn not from it to the right hand or to the left, that thou mayest prosper whithersoever thou goest (Josh. 1:6-7).

These things I have spoken unto you, that in me ye might have peace. In the world ye shall have tribulation: but be of good cheer; I have overcome the world (John 16:33).

This is the confidence that we have in him, that, if we ask any thing according to his will, he heareth us: and if we know that he hear us, whatsoever we ask, we know that we have the petitions that we desired of him (1 John 5:14-15).

He that committeth sin is of the devil; for the devil sinneth from the beginning. For this purpose the Son of God was manifested, that he might destroy the works of the devil (1 John 3:8).

PRAYER FOCUS
- To thank the Lord, my defense, for "en-couraging" me
- To see the Lord arise against all hopelessness and works of darkness in my life, family, and destiny

PRAYER GUIDES
1. Thank You, Lord for being my guide and my defense against hopelessness, in the name of Jesus Christ.
2. O Lord, arise and reposition me for the breakthrough that refutes hopelessness, in the name of Jesus Christ.
3. O Lord, arise and destroy the works of the devil in my life and destiny today, in the name of Jesus Christ.
4. Lord Jesus, You manifested on Earth to destroy the works of the devil; manifest now in my life and destroy every planting of darkness therein.
5. Lord Jesus, You manifested on Earth to destroy the works of the devil; manifest now in my body and destroy every sickness and disease therein (name the problems to be destroyed.)
6. Lord Jesus, You manifested on Earth to destroy the works of the devil; manifest now in my family and destroy every problem therein (name the problems to be destroyed.)

7. Thank You, Lord, for answering my prayers. Amen.

✞ PRAYERS FOR THE COURAGE THAT OVERCOMES HOPELESSNESS — PART 3

BIBLE PRAYER LINKS

Be strong and of a good courage, fear not, nor be afraid of them: for the LORD thy God, he it is that doth go with thee; he will not fail thee, nor forsake thee (Deut. 31:6).

Therefore the redeemed of the LORD shall return, and come with singing unto Zion; and everlasting joy shall be upon their head: they shall obtain gladness and joy; and sorrow and mourning shall flee away. I, even I, am he that comforteth you... (Isa. 51:11-12).

They that wait upon the LORD shall renew their strength; they shall mount up with wings as eagles; they shall run, and not be weary; and they shall walk, and not faint (Isa. 40:31).

PRAYER FOCUS
- To wait upon the Lord in prayer; to be comforted, encouraged, and empowered
- To declare the setting right of God's path for me, and to courageously follow Him on it

PRAYER GUIDES
1. Father Lord, I thank You for setting this time to comfort and encourage me, in the name of Jesus Christ.
2. O Lord, as I wait upon You in this prayer program, let my strength be renewed, in the name of Jesus Christ.
3. O Lord, as I wait upon You in this prayer program, let me mount up with wings as eagles, in the name of Jesus Christ.
4. O Lord, as I wait upon You in this prayer program, let me run and not be weary, in the name of Jesus Christ.

5. O Lord, as I wait upon You in this prayer program, let me walk and not faint, in the name of Jesus Christ.

6. O Lord, as I wait upon You in this prayer program, I receive the courage that overcomes hopelessness, in the name of Jesus Christ.

7. O Lord of Hosts, as I wait upon You in this prayer program, You shall bring to an end all pains and sorrows of my life, in the name of Jesus Christ.

8. O Lord, arise by the greatness of Your power and bring to an end every conflict that obstructs my life and destiny, in the name of Jesus Christ.

9. O, voice of God, speak comfort and courage to my agonizing soul, in the name of Jesus Christ.

10. In the name of Jesus Christ, I proclaim that every valley of my life and destiny shall be exalted.

11. In the name of Jesus Christ, I proclaim that every mountain and hill of my life and destiny shall be made low.

12. In the name of Jesus Christ, I proclaim that the crooked places of my life and destiny shall be made straight.

13. In the name of Jesus Christ, I proclaim that the rough places of my life and destiny shall be made smooth.

14. Let the glory of the Lord be revealed in my life and destiny now, for the world to see, in the name of Jesus Christ.

15. Thank You, Lord, for answering my prayers. Amen.

Embracing the Blessing of God

✙ Prayers for the Lord to Bless Me and Change My Story to Glory

Bible Prayer Link

It shall come to pass, if thou shalt hearken diligently unto the voice of the Lord thy God, to observe and to do all his commandments which I command thee this day, that the Lord thy God will set thee on high above all nations of the earth: and all these blessings shall

*come on thee, and overtake thee, if thou shalt hearken
unto the voice of the* LORD *thy God* (Deut. 28:1-2).

PRAYER FOCUS
- To invoke God's manifold blessing in my life
- To establish paths of blessing in my life and destiny

PRAYER GUIDES
1. O God from whom all blessings flow, glory be to Your name, in the name of Jesus Christ.
2. O God from whom all blessings flow, bless me today and make me a blessing to my generation, in the name of Jesus Christ.
3. O God from whom all blessings flow, arise today and turn every curse operating against my life and destiny into blessing, in the name of Jesus Christ.
4. Father God, as You have chosen Zion in Your mercy and blessed her provision, choose me and bless my provision, in the name of Jesus Christ.
5. Every demonic power using subtlety to steal my blessing, the Lord rebuke you. Be destroyed now, in the name of Jesus Christ.
6. O Lord, let Your blessing come upon me and neutralize every foundational curse that is oppressing my life and destiny, in the name of Jesus Christ.
7. Bless me, O Lord, and let my story change to glory today, in the name of Jesus Christ.
8. Father Lord, arise today and command Your blessing upon all that I lay my hands on, in the name of Jesus Christ.
9. Thank You, Lord, for answering my prayers. Amen.

Establishing and Continuing in Divine Purpose

✝ PRAYERS ESTABLISHING MY DIVINE PURPOSE

Note: The heaven of heavens is the third heaven, the throne of Almighty God (see Deut. 10:14), the place of ultimate power controlling all that exists. You can enter into the heaven of heavens by prayer, worship, holiness, deep humility, the blood of Jesus Christ, and the Word of God.

BIBLE PRAYER LINKS

I have set watchmen upon thy walls, O Jerusalem, which shall never hold their peace day nor night: ye that make mention of the LORD, keep not silence, and give him no rest, till he establish, and till he make Jerusalem a praise in the earth (Isa. 62:6-7).

Thus saith the LORD the maker thereof, the LORD that formed it, to establish it; the LORD is his name (Jer. 33:2).

Let the beauty of the LORD our God be upon us: and establish thou the work of our hands upon us; yea, the work of our hands establish thou it (Ps. 90:17).

PRAYER FOCUS

- To rest in the names of God and to raise them as my banner

PRAYER GUIDES

1. O God of all possibilities, let my divine purpose be established to Your glory, in the name of Jesus Christ.
2. Father God, arise in the power of Your Creation and restore my dominion blessing to me, in the name of Jesus Christ.
3. Father God, arise by the power for which You are known as God Almighty and let me fulfill my divine purpose, in the name of Jesus Christ.
4. Father God, arise in the power of Your name *Jehovah* and destroy the evil hosts enforcing the bondage of addictions in my life, including (<u>name them</u>).
5. Father God, arise in the power of Your name *Jehovah Jireh* and break the yoke of poverty in my life.
6. Father God, arise in the power of Your name *I AM THAT I AM* and establish the fullness of Your goodness in my life.

7. God of wonders, arise in the power of Your wonders and deliver my glory from demonic oppression, in the name of Jesus Christ.
8. Thank You, Lord, for answering my prayers. Amen.

✝ PRAYERS FOR THE LORD TO ARISE AND MAGNIFY ME

To magnify is to make great, enlarge, expand, increase, or exalt. We do not seek any greatness achieved by or in our flesh. In prayer, we seek only the greatness ordained for us in and by God, which is the fullness of our God-given purpose. By His mercy and grace, the Lord magnified Joshua, Solomon, and Hezekiah. He will do same for you, in Jesus Christ's name.

BIBLE PRAYER LINKS

The Lord said unto Joshua, This day will I begin to magnify thee in the sight of all Israel, that they may know that, as I was with Moses, so I will be with thee (Josh. 3:7).

On that day the Lord magnified Joshua in the sight of all Israel; and they feared him, as they feared Moses, all the days of his life (Josh. 4:14).

The Lord magnified Solomon exceedingly in the sight of all Israel, and bestowed upon him such royal majesty as had not been on any king before him in Israel (1 Chron. 29:25).

Solomon the son of David was strengthened in his kingdom, and the Lord his God was with him, and magnified him exceedingly (2 Chron. 1:1).

Many brought gifts unto the Lord to Jerusalem, and presents to Hezekiah king of Judah: so that he was

magnified in the sight of all nations from thenceforth
(2 Chron. 32:23).

PRAYER FOCUS
- To ask the Father to magnify His goodness and promises in and through my life

PRAYER GUIDES
1. O God of grace and mercy, I thank You for bringing me to this day, in the name of Jesus Christ.
2. O God of time and purpose, I thank You for Your purpose for my life at this time, in the name of Jesus Christ.
3. O Lord, in the mighty name of Jesus Christ, let this be a day of change in my life as You magnify me in the sight of those who have written me off.
4. This day, O Lord, arise and magnify my divine purpose in the sight of my foundational enemies, in the name of Jesus Christ.
5. This day, O Lord, arise and magnify my calling, ministry (business, career, etc.), in the sight of all the environmental powers standing against it, in the name of Jesus Christ.
6. This day, O Lord, arise and magnify my glory in the sight of those who seek to belittle me, in the mighty name of Jesus Christ.
7. This day, O Lord, arise and magnify my excellency, to the shame of my evil detractors, in the name of Jesus Christ.
8. This day, O Lord, arise and magnify the labor of my hands. Do it in the sight of any demonic oppressors, in the name of Jesus Christ.
9. O Lord, in the name of Jesus Christ, arise today and magnify in my life anything that has depreciated due to demonic attacks.
10. O Lord, in the name of Jesus Christ, arise today and magnify in my marriage anything (i.e., love, commitment, mutual respect, etc.) that has been depreciated by demonic attacks, in the name of Jesus Christ.
11. This day, O Lord, arise and magnify my marital destiny in the sight of the powers that vowed to oppress it, in the name of Jesus Christ.

12. This day, O Lord, arise and magnify my physical health in the sight of those who deny hope for my healing, in the name of Jesus Christ.
13. Father Lord, in the name of Jesus Christ, magnify me today so that the eyes of those who have despised me in the past may see, and so glory may be given to Your name.
14. Father Lord, by the Holy Spirit bestow on me the spiritual power and wisdom that will bring increase into my life, destiny, household, and family, in the name of Jesus Christ.
15. Thank You, Lord, for answering my prayers. Amen.

✟ PRAYERS FOR THE LORD TO PERFECT THAT WHICH CONCERNS ME — PART 1

This section draws from the prayer of David asking the Lord to (1) accomplish all things concerning his life, destiny, and all that is his, and (2) to finish every good thing He started on David's behalf. Praying these prayers will bring divine supervision for your activities and will prevent the tools of the wicked from prevailing against you.

BIBLE PRAYER LINKS

Though I walk in the midst of trouble, thou wilt revive me: thou shalt stretch forth thine hand against the wrath of mine enemies, and thy right hand shall save me. The LORD will perfect that which concerneth me: thy mercy, O LORD, endureth for ever: forsake not the works of thine own hands (Ps. 138:7-8).

Being confident of this very thing, that which hath begun a good work in you will complete it until the day of Jesus Christ (Phil. 1:6).

I will cry unto God most high, unto God that performeth all things for me (Ps. 57:2).

PRAYER FOCUS

- To attain to the higher places in my life
- To request God's perfection and completion of His will for me

PRAYER GUIDES

1. Thank You, Jesus Christ, for being my guide.
2. Lord, perfect that which concerns my life, destiny, calling, marriage, marital destiny, business, finances, etc., in the name of Jesus Christ.
3. Lord, arise and perfect the good work You began in my life, destiny, calling, marriage, marital destiny, business, finances, etc., in the name of Jesus Christ.
4. Every enemy of my divine perfection, healing, calling, destiny, etc., the Lord rebuke you. Be paralyzed, in the name of Jesus Christ.
5. Let the blood of Jesus Christ break the hold of any evil power over my life, destiny, finances, health, promotion, and elevation, etc., in the name of Jesus Christ.
6. Lord, let every mountain of satanic resistance to my financial, marital, health, material, and other breakthroughs be removed now, in the name of Jesus Christ.
7. Lord, arise today and let every satanic battle confronting my life and destiny, my progress and advancement, etc., fall apart, in the name of Jesus Christ.
8. Father Lord, let the spirit of excellence (spirit of success) manifest in every area of my life, in the name of Jesus Christ.
9. O Lord, arise and bring breakthroughs in all areas of my life, in the name of Jesus Christ.
10. O Lord, arise and perfect my complete deliverance from poverty, lack, anger, addiction, backwardness, etc., in the name of Jesus Christ.
11. Lord, arise and reorganize my life to confuse demonic observers, in the name of Jesus Christ.
12. Thank You, Jesus Christ, for answering my prayers. Amen.

✠ Prayers for the Lord to Perfect That Which Concerns Me — Part 2

Bible Prayer Links

> *Though I walk in the midst of trouble, thou wilt revive me: thou shalt stretch forth thine hand against the wrath of mine enemies, and thy right hand shall save me. The Lord will perfect that which concerneth me: thy mercy, O Lord, endureth for ever: forsake not the works of thine own hands* (Ps. 138:7-8).

> *Ye shall not go out with haste, nor go by flight: for the Lord will go before you; and the God of Israel will be your rereward* (Isa. 52:12).

Prayer Focus
- To trust the Lord's keeping power on my behalf
- To oppose and destroy all satanic blockage to the perfection and completion of God's will for me

Prayer Guides
1. Thank You, Jesus Christ, for being my everlasting strength, so I will not take flight and abort my divine destiny.
2. Lord, arise in Your wonder-working power and change my story to glory today, in the name of Jesus Christ.
3. Holy Spirit, release the anointing that destroys every evil yoke and secures the divine liberty needed to complete my course, in the name of Jesus Christ.
4. Any demonic power on assignment to intercept my angel of help and stymie my divine progress, the Lord rebuke you. Give way now, in the name of Jesus Christ.
5. Lord, arise now and terminate every evil cycle in my life, destiny, calling, and finances, in the name of Jesus Christ.
6. As Moses did, by the power of the Holy Spirit, I command tenfold judgments of God upon the enemies of my divine

destiny, life, family, calling, finances, etc., in the name of Jesus Christ.

7. As Moses did, by the power of the Holy Spirit, I command tenfold judgments of God upon the demonic powers assigned to put me in any bondage (spiritual, physical, financial, or material), in the name of Jesus Christ.

8. Every decision made in the second heaven against me and my divine purpose in life, be rendered null and void now by the redeeming blood of the Lord Jesus Christ.

9. Every satanic yoke mocking my faith in the Lord Jesus Christ or denying His promises for my life, be broken by the powerful blood of the Lamb, Jesus Christ.

10. Let the resurrection power of the Lord Jesus Christ come upon me now and revive me physically and spiritually to complete my course, in the name of Jesus Christ.

11. O God of times and seasons, arise now and neutralize every satanic decree programmed to afflict my divine destiny, in the name of Jesus Christ.

12. O God of times and seasons, arise now and decree immediate manifestation of my breakthroughs (financial, blessings, etc.) in the name of Jesus Christ.

13. O God of times and seasons, arise now and destroy anything that is aborting my progress toward my destiny, and perfect all that concerns me, in the name of Jesus Christ.

14. Good things belonging to my destiny but stolen from my life even when I was in my mother's womb, I recover you now by the power of the Holy Ghost, in the name of Jesus Christ.

15. Thank You, Jesus Christ, for answering my prayers. Amen.

Overcoming Difficulty

✝ PRAYERS OF WARFARE TO OVERCOME DIFFICULT CIRCUMSTANCES

Difficult circumstances include hard, burdensome situations or problems that defy all reasonable attempts to solve and resolve them. Most often, forces of darkness are behind these challenges. However, in the name of Jesus Christ and by the power of the Holy Spirit, difficult circumstances disintegrate and are no more!

BIBLE PRAYER LINK

The LORD is my light and my salvation; whom shall I fear? The LORD is the strength of my life; of whom shall I be afraid? When the wicked, even mine enemies and my foes, came upon me to eat up my flesh, they stumbled and fell. Though an host should encamp against me, my heart shall not fear: though war should rise against me, in this will I be confident. One thing have I desired of the LORD, that will I seek after; that I may dwell in the house of the LORD all the days of my life, to behold the beauty of the LORD, and to inquire in his temple. For in the time of trouble he shall hide me in his pavilion: in the secret of his tabernacle shall he hide me; he shall set me up upon a rock. And now shall mine head be lifted up above mine enemies round about me: therefore will I offer in his tabernacle sacrifices of joy; I will sing, yea, I will sing praises unto the LORD. Hear, O LORD, when I cry with my voice: have mercy also upon me, and answer me. When thou saidst, Seek ye my face; my heart said unto thee, Thy face, LORD, will I seek. Hide not thy face far from me; put not thy servant away in anger: thou hast been my help; leave me not, neither forsake me, O God of my salvation. When my father and my mother forsake me, then the LORD will take me up. Teach me thy way, O LORD, and lead me in a plain path, because of mine enemies. Deliver me not over unto the will of mine enemies: for false witnesses are risen up against me, and such as breathe out cruelty. I had fainted, unless I had believed to see the goodness of the LORD in the land of the living. Wait on the

LORD: *be of good courage, and he shall strengthen thine heart: wait, I say, on the* LORD (Ps. 27:1-14).

PRAYER FOCUS

- To proclaim my divine connection to the kingdom of God and all of His goodness
- To dismantle all wicked schemes, tools, and assignments deployed to create difficult circumstances in my life

PRAYER GUIDES

1. Thank You, Lord Jesus Christ, for granting me blessings and breakthroughs through this prayer program, by the Holy Spirit.
2. I repent of my sins and I confess my known sins to You now: (name them).
3. Any wicked power or agent of the kingdom of darkness projecting difficulty against my life, destiny, business, family, finances, etc., on a daily basis, I command your wickedness and your tools to boomerang and afflict you, in the mighty name of the Lord Jesus Christ.
4. By the power of the Holy Spirit, I take authority and overcome all demonic resistance to my success in life, in the name of Jesus Christ.
5. By the power of the Holy Spirit, I declare that I am divinely connected to success, glory, and victory, in the name of Jesus Christ.
6. I hold up the blood of Jesus Christ to destroy any voodoo that has been invoked to confine me to failure and hardship, in the mighty name of the Lord Jesus Christ.
7. By the blood and name of our Lord Jesus Christ, I terminate the potency of any demonic object created to afflict my body, life, and destiny, in the name of Jesus Christ.
8. O Lord, arise and strike with Your rod of judgment those who vowed to prevent my success in life. Cast them into outer darkness, in the mighty name of Jesus Christ.
9. Every demonic wind of frustration stirred up against me, (insert your name), from any evil domain, stop, turn back, and afflict your sender, in the name of Jesus Christ.

10. In the name of Jesus Christ, I command all evil transmissions from the kingdom of darkness against my life, well-being, business, finances, etc., to be cut off now with the blood of Jesus Christ.

11. Father God, as You did to Pharaoh and the Egyptians, turn to blood the waters of demonic powers that desire to thwart my success in life, so that I can freely serve You, in the name of Jesus Christ.

12. Father God, as You did to Pharaoh and the Egyptians, afflict with boils those who have vowed to resist my financial breakthrough, in the name of Jesus Christ.

13. Thank You, Jesus Christ, for Your name shall be glorified as my difficult circumstances recede and Your promise of abundant life is made manifest (see John 10:10). Amen.

✞ Prayers for My Savior to Terminate My Affliction

Affliction is any physical or spiritual issue, such as illness, loss, or misfortune, that causes pain or sorrow. Affliction is a spirit. It can come from the Lord, Satan, or the hosts of darkness. When it comes from the Lord, it is an investment, a positive input that results in a favorable outcome. Such "training drills" end in testimonies to the faithfulness and greatness of God (see Ps. 66:10-12).

When Satan or his hosts bring affliction, they leave lives shattered and disorganized. Their motive it is to mock your trust in the Lord and to ask, "Where is your God?" (see Ps. 42:10).

By the power of the Holy Spirit and in the name of Jesus Christ the affliction caused by the wicked will end when you pray in faith. Begin by making this confession: In the name of Jesus Christ, affliction shall not rise up a second time in my life (Nah. 1:9). Amen.

BIBLE PRAYER LINKS

In all their affliction he was afflicted, and the angel of his presence saved them: in his love and in his pity he redeemed them; and he bare them, and carried them all the days of old (Isa. 63:9).

What do ye imagine against the Lord? he will make an utter end: affliction shall not rise up the second time (Nahum 1:9).

Nevertheless he regarded their affliction, when he heard their cry (Ps. 106:44).

Judah is gone into captivity because of affliction, and because of great servitude: she dwelleth among the heathen, she findeth no rest: all her persecutors overtook her between the straits (Lam. 1:3).

PRAYER FOCUS
- To receive the Lord's grace to overcome affliction
- To expose and terminate all schemes to afflict me

PRAYER GUIDES
1. Thank You, Lord, for Your grace to me today.
2. Father God, let the glory of divine liberty be seen on me today and forever, in the name of Jesus Christ.
3. As I cry out to You, O Lord my God, be touched by my affliction as You were for the people of Judah, in the name of Jesus Christ.
4. All affliction of poverty established and supervised by environmental demons, expire now, in the mighty name of Jesus Christ.
5. Every affliction designed to lead me into captivity, expire now, in the name of Jesus Christ.
6. Every bitter affliction that has removed my helpers, expire now, in the name of Jesus Christ.

7. Every bitter affliction that has shut the door to my (financial, marital, spiritual, etc.) blessings and breakthroughs, expire now, in the name of Jesus Christ.

8. Demonic powers fanning sickness and affliction in my life, be paralyzed now, in the name of Jesus Christ.

9. Father Lord, in Your love and pity, redeem my life from the hold of bitter affliction, in the name of Jesus Christ.

10. O Lord, assign Your angels to deliver me from the hold of any affliction sent to abbreviate my life, in the mighty name of my Lord Jesus Christ.

11. Let the blood of Jesus Christ arise now and destroy every affliction fashioned against my glory, in the name of Jesus Christ.

12. Every river of affliction that is flowing into my life and destiny, I command you to dry up now, in the name of Jesus Christ.

13. Altars of affliction raised up against me, be consumed by the fire of God, in the name of Jesus Christ.

14. Thank You, Jesus Christ, for answering my prayers. Amen.

✞ PRAYERS TO ESTABLISH FREEDOM FROM AFFLICTION

BIBLE PRAYER LINKS

If they be bound in fetters, and be holden in cords of affliction... (Job 36:8).

Say, Thus saith the king, Put this fellow in the prison, and feed him with bread of affliction and with water of affliction, until I return in peace (2 Chron. 18:26)

Such as sit in darkness and in the shadow of death, being bound in affliction and iron;... Again, they are minished and brought low through oppression, affliction, and sorrow (Ps. 107:10, 39).

PRAYER FOCUS
- To bind all wicked means and powers of affliction
- To loose my life and destiny from all forms of affliction

PRAYER GUIDES

1. Thank You, Jesus Christ! By Your Word You have decreed my liberty today.

2. Father God, let the glory of divine liberty be seen on me today and forever, in the name of Jesus Christ.

3. I cry out to You, O God. Visit me today and break the power of any affliction over my life and destiny, in the name of Jesus Christ.

4. By the blood of Jesus Christ, and in His name, I subdue, overthrow, and refuse to be bound by any evil powers assigned to bind me in affliction (in my finances, marital status, and spiritual life, etc.). I am free!

5. Powers assigned to bind me in any affliction, the Lord rebuke you. Be paralyzed, in the name of Jesus Christ.

6. With the rod of God in my hand, I break the bonds of affliction designed to seat me in darkness or in the shadow of death, in the mighty name of the Lord Jesus Christ.

7. O God who delivered Job from his affliction, deliver me today from every affliction opposing my life and destiny, in the name of Jesus Christ.

8. Every bond of affliction that has limited my enlargement, be consumed by Holy Ghost fire, in the name of Jesus Christ.

9. Afflictions of poverty and failure, the Lord rebuke you. Be permanently severed from my life, in the name of Jesus Christ.

10. Afflictions of disease and sickness, the Lord rebuke you. Be permanently severed from my life, in the name of Jesus Christ.

11. Marital destruction, the Lord rebuke you. Be permanently severed from my life, in the name of Jesus Christ.

12. Glory of God, overshadow me now. Break the bonds of affliction assigned over my life (my marriage, health, career, etc.), in the name of Jesus Christ.

13. Father God, by Your name *Jehovah*, arise and visit with instant deliverance the afflictions that have kept me below my divinely-appointed position, in the mighty name of Jesus Christ.

14. O Lord, if I am being bound in any affliction, in Your mercy, release me now, in the name of Jesus Christ.

15. Thank You, Jesus, for answering my prayers. Amen.

✝ Prayers to Break Cycles of Destruction

A cycle of destruction can be defined as the progressive, repetitive process of destruction leading to a predetermined, wicked destination.

Bible Prayer Links

Destruction upon destruction is cried; for the whole land is spoiled: suddenly are my tents spoiled, and my curtains in a moment (Jer. 4:20).

Who redeemeth thy life from destruction; who crowneth thee with lovingkindness and tender mercies (Ps. 103:4).

Prayer Focus
- To appeal to the power of God and the blood of Jesus Christ to terminate cycles of destruction in my life
- To assert my authority, in the name of Jesus Christ, to terminate cycles of destruction

Prayer Guides
1. Thank You, O Lord, for breaking all cycles of destruction that have been arrayed against my life, in the name of Jesus Christ.
2. Father God, let the glory of divine liberty be seen on me today and forever, in the name of Jesus Christ.
3. Blood of Jesus, nullify now the legal ground from which cycles of destruction are operating against my life and destiny, in the name of Jesus Christ.
4. By the anointing of the Holy Spirit, I receive the divine power to break up cycles of destruction in my life and destiny, in the name of Jesus Christ.
5. O God who created the heavens and the earth, expose and destroy all hidden cycles of destruction in my life, in the name of Jesus Christ.

6. O Lord, arise now and arrest all daily, weekly, monthly, and yearly cycles of destruction arrayed to frustrate my life, in the name of Jesus Christ.

7. Cycles of destruction arrayed against my prosperity, be permanently disrupted now, in the name of Jesus Christ.

8. Demonic powers enforcing cycles of destruction in my life and destiny, the Lord rebuke you. Surrender your ground of enforcement, in the name of Jesus Christ.

9. Any demonic power positioning me for cycles of destruction, the Lord rebuke you. Perish by the arrow of God, in the name of Jesus Christ.

10. Every seed of destruction sown into my life, and every future-scheduled cycle of destruction, die now, in the name of Jesus Christ.

11. Thank You, Jesus, for answering my prayers. Amen.

✟ Prayers for Fearless Victory over Spirits and Cycles of Destruction

Bible Prayer Links

At destruction and famine thou shalt laugh: neither shalt thou be afraid of the beasts of the earth (Job 5:22).

O death, where is thy sting? O grave, where is thy victory? The sting of death is sin; and the strength of sin is the law. But thanks be to God, which giveth us the victory through our Lord Jesus Christ (1 Cor. 15:55-57).

When I cry unto thee, then shall mine enemies turn back: this I know; for God is for me (Ps. 56:9).

Notice that in asking, "O death, where is thy sting? O grave, where is thy victory?" the apostle Paul laughed at destruction and rebuked fear!

PRAYER FOCUS

- To proclaim victory and operate in the trust that breaks the spirit of fear
- To suffocate the spirits assigned to bring destruction

PRAYER GUIDES

1. Thank You, Lord, for giving me victory and removing all fear, through my Lord Jesus Christ.
2. Father God, let the glory of divine liberty be seen on me today and forever, in the name of Jesus Christ.
3. By the Word of God, I shall laugh at all cycles of destruction arrayed to bring fear, in the name of Jesus Christ.
4. I receive Holy Ghost power to conquer cycles of destruction and the spirits behind them, in the name of Jesus Christ.
5. In the name of Jesus Christ, I receive angelic assistance to fight and overcome every demonic contingent arrayed against my life and destiny.
6. Evil spirits behind cycles of financial destruction, suffocate and die now, in the name of Jesus Christ.
7. Evil spirits behind cycles of marital destruction, suffocate and die now, in the name of Jesus Christ.
8. Evil spirits behind recurring stagnation and the hindering of my progress, suffocate and die now, in the name of Jesus Christ.
9. Evil spirits behind all cycles of destruction in my career and business, suffocate and die now, in the name of Jesus Christ.
10. Evil spirits behind sickness and all destruction of bodily organs or function, suffocate and die now, in the name of Jesus Christ.
11. Evil weapons fashioned to destroy my marital destiny, be consumed now in the fire of God, in the name of Jesus Christ.
12. I command the strength and wickedness of the enemy that has been set against my life to fail and wither, in the name of Jesus Christ.
13. Every recurring evil in my life, be terminated by Holy Ghost fire, in the name of Jesus Christ.

14. Every persistent spirit of the valley assigned against my life and destiny, be paralyzed now, in the name of Jesus Christ.
15. O Lord of Hosts, I thank You that You are ordering my life for outstanding blessings that cannot be destroyed or revoked, in the name of Jesus Christ.
16. Thank You, Jesus, for answering my prayers. Amen.

Overcoming Evil Ancestral Works

✝ PRAYERS AGAINST ANY HINDRANCE BY ANCESTRAL POWERS

Ancestral powers are bloodline demons that rule families from generation to generation by posing as the spirits of dead family members. Their wicked tasks include the following:

- They attack those who choose to breach or break ancestral covenants, vows, or agreements made with occults or demon gods.
- They oversee afflictions, limitations, hard struggles, misfortunes, and illnesses in a family line.
- They work to enforce any generational curses that have been pronounced upon a family.

By the power of the Holy Spirit and the blood of Jesus Christ, evil ancestral works are neutralized when prayers such as those below are prayed in faith and in the name of Jesus Christ.

BIBLE PRAYER LINK

The rest of the people, the priests, the Levites, the porters, the singers, the Nethinims, and all they that had separated themselves from the people of the lands unto the law of God, their wives, their sons, and their daughters, every one having knowledge, and having understanding; they clave to their brethren, their nobles, and entered into a curse, and into an oath, to walk in God's law, which was given by Moses the

293

servant of God, and to observe and do all the com-
mandments of the Lord our Lord, and his judgments
and his statutes (Neh. 10:28-29).

PRAYER FOCUS
■ To eradicate all vestiges of the wickedness established by my ancestors

PRAYER GUIDES
1. Lord, I worship You, and thank You for Your grace and mercy.
2. Redeeming blood of Jesus Christ, cancel all personal and ancestral sins that have exposed me to the hold of ancestral powers, in the mighty name of Jesus Christ.
3. Ancestral powers assigned to demote me, your time is up. Be paralyzed, in the name of Jesus Christ.
4. If, by their idol worship and other evil engagements, my ancestors and/or parents undermined or sold me out, I plead the blood of Jesus Christ, which redeems me now, in His name.
5. Blood of Jesus Christ, break any evil covenants by which my ancestors sold me out. Redeem me now, in the mighty name of Jesus Christ.
6. Evil allegiances and dedications offered by my past generations, I separate myself from you now, by the redeeming blood of Jesus Christ.
7. Evil spiritual hands that hold me down, be paralyzed now, in the name of Jesus Christ.
8. Every idol spirit in my ancestral lineage assigned to hinder my spiritual growth, be separated from me now, in the name of Jesus Christ.
9. Every idol spirit in my ancestral lineage assigned to kill what is good in my life and destiny, the Lord rebuke you. Depart from me now, in the name of Jesus Christ.
10. Every idol spirit in my ancestral lineage assigned to enforce sickness, poverty, etc., in my life and destiny, the Lord rebuke you. Loose your hold and depart from me now, in the name of Jesus Christ.

11. Every idol spirit in my ancestral lineage assigned to lead me into error and keep me in the bondage of poverty, lack, hardship, limitation, and nonachievement, the Lord rebuke you. Loose your hold and depart from me now, in the mighty name of Jesus Christ.

12. Thank You, Jesus, for answering my prayers. Amen.

✟ Prayers to Conquer Generational Battles

Just as physical characteristics can be passed down from parents to their offspring, spiritual battles can be handed down to generations yet unborn.

Generational battles can have indirect and direct effects, including frustration, poverty, scandals, lack of growth, sluggish progress, disunity, constant infirmity, tragedy, troublesome spouses or children, or patterns of "going around in circles."

Remember, the more we pray, the more the Holy Spirit reveals. The more revelation we have, the more ground we can reclaim from the enemy. The more ground we reclaim, the more assurance we have of destiny fulfillment.

Bible Prayer Links

The Lord said unto Moses, Write this for a memorial in a book, and rehearse it in the ears of Joshua: for I will utterly put out the remembrance of Amalek from under heaven. And Moses built an altar, and called the name of it Jehovah-nissi: for he said, Because the Lord hath sworn that the Lord will have war with Amalek from generation to generation (Exod. 17:14-16).

Thou shalt not bow down thyself to them, nor serve them: for I the Lord thy God am a jealous God, visiting the iniquity of the fathers upon the children unto the third and fourth generation of them that hate me (Exod. 20:5).

Keeping mercy for thousands, forgiving iniquity and transgression and sin, and that will by no means clear the guilty; visiting the iniquity of the fathers upon the children, and upon the children's children, unto the third and to the fourth generation (Exod. 34:7).

The leprosy therefore of Naaman shall cleave unto thee, and unto thy seed for ever. And he went out from his presence a leper as white as snow (2 Kings 5:27).

His mercy is on them that fear him from generation to generation (Luke 1:50).

PRAYER FOCUS
- To take authority over the wicked and their works in my generational foundation
- To uproot all unholy decisions and acts in my generations past

PRAYER GUIDES
1. Father Lord, I thank You for the mercy I am about to receive from You during this prayer program.
2. Father Lord, by Your grace, empower me to conquer every battle that my past generations failed to conquer, in the name of Jesus Christ.
3. In the name of Jesus Christ, every generational battle that has defied solution in the past, I conquer you today by the redeeming blood of Jesus, my Lord.
4. O God of mercy and grace, arise and crush all oppressive generational battles confronting me, in the name of Jesus Christ.
5. Generational battles that cut short the glory of my ancestors, I overcome you now by the blood of Jesus Christ, and in His name.

6. Ancestral evil covenants and vows that have given demonic powers the legal ground to operate against my divine purpose, be broken now by the blood of my Lord Jesus Christ.

7. Every unholy agreement entered into with demonic powers or deities by my ancestors or parents, be canceled with the blood of Jesus. All negative impact on my life, destiny, progress, finances, etc., be reversed now, in Jesus Christ's name.

8. Every unholy decision, vow, or promise made by my ancestors or parents that is contrary to my peace and well-being, I loose your hold over my life now, in the name of Jesus Christ.

9. Blood of Jesus Christ, neutralize all curses in my foundation and set me free from them, in the name of Jesus Christ.

10. O Lord, release divine water into my generational foundation so that I may bear pure, uncontaminated fruit, in the mighty name of Jesus Christ.

11. Every battle in the foundation of my life, crumble and die, to the glory of God, in the mighty name of Jesus Christ.

12. Thank You, Jesus, for answering my prayers. Amen.

✟ PRAYERS FOR RELEASE FROM EVIL ANCESTRAL RESTRAINTS

BIBLE PRAYER LINK

Behold, we are servants this day, and for the land that thou gavest unto our fathers to eat the fruit thereof and the good thereof, behold, we are servants in it: and it yieldeth much increase unto the kings whom thou hast set over us because of our sins: also they have dominion over our bodies, and over our cattle, at their pleasure, and we are in great distress (Neh. 9:36-37).

PRAYER FOCUS
- To dismantle and destroy all forms of ancestral agreement with wickedness
- To cancel and reverse all effects of evil restraints established by my ancestors

PRAYER GUIDES

1. I cover myself, my environment, and my family line with the blood of Jesus Christ.

2. Any power prepared to resist my blessings and breakthroughs in this prayer program, the Lord rebuke you now, in the name of Jesus Christ.

3. O Lord, break the hold of any evil consequence upon my life stemming from the ancestral worship of any deity, in the name of Jesus Christ.

4. In the name of Jesus Christ and by the power of His blood, I break the power of any unconscious covenant with evil family guardian spirits.

5. Any unconscious evil soul tie or covenant formed with my dead grandparents, occult uncles and aunts, custodians of family gods/oracles/shrines, be broken by the blood of Jesus Christ.

6. I disconnect myself from any decisions, vows, and promises made by any of my forefathers or foremothers contrary to my divine destiny. Loose your hold now, in the mighty name of the Lord Jesus Christ.

7. O Lord, arise and cut off every evil ancestral life pattern that was established for me through evil vows, promises, or covenants of my forefathers and foremothers, in the name of Jesus Christ.

8. Father Lord, by the blood of Jesus Christ, let any legal grounds occupied by ancestral guardian spirits to impair my life and destiny be destroyed now.

9. Every generational curse of God resulting from the idolatry of my forefathers and foremothers, loose your hold upon my life, marital and family destiny, and professional destiny, etc., in the name of Jesus Christ.

10. O Rock of Ages, strike and break to pieces every ancestral evil altar that is functioning against me or my ministry, marriage, finances, etc., in the mighty name of Jesus Christ.

11. Evil sacrifices offered on my behalf by any member of my family, loose your hold. I declare your power dead, in the name of Jesus Christ.

12. In the mighty name of Jesus Christ, let the fire of the God of Elijah fall upon and burn to ashes any garment of ancestral infirmity, disease, sickness, untimely death, poverty, disfavor, dishonor, shame, or failure at the edge of breakthrough that has been passed down to my generation.

13. O Lord, cut off every evil ancestral river from flowing into my life and destiny, in the name of Jesus Christ.

14. Any demonic power from my roots that seeks to frustrate any area of my life and destiny and discourage me from following the Lord Jesus Christ, be consumed in the fire of the God of Elijah, in the name of Jesus Christ.

15. All damage done to my life and destiny by ancestral evil powers, be restored and made whole now by the redeeming blood and name of the Lord Jesus Christ.

16. Thank You, Jesus Christ, for answering my prayers. Amen.

Overcoming Persistent Enemies

✞ Prayers to Overcome Persistent Enemies

Persistent enemies are unrepentant opponents such as the ancient Midianites who repeatedly attacked the Israelites and the increase of their land. To overcome wicked foes in your life, cry to the Lord for His intervention using the following prayers. As you pray, deliverance must come.

Bible Prayer Link

The Lord said unto him [Gideon], *Surely I will be with thee, and thou shalt smite the Midianites as one man* (Judg. 6:16).

Prayer Focus
- To cry out to the Lord and receive His deliverance
- To uproot unrelenting enemies and their recurring attacks

PRAYER GUIDES

1. Thank You, Lord, for being in our midst and delivering us from the wiles of the enemy, in the name of Jesus Christ.

2. O Lord, thank You for Your faithfulness to those who genuinely cry out to You for their deliverance.

3. O Lord, in the name of Jesus Christ, hear my cries as You heard the cries of the Israelites over the destruction wrought by Midian.

4. Every satanic gate opened wide for my destruction, be closed now in the name of Jesus Christ.

5. Satanic fire ignited for my destruction, be quenched now by the fire of the Holy Ghost, in the name of Jesus Christ.

6. I declare that my persistent enemy cannot turn my achievements into sources of destruction, in the name of Jesus Christ.

7. Father God, let the glory of divine liberty be seen on me today and forever, in the name of Jesus Christ, to prophesy victory against my persistent enemy.

8. My Father and my God, empower me to overthrow the ongoing assignment against my increase. Thank You for increase, year after year, in the name of Jesus Christ.

9. Recurring troubles and pains, persistent attackers, and all cycles of destruction in my life, your end has come today. Vanish, in the name of Jesus Christ.

10. O Lord, redeem my life from every evil seasonal attack that brings pain and sorrow, and disconnect my body and life from all cycles of destruction, in the name of Jesus Christ.

11. Every evil or sin in my life that serves as a magnet to persistent attacks, be removed now by the blood of Jesus Christ.

12. Thank You, Lord Jesus Christ, for answering my prayers. Amen.

✠ PRAYERS FOR GOD'S POWER AND MIGHT TO TURN THE TIDE OF BATTLE

BIBLE PRAYER LINK

Cast thy burden upon the LORD, and he shall sustain thee: he shall never suffer the righteous to be moved.

But thou, O God, shalt bring them down into the pit of destruction: bloody and deceitful men shall not live out half their days; but I will trust in thee (Ps. 55:22-23).

PRAYER FOCUS
- To seek the Lord's deliverance
- To arrest and prevent the works of those who harbor evil against me

PRAYER GUIDES
1. I thank You, Lord Jesus Christ, for Your faithfulness.
2. In the name of Jesus Christ, I, (insert your name), now call upon my God, and He shall deliver me (see Ps. 55:16).
3. Regarding those assigned against my life and staff of bread, O Lord, destroy their schemes and confuse their tongues, in the name of Jesus Christ (see Ps. 55:9).
4. Father God, let those satanic powers that harbor evils against me be afflicted with their evils, in the name of Jesus Christ.
5. Father God, let those satanic powers that harbor wickedness against me, be afflicted with their wickedness, in the name of Jesus Christ (see Ps. 55:19).
6. Father God, let all agents of darkness that harbor evils and wickedness against me be cut off forever, in the name of Jesus Christ (see Ps. 55:15).
7. Father God, let those who are perpetuating wickedness against me be brought down into the pit of destruction, and let their tools turn against them, in the name of Jesus Christ (see Ps. 55:23).
8. In the name of Jesus Christ, I declare that the counsel of the wicked against my life and destiny shall not stand.
9. By authority of my divine ordination as God's child, I reverse every evil decree fashioned against my life, family, and household, in the name of Jesus Christ.
10. Every program of failure and disfavor fashioned against my life and destiny, be cut off now, in the name of Jesus Christ.

11. Every agent of darkness using witchcraft power to manipulate my body, spirit, and soul for pain and sorrow, receive the judgment of God now, in the name of Jesus Christ.

12. Every evil champion lurking in my environment to attack me, be exposed and permanently cut off, in the name of Jesus Christ.

13. Every mouth speaking stagnancy to my progress and prosperity, receive an angelic slap and be paralyzed, in the name of Jesus Christ.

14. O Lord, defeat all demonic assaults and revive Your works in my church/ministry, (insert church/ministry name), to Your glory, in the name of Jesus Christ.

15. O Lord, in the name of Jesus Christ, overwhelm the enemy and bring revival to this congregation, as You brought revival on the day of Pentecost.

16. O Lord, thwart the enemy and let the glory of divine liberty be seen on this church/ministry forever, in the mighty name of Jesus Christ.

17. Thank You, Jesus Christ, for answering my prayers. Amen.

Overthrowing Evil Consultations

✞ PRAYERS TO OVERTHROW EVIL CONSULTATIONS AGAINST ME — PART 1

As a rule, the wicked consult and collaborate with one another in committing evil works. Prayers such as the Holy Spirit has provided here will dismantle evil consultations, in the name of Jesus Christ.

BIBLE PRAYER LINK

They only consult to cast him down from his excellency: they delight in lies: they bless with their mouth, but curse inwardly (Ps. 62:4).

PRAYER FOCUS
- To uproot evil consultations and their effects

PRAYER GUIDES
1. Thank You, Lord, for helping me through times of trouble, in the name of Jesus Christ.
2. In the name of Jesus Christ, I use my divine ordination as a child of God to reverse every evil decree against my life and destiny.
3. O Lord, arise and destroy any works of evil consultation against my life and staff of bread. Confuse their tongues, in the name of Jesus Christ (see Ps. 55:9).
4. Father Lord, let those who harbor evil and wickedness against me in their hearts and habitations be forever cut off from harming me, in the name of Jesus Christ (see Ps. 55:15).
5. Father Lord, let the powers executing wickedness against me be lowered into the pit of destruction. Let their tools turn against them, in the name of Jesus Christ (see Ps. 55:23).
6. Evil consultations stirring limitation, frustration, and failure in my life (my health, finances, etc.), I command you to be scattered like dust, in the name of Jesus Christ.
7. In the name of Jesus Christ, I command the intents, plans, and beings of all satanic consultants hired against my life and destiny to be paralyzed now by Holy Ghost fire, in the name of Jesus Christ.
8. Every champion consulting against my life, be exposed and cut off permanently, in the name of Jesus Christ.
9. Any satanist planning daily sorrows for my life, I command your tools to turn against you, in the name of Jesus Christ.
10. Let every organized strategy of wicked powers against my life (my marriage, family, etc.) be rendered powerless, in the name of Jesus Christ.
11. Let every demonic influence targeted at destroying my life and destiny become null and void, in the name of Jesus Christ.
12. My Father and my God, arise today. Contend with those who contend against my life and destiny in the heavenlies, in the earth, and in the waters, in the name of Jesus Christ.

13. Thank You, Lord, for answering my prayers. Amen.

✞ PRAYERS TO OVERTHROW EVIL CONSULTATIONS AGAINST ME — PART 2

BIBLE PRAYER LINKS

The chief priests consulted that they might put Lazarus also to death; because that by reason of him many of the Jews went away, and believed on Jesus (John 12:10-11).

How long will ye imagine mischief against a man? Ye shall be slain all of you: as a bowing wall shall ye be, and as a tottering fence. They only consult to cast him down from his excellency: they delight in lies: they bless with their mouth, but they curse inwardly. Selah (Ps. 62:3-4).

PRAYER FOCUS
- To dismantle, frustrate, and scatter like dust all evil consultations set to hinder my life and destiny

PRAYER GUIDES
1. Thank You, Lord, for causing me to sit with You in heavenly places (see Eph. 1:3).
2. Thank You, Father, for blessing me with all spiritual blessings in heavenly places in Christ Jesus (see Eph. 1:3).
3. Today, to the glory of God, power is changing hands in favor of my life and destiny, in the name of Jesus Christ.
4. Today, let the heavens declare the glory of God over my life (my destiny, career, family), in the name of Jesus Christ (see Ps. 19:1).
5. O God to whom power belongs, arise today and exercise Your power of judgment against those who are consulting to cast me down from my excellency and my position in heavenly places with You, in the name of Jesus Christ.

6. O Lord arise and send confusion into the midst of the powers consulting against my breakthrough (my healing, success, etc.), in the name of Jesus Christ.

7. Satan, the Lord rebuke you and all your consultations against my life and family, in the name of Jesus Christ.

8. In the name of Jesus Christ, I overthrow and command to backfire all evil consultations occurring in the second heaven against my life and destiny.

9. Demonic powers consulting together to kill me because of God's manifested glory in my life, the Lord rebuke you. Be scattered, in the name of Jesus Christ.

10. Demonic powers consulting together to reverse my break-throughs, the Lord rebuke you. Be frustrated, in the name of Jesus Christ.

11. O Lord, arise and reveal Yourself whenever and wherever the wicked are consulting against Your wonders in my life and destiny, in the name of Jesus Christ.

12. Today, the miracle of "Come and see" will take place in my life (my ministry, finances, etc.), in the name of Jesus Christ (see John 1:46).

13. *Point to the sky and pray the following words*: Wickedness put together in the second heaven to be launched against me, scatter like dust, in the name of Jesus Christ.

14. Thank You, Lord, for answering my prayers. Amen.

Petitioning Divine Intervention

✟ Prayers for the Lord's Rebuke of Those Opposing My Divine Liberty

Bible Prayer Links

> *Yet Michael the archangel, when contending with the devil he disputed about the body of Moses, durst not bring against him a railing accusation, but said, The Lord rebuke thee* (Jude 1:9).

The LORD said unto Satan, The LORD rebuke thee, O Satan; even the LORD that hath chosen Jerusalem rebuke thee: is not this a brand plucked out of the fire? (Zech. 3:2).

At thy rebuke, O God of Jacob, both the chariot and horse are cast into a dead sleep (Ps. 76:6).

I will rebuke the devourer for your sakes, and he shall not destroy the fruits of your ground; neither shall your vine cast her fruit before the time in the field, saith the LORD of hosts (Mal. 3:11).

PRAYER FOCUS
- To assert the Lord's rebuke of the enemy
- To assert God's protection and power on my behalf

PRAYER GUIDES
1. O Lord, I thank You that Your rebuke of the enemy will set me free today, in the name of Jesus Christ.
2. Father Lord, let the glory of divine liberty be seen on me today and forever, in the name of Jesus Christ.
3. Let the rebuke of the Lord arise with flames of fire to destroy the adversary of my divine liberty, in the name of Jesus Christ.
4. Satan, chief adversary of my divine liberty, the Lord rebuke you with flames of fire. Let me go, in the name of Jesus Christ.
5. Leviathan spirit sent (in all your manifesting forms) to attack me and my life, destiny, finances, progress, and prosperity, etc., the Lord rebuke you now with flames of fire. You are defeated, in the name of Jesus Christ.
6. Queen of Heaven/Queen of the Coast sent (in all your manifesting forms) to oppress me and my life, destiny, finances, progress, and prosperity, etc., the Lord rebuke you now with flames of fire. You are overthrown, in the name of Jesus Christ.
7. Python spirits sent (in all your manifesting forms) to hinder me and my life, destiny, finances, progress, and prosperity,

306

etc., the Lord rebuke you now with flames of fire. I trample you, in the name of Jesus Christ.

8. Demonic powers operating from the second heaven against my life and destiny, the Lord rebuke you now with flames of fire. You are hindered from performing your operations, in the name of Jesus Christ.

9. Demonic night caterers, force-feeding me with demonic food and drink in my dreams, the Lord rebuke you now with flames of fire. You must lose your powers, in the name of Jesus Christ.

10. Demonic night raiders stealing my goods and blessings, the Lord rebuke you now with flames of fire. Your route of invasion is blocked, in the mighty name of Jesus Christ.

11. Powers of the night responsible for planting evils, sicknesses, and diseases in my body, the Lord rebuke you now with flames of fire. Your power now becomes null and void, in the mighty name of Jesus Christ.

12. Destruction at noonday that wastes my opportunities, the Lord rebuke you now with flames of fire, in the name of Jesus Christ (see Ps. 91:6).

13. Demonic pestilence that walks in darkness to afflict me and my goods, the Lord rebuke you now with flames of fire. In the name of Jesus Christ, I declare that both I and my goods are rendered invisible to you (see Ps. 91:6).

14. Evil arrows flying during the day, the Lord rebuke you now with flames of fire (see Ps. 91:5). You shall not locate me, in the mighty name of Jesus Christ.

15. Satanists and satanic agents in my family who are behind my struggles, the Lord rebuke you now with flames of fire. Become powerless and be put to shame, in the name of Jesus Christ.

16. Thank You, Jesus Christ, for answering my prayers. Amen.

✝ PRAYERS FOR GOD TO REPAIR ALL DAMAGE, MISTAKES, AND BROKEN DESTINIES

BIBLE PRAYER LINK

To appoint unto them that mourn in Zion, to give unto them beauty for ashes, the oil of joy for mourning, the garment of praise for the spirit of heaviness; that they might be called trees of righteousness, the planting of the Lord, that he might be glorified. And they shall build the old wastes, they shall raise up the former desolations, and they shall repair the waste cities, the desolations of many generations (Isa. 61:3-4).

To repair something is to restore, renew, or revive it—to return it to a former, superior condition, undoing damage or decay.

- Health can be repaired.
- Mistakes can be remedied.
- Destinies, marital destinies, careers, businesses, etc., can be repaired by the power of the Lord.

PRAYER FOCUS
- To access in prayer repair of all damage done through wicked means

PRAYER GUIDES
1. Thank You, O Lord, for repairing all damages I have experienced in my life.
2. Father Lord, let the glory of divine liberty be seen on me today and forever, in the name of Jesus Christ.
3. O Lord, repair now all damage done to my life and destiny through witchcraft and other wicked means, in the name of Jesus Christ.
4. O Lord, repair now all damage done to my health through witchcraft plantings and programming, and through demonic attacks and possessions, in the name of Jesus Christ.

5. Damages done by the serpent spirit to any organ of my body, be repaired now by the blood of Jesus Christ.

6. Blood of Jesus Christ, begin to erase now every witchcraft jinx and spell assigned to abort my divine purposes, in the name of Jesus Christ.

7. O Lord, arise now and reverse every demonic transaction (involving virtues, progress, promotions, prosperity, etc.), that has occurred in my life and destiny, in the name of Jesus Christ.

8. Perversions and diversions manifesting in my life and destiny because of witchcraft attacks and programming, be neutralized now by the fire of the Holy Ghost, in the name of Jesus Christ.

9. By the word of prophecy, I command all of my divine potential that has been stifled or deadened by the Leviathan spirit to resurrect now, in the name of Jesus Christ.

10. By the word of prophecy, I command my fragmented soul to come together now and prosper, in the mighty name of our Lord and Savior, Jesus Christ.

11. All good things in my life choked by the spirit of the serpent, receive the resurrection power of Jesus Christ and come back to life now, in Jesus' name.

12. In the name of Jesus Christ and by the power of the Holy Spirit, I recover now all blessings, fruitfulness, and opportunities that were swallowed by demonic powers.

13. Thank You, Jesus Christ, for answering my prayers. Amen.

✟ PRAYERS TO LIFT DEMONIC EMBARGOES

Note that, spiritually speaking, *embargo* refers to any wicked restriction or restraint designed to stifle destiny and the testimony of God's goodness.

BIBLE PRAYER LINKS

And he shewed me Joshua the high priest standing before the angel of the Lord, and Satan standing at his right hand to resist him. And the Lord said unto Satan, The Lord rebuke thee, O Satan; even the Lord that hath chosen Jerusalem rebuke thee: is not this a brand plucked out of the fire? Now Joshua was clothed with filthy garments, and stood before the angel. And he answered and spake unto those that stood before him, saying, Take away the filthy garments from him. And unto him he said, Behold, I have caused thine iniquity to pass from thee, and I will clothe thee with change of raiment (Zech. 3:1-4).

He that committeth sin is of the devil; for the devil sinneth from the beginning. For this purpose the Son of God was manifested, that he might destroy the works of the devil (1 John 3:8).

Prayer Focus
- To seek the Lord's power to break all demonic embargoes
- To loose my life and destiny from all wicked restrictions

Prayer Guides
1. Thank You, O Lord, for manifesting Your will to destroy the devil's restricting works in my life and destiny.
2. Demonic embargo imposed upon the glory of my divine liberty, be lifted now by the decree of Almighty God, in the name of Jesus Christ.
3. Father Lord, let the glory of divine liberty be seen on me today and forever, in the name of Jesus Christ.
4. O Lord, if my life journey has been altered or embargoed through demonic interference, correct it by Your power, in the name of Jesus Christ.
5. O Lord, arise in the greatness of Your power and cancel any embargo imposed upon my life and destiny by Satan, in the name of Jesus Christ.
6. O Lord, send forth Your rebuke against any demonic embargo imposed upon my healing, blessings, breakthrough, success,

progress, etc. Let the glory of divine liberty manifest now in my life, in the name of Jesus Christ.

7. O God who delivered Israel from the limitations (embargo) of the Red Sea, arise now to deliver me from the "Red Sea" that confronts my rising to glory, in the name of Jesus Christ.

8. Every bitter problem that has embargoed my advancement, receive divine solution and vanish now, in the name of Jesus Christ.

9. Every embargo established in the heavenlies by the Leviathan spirit or the Queen of Heaven to block my open heaven, shatter now, in the name of Jesus Christ.

10. Holy Ghost fire, shatter every blockage erected by demonic powers against my spiritual vision, in the name of Jesus Christ.

11. Demonic embargo imposed upon my prosperity, be removed now by the finger of God, in the name of Jesus Christ.

12. Demonic powers assigned to enforce any embargo against my life and destiny, the Lord rebuke you. Be overthrown, in the name of Jesus Christ.

13. With the blood of Jesus Christ, I challenge every demonic restriction imposed upon my physical and spiritual enlargement, in the name of Jesus Christ.

14. With the blood of Jesus Christ, I challenge every demonic restriction imposed upon my divine purpose, in the name of Jesus Christ.

15. Let the blood of Jesus Christ nullify every embargo enacted to produce my untimely death or that of other members of my household, in the name of Jesus Christ.

16. Thank You, Jesus Christ, for answering my prayers. Amen.

✟ PRAYERS FOR DIVINE REVERSALS

BIBLE PRAYER LINK

We acknowledge, O LORD, our wickedness, and the iniquity of our fathers: for we have sinned against thee. Do not abhor us, for thy name's sake, do not disgrace the throne of thy glory: remember, break not thy covenant with us. Are there any among the vanities of the Gentiles that can cause rain? or can the heavens give showers? Art not thou he, O LORD our God? therefore we will wait upon thee: for thou hast made all these things (Jer. 14:20-22).

PRAYER FOCUS

- To acknowledge and worship the One and Only Almighty One
- To seek the Lord's might and power on my behalf

PRAYER GUIDES

1. Lord God, I praise and worship You, the one true and mighty God!
2. Thank You, Lord, for Your mighty acts and for the excellency of Your greatness in my life (see Ps. 150:2).
3. O God who made Daniel celebrated, thank You for making me celebrated, in the name of Jesus Christ.
4. O God who destroyed the garment of shame assigned to blind Bartimaeus, hear my cry. Remove the garment of shame assigned to me (my marriage, progress, family, finances, etc.), in the name of Jesus Christ.
5. Father Lord, let Your favor crown my efforts in life, in the name of Jesus Christ.
6. O Lord, balance my life's account. Compensate me for the times and seasons wasted by my enemies through hindrance, sickness, poverty, demonic obstruction, etc., in the name of Jesus Christ.
7. All wasted, desolate, and ruined places of my life and destiny, receive divine restoration now, in the name of Jesus Christ.
8. O God of Elijah, arise now and turn my disappointments into divine appointments, in the name of Jesus Christ.
9. O God of Elijah, arise now and turn my disgrace to glory, in the name of the Lord Jesus Christ.
10. Thank You, Jesus, for answering my prayers. Amen.

Petitioning the Finger of God

✝ PRAYERS TO PETITION THE FINGER OF GOD—PART 1

The finger of God casts out demons and stops the hands of Satan and his agents from performing their enterprises (see Job 5:12). The finger of God also writes instructions (divine laws) and judgments, as He did against the king of Babylon (see Dan. 5:5). When this spiritual weapon is used against the wicked one and his agents, they are subdued and their agendas are destroyed, in the name of Jesus Christ.

BIBLE PRAYER LINK

The magicians did so with their enchantments to bring forth lice, but they could not: so there were lice upon man, and upon beast. Then the magicians said unto Pharaoh, This is the finger of God: and Pharaoh's heart was hardened, and he hearkened not unto them; as the Lord had said (Exod. 8:18-19).

PRAYER FOCUS
- To request and give thanks for the mighty finger of God working on my behalf

PRAYER GUIDES
1. Father God, I thank You that Your finger comes against the adversaries of my soul today.
2. Father God, let the glory of divine liberty be seen on me today and forever, in the name of Jesus Christ.
3. O Lord, arise today and teach my fingers to fight as David fought, in the name of Jesus Christ.
4. Power of God that defeated the purposes of Egypt's magicians, arise now and defeat the purposes of the enemy in my life, in the name of Jesus Christ (see Exod. 7).

5. Finger of God, arise now. Pursue to destruction the powers hindering the fulfillment of my divine purpose, in the name of Jesus Christ.

6. O Lord, arise today and let Your finger oppose and put to shame the powers determined to destroy me (my marriage, destiny, life, and ministry), in the name of Jesus Christ.

7. O Lord, stretch forth Your finger against any demon or power occupying my throne of glory. Cast it out, in the name of Jesus Christ.

8. Finger of God, come against and kill any sickness and disease in my body, in the name of Jesus Christ.

9. My Father, with Your finger begin Your work in my life. Let the enemy recognize what You are doing and bow in fear of You, in the name of Jesus Christ.

10. Finger of God, work now for my deliverance from addictions to (name the addictions) and demonic possessions by (name the spirits/conditions), in the name of Jesus Christ.

11. Every satanic clock assigned to govern the affairs of my life, destiny, marital destiny, and prosperity, etc., be shattered to pieces by the finger of God, in the name of Jesus Christ.

12. Finger of God, stop any powers that are stealing good things from the garden of my life and destiny, in the name of Jesus Christ.

13. Finger of God, dismantle and cast out the powers sowing and watering evil in the garden of my life and destiny, in the name of Jesus Christ.

14. Finger of God, oppose and cast out every spirit that is behind any pain or sorrow in my life and destiny, in the name of Jesus Christ.

15. Finger of God, begin to write good things for my life and destiny, in the mighty name of Jesus Christ.

16. Finger of God, write out the divine decrees that will bring glorious changes into my life and destiny, in the name of Jesus Christ.

17. Thank You, Jesus Christ, for answering my prayers. Amen.

✢ PRAYERS TO PETITION THE FINGER OF GOD — PART 2

BIBLE PRAYER LINK

> *But if I with the finger of God cast out devils, no doubt the kingdom of God is come upon you* (Luke 11:20).

PRAYER FOCUS

- To give thanks for the mighty finger of God and for His goodness and mercy
- To seek God's mighty finger to operate on my behalf against all forms of darkness

PRAYER GUIDES

1. I bless You, Lord, for Your goodness and mercy.
2. I plead the blood of Jesus Christ over myself and my environment.
3. Divine finger of God, arise and pursue the powers that seek to bind me away from my divine purpose, in the name of Jesus Christ.
4. Divine finger of God, arise and pursue my pursuers, in the name of Jesus Christ.
5. Lord, by Your divine finger and Your name *Jehovah*, arise and fight my battles as You did for the Israelites in their Egyptian captivity, in the name of Jesus Christ.
6. Lord, arise and lift Your finger against the powers that have purposed to distort, corrupt, or confuse my destiny, life, marriage, ministry, and finances, in the name of Jesus Christ.
7. Lord, stretch forth Your finger against any demon occupying my throne of glory. Cast it out, in the name of Jesus Christ.
8. Every limitation established in the second heaven against me or my life, destiny, family, progress, etc., be scattered now by the finger of God, in the mighty name of Jesus Christ.
9. Thank You, Jesus Christ, for answering my prayers. Amen.

Proclaiming God's Glory in My Life

✟ PRAYERS TO PROCLAIM, "HE HAS CREATED ME FOR HIS GLORY!"

BIBLE PRAYER LINKS

I am the Lord thy God, the Holy One of Israel, thy Saviour: I gave Egypt for thy ransom, Ethiopia and Seba for thee. Since thou wast precious in my sight, thou hast been honourable, and I have loved thee: therefore will I give men for thee, and people for thy life. Fear not: for I am with thee: I will bring thy seed from the east, and gather thee from the west; I will say to the north, Give up; and to the south, Keep not back: bring my sons from far, and my daughters from the ends of the earth; even every one that is called by my name: for I have created him for my glory, I have formed him; yea, I have made him (Isa. 43:3-7).

Behold, the former things are come to pass, and new things do I declare: before they spring forth I tell you of them (Isa. 42:9).

PRAYER FOCUS
- To proclaim the reality of God's glory in my life
- To reflect His glory in every area of my life

PRAYER GUIDES
1. O Lord, I praise and worship You!
2. Thank You, Lord, for Your mighty acts and excellent greatness in my life (see Ps. 150:2).
3. The Lord has created me for His glory. Therefore, wherever I go, I radiate His glory, which shall be seen upon me, in the name of Jesus Christ.
4. *The Lord has created me for His glory; therefore I command:*

5. Sickness, hear the Word of the Lord and be destroyed in my body.
6. Poverty, hear the Word of the Lord and be destroyed in my life.
7. Failure, hear the Word of the Lord and be destroyed in my life.
8. The Lord has created me for His glory. Therefore, my walls, body, spirit, and soul shall be delivered from all evil. In Him, I enjoy prosperity and good health, in the mighty name of our Lord and Savior, Jesus Christ.
9. Father Lord, as the heavens declare Your glory, let my life, calling, ministry, body, finances, family, etc., declare Your glory, in the name of Jesus Christ.
10. Father Lord, as the heavens declare Your glory, let everything I put my hands to declare Your glory, in the mighty name of myLord and Savior, Jesus Christ.
11. By the Word of God, the power of the oppressor shall be broken. My life shall declare the glory of the Lord, in the mighty name of my Lord and Savior, Jesus Christ.
12. Thank You, Jesus Christ, for answering my prayers. Amen.

✝ PRAYERS FOR GOD'S MANIFESTED GLORY IN MY MARITAL DESTINY

Begin this prayer journey with the following confession:

I confess that any words or actions (from me or my ancestors) that have given Satan and his demonic hosts any legal ground to oppress and manipulate my life and marital destiny are now covered with the blood of Jesus Christ and rendered null and void.

I submit my life to the Lord Jesus. Satan, I resist you in my life and marital destiny and I command you to flee from me, in the name of Jesus. I confess that I have the mark of the Lord Jesus on my spirit, soul, and body. Henceforth, let every demonic hindrance to my marital breakthrough be removed, in the name of Jesus Christ. Amen.

BIBLE PRAYER LINK

> *Shall the prey be taken from the mighty, or the lawful captive delivered? But thus saith the LORD, Even the captives of the mighty shall be taken away, and the prey of the terrible shall be delivered: for I will contend with him that contendeth with thee, and I will save thy children* (Isa. 49:24-25).

PRAYER FOCUS

- To release my God-given marital destiny from all hindrance
- To cast down all wicked schemes aimed at my marital destiny

PRAYER GUIDES

1. Father Lord, I thank You because You have already given me victory in this prayer program.
2. Every evil power holding my marital destiny and defying Almighty God's command to release it, be slain by the sword of God, in the name of Jesus Christ.
3. Foundational strong man holding my marital destiny captive, I bring the sword of God against you. Be slain, in the name of Jesus Christ.
4. By fire, Father Lord, execute judgment upon the strong man and the host of dark powers attacking my marital breakthrough, in the name of Jesus Christ.
5. Father Lord, assign pestilence against the host of wicked spirits summoned to prevent my getting married and having my own children, in the name of Jesus Christ.
6. Powers that have singled me out for marital affliction, receive the sword of God and be slain, in the name of Jesus Christ.
7. Evil powers assigned to frustrate my life and marital destiny, be paralyzed, in the name of Jesus Christ.
8. Any member of my household using familiar spirits to hinder my getting married, the Lord rebuke you. Be cut off from me, in the name of Jesus Christ.

9. O Lord, burn to ashes with Your fire any family or house seen repeatedly in my dreams and arranged for me in the spirit realm by the wicked, in the name of Jesus Christ.
10. O Lord, connect me now to my husband/wife and let my marriage be established before You, in the name of Jesus Christ.
11. Holy Spirit, build Your fire around me so familiar spirits cannot come against my marital destiny, in the name of Jesus Christ.
12. Satan, I resist and rebuke you in my life and marital destiny, in the name of Jesus Christ.
13. Thank You, Jesus, for answering my prayers. Amen.

Pursuing Divine Enlargement

✞ PRAYERS FOR ENLARGEMENT

BIBLE PRAYER LINKS

Jabez was more honourable than his brethren.... And Jabez called on the God of Israel, saying, Oh that thou wouldest bless me indeed, and enlarge my coast, and that thine hand might be with me, and that thou wouldest keep me from evil, that it may not grieve me! And God granted him that which he requested (1 Chron. 4:9-10).

The blessing of the Lord, it maketh rich, and he addeth no sorrow with it (Prov. 10:22).

Thou preparest a table before me in the presence of mine enemies: thou anointest my head with oil; my cup runneth over. Surely goodness and mercy shall follow me all the days of my life: and I will dwell in the house of the LORD for ever (Ps. 23:5-6).

Then thou shalt see, and flow together, and thine heart shall fear, and be enlarged; because the abundance

*of the sea shall be converted unto thee, the forces of
the Gentiles shall come unto thee* (Isa. 60:5).

PRAYER FOCUS

■ To seek and receive enlargement by faith

PRAYER GUIDES

1. Thank You, Jesus, for hearing my prayers as You heard the prayers of Jabez.
2. O Lord my God, I call upon You as Jabez did. Bless me indeed, and make me and my household rich, prosperous, and fruitful for the kingdom of heaven, in the name of Jesus Christ.
3. O Lord my God, I call upon You as Jabez did. Arise and enlarge my and my household's coast (spiritually, physically, financially, and materially), in the name of Jesus Christ.
4. O Lord my God, I call upon You as Jabez did. Arise and let Your hand be upon me and my household for good success, blessings, breakthroughs, promotion, progress, financial progress, and excellence, in the mighty name of Jesus Christ.
5. O Lord my God, I call upon You as Jabez did. Keep me from the evils of poverty, lack, hardship, sickness, limitations, failure, backwardness, rejection, and nonachievement, in the name of Jesus Christ.
6. Bless me O Lord, and make me rich (financially and materially), to Your glory, in the name of Jesus Christ.
7. In the name of Jesus Christ, I declare that the blessing of God to me and my household (spiritually, physically, financially, and materially), brings riches with no sorrow, in the mighty name of Jesus Christ.
8. O Lord, let your beauty rest upon my life, destiny, children, calling, and household members, just as Your beauty rested upon King David and the early apostles, in the name of Jesus Christ.
9. O Lord my God, arise now and anoint my head with the oil of joy, gladness, blessings, abundance, breakthroughs, success, prosperity, promotion, and elevation, in the name of the Lord Jesus Christ.

10. O Lord my God, let Your goodness and mercy begin to follow me all the days of my life, in the name of Jesus Christ.

11. O Lord my God, I beseech You today, send Your prosperity, blessings, and breakthroughs to me and my household, in the name of Jesus Christ.

12. O Lord my God, arise now and convert the abundance of the sea and land to me and my household, in the mighty name of Jesus Christ.

13. Thank You, Lord, for answering my prayers. Amen.

✠ PRAYERS TO GO UP AND POSSESS THE LAND

As it is used here, *the land* represents destiny, divine purpose, career, blessing, a good marriage, and all the good that is contained in God's plan at the time of a person's birth.

BIBLE PRAYER LINKS

Caleb stilled the people before Moses, and said, Let us go up at once, and possess it; for we are well able to overcome it (Num. 13:30).

But now I will not be unto the residue of this people as in the former days, saith the LORD of hosts. For the seed shall be prosperous; the vine shall give her fruit, and the ground shall give her increase, and the heavens shall give their dew; and I will cause the remnant of this people to possess all these things. And it shall come to pass, that as ye were a curse among the heathen, O house of Judah, and house of Israel; so will I save you, and ye shall be a blessing: fear not, but let your hands be strong (Zech. 8:11-13).

PRAYER FOCUS
- To pursue and recover my divine allocations

PRAYER GUIDES

1. Thank You, O Lord, for the restoration and enlargement that will take place in my life today, in the name of Jesus Christ.
2. Spirit of faith in God, possess me now, in the name of Jesus Christ.
3. O God of grace and mercy, visit me today and destroy every yoke assigned to deny me my divine possession, in the name of Jesus Christ.
4. O Lord, by the Holy Spirit, empower me today to possess my promised land, in the name of Jesus Christ.
5. O Lord, arise and break the power of passivity that keeps me from entering my land of promise, in the name of Jesus Christ.
6. By the power of the Holy Spirit, I arise and possess all the good things the Lord established for me at the Creation, in the name of Jesus Christ.
7. All demonic powers in possession of my blessings and blocking my promised land, you must release them to me now, in the name of Jesus Christ.
8. By the power of the Holy Spirit, I overcome all demonic opposition to my destiny fulfillment, in the name of Jesus Christ.
9. By the power of the Holy Spirit, I break down every demonic wall erected against my progress, enlargement, and fruitfulness, in the name of Jesus Christ.
10. By the power of the Holy Spirit, my hands shall be strong against the enemy of my divine accomplishments, in the name of Jesus Christ.
11. Thank You, Lord, for answering my prayers. Amen.

Removing Reproach

✝ PRAYERS FOR THE LORD TO ROLL AWAY ALL REPROACH

Reproach is the bringing of shame, disgrace, or stigma upon one's life. Sin brings reproach, but so does Satan, the accuser of the brethren (see Rev. 12:10).

BIBLE PRAYER LINKS

The Lord said unto Joshua, This day have I rolled away the reproach of Egypt from off you. Wherefore the name of the place is called Gilgal unto this day (Josh. 5:9).

She conceived, and bare a son; and said, God hath taken away my reproach (Gen. 30:23).

Hear, O our God; for we are despised: and turn their reproach upon their own head, and give them for a prey in the land of captivity (Neh. 4:4).

Deliver me from all my transgressions: make me not the reproach of the foolish (Ps. 39:8).

As with a sword in my bones, mine enemies reproach me; while they say daily unto me, Where is thy God? (Ps. 42:10).

Reproach hath broken my heart; and I am full of heaviness: and I looked for some to take pity, but there was none; and for comforters, but I found none (Ps. 69:20).

O God, how long shall the adversary reproach? Shall the enemy blaspheme thy name for ever? (Ps. 74:10)

Turn away my reproach which I fear: for thy judgments are good (Ps. 119:39).

PRAYER FOCUS
- To turn away, by faith, all reproach of the wicked
- To turn back all wicked schemes to bring reproach

323

PRAYER GUIDES

1. As I begin in prayer, I plead the blood of Jesus Christ over my petitions and my life.
2. Thank You, Lord, for delivering me this day from every form of reproach to Your glory, in the name of Jesus Christ.
3. This day, O Lord, arise and roll away from me all financial reproach, in the name of Jesus Christ.
4. This day O Lord, arise and roll away from me all reproach where my health is concerned, in the name of Jesus Christ.
5. This day O Lord, arise and roll away from me the reproach of all bondages including (name them), in the name of Jesus Christ. (Examples: addiction, poverty, backwardness, etc.)
6. All reproach assigned to break my heart, honor me instead, in the name of Jesus Christ.
7. By the power of the Holy Spirit, the reproach of the foolish shall not be upon me, in the name of Jesus Christ.
8. O Lord my God, arise now and turn any reproach of my enemies (as regards my life and destiny, including financial, spiritual, and marital destiny) upon their own heads, in the name of Jesus Christ.
9. This day, O Lord, arise and terminate the means of demonic forces empowering reproach against my life and destiny, in the name of Jesus Christ.
10. Father Lord, undertake for me today and let all reproach assigned to bring heaviness into my soul be rolled away from me, in the name of Jesus Christ.
11. Every affliction, sickness, or disease that is bringing reproach to my life and destiny, be terminated today, in the name of Jesus Christ.
12. By the Word of God, I command all demonic powers that are incensed against me to become ashamed, confounded, and rendered as nothing today. Perish, in the name of Jesus Christ (see Isa. 41:11).
13. Father Lord, send blindness and confusion into the midst of demonic powers seeking to bring reproach by arresting my life and destiny, in the name of Jesus Christ.

14. Father Lord, let all satanic agents, including the Sanballats and Tobiahs of this day who are assigned to despise and reproach me, be given for a prey to their enemies, in the name of Jesus Christ.
15. Thus says the Lord God concerning me, (insert name): I shall be like a tree planted by the rivers of water, that brings forth his fruit in his season; his leaf also shall not wither and whatsoever I do shall prosper, in the name of Jesus Christ (see Ps.1:3).
16. Thank You, Jesus, for answering my prayers. Amen.

Renewing God's Creation Blessings in My Life

✟ Prayers for Renewed Fruitfulness, Multiplication, Replenishment, Subduing, and Dominion — Part 1

In the beginning, God blessed the man and the woman and said "Be fruitful, and multiply, and replenish the earth, and subdue it: and have dominion over the fish of the sea," and so on (Gen. 1:28). These blessings remain operative, but in some lives they have been suppressed by the wicked. Prayer can relieve the suppression and release a turnaround so that failure is replaced by success and any casting down is replaced by a lifting up.

Bible Prayer Link

So God created man in his own image, in the image of God created he him; male and female created he them. And God blessed them, and God said unto them, Be fruitful, and multiply, and replenish the earth, and subdue it: and have dominion over the fish of the sea, and over the fowl of the air, and over every living thing that moveth upon the earth (Gen. 1:27-28).

Prayer Focus
- To confess and repent of sins and the restriction they create
- To restore the blessings God granted to mankind at the Creation

PRAYER GUIDES

1. Thank You, Jesus Christ, for undoing the enemy's works in my life, in the name of Jesus Christ.

2. Lord, I confess and repent of any ancestral or other sin that has hindered the manifestation of Your Creation blessings (fruitfulness, multiplication, replenishment, subduing, and dominion) in my life.

3. Blood of Jesus Christ, wipe away my confessed sins and manifest Creation blessings (fruitfulness, multiplication, replenishment, subduing, and dominion) in my life and destiny today, in the name of Jesus Christ.

4. By the blood of our Lord Jesus Christ, I break the power of all ancestral and other sins that have restricted the manifestation of Creation blessings (fruitfulness, multiplication, replenishment, subduing, and dominion) in my life and destiny, in the name of Jesus Christ.

5. Father God, grant me the grace of a new beginning and revive Your Creation blessings (fruitfulness, multiplication, replenishment, subduing, and dominion) in my life and destiny, in the name of Jesus Christ.

6. Let the Shekinah glory of God appear now to scatter every cloud of confusion and ignorance that is restricting any Creation blessings (fruitfulness, multiplication, replenishment, subduing, and dominion), in the name of Jesus Christ. *Lay hold of this truth and stand fast on it!*

7. Let the Shekinah glory of God attack and destroy the enemy of my divine destiny and dominion, in the name of Jesus Christ.

8. In the name of Jesus Christ, let the holy fire of God possess me and dissolve any demonic plantings in my life that have hindered the manifestation of Creation blessings (fruitfulness, multiplication, replenishment, subduing, and dominion) in my life.

9. In the name of Jesus Christ, let the holy fire of God possess me now to revive the Creation blessings (fruitfulness, multiplication, replenishment, subduing and dominion) in my life.

10. Thank You, Lord, for answering my prayers. Amen.

✞ Prayers for Renewed Fruitfulness, Multiplication, Replenishment, Subduing, and Dominion — Part 2

Bible Prayer Link

God blessed Noah and his sons, and said unto them,
Be fruitful, and multiply, and replenish the earth
(Gen. 9:1).

Prayer Focus
- To receive God's blessing and grace for new beginnings
- To restore the blessings God granted to mankind at Creation

Prayer Guides
1. Thank You, Jesus Christ for undoing the enemy's works in my life.
2. O Lord, grant me the blessings of new beginnings as You did for Noah and his household after the flood, in the name of Jesus Christ.
3. Father God, as You granted Noah Your grace, please grant it to me. In the name of Jesus Christ, revive Your Creation blessings (fruitfulness, multiplication, replenishment, subduing, and dominion) in my life and destiny.
4. Father God, as Noah found grace in Your eyes, let me also find it. In the name of Jesus Christ, please manifest my healing, deliverance, prosperity, promotion, elevation, etc.
5. O Lord, in the name of Jesus Christ, let every visitation of darkness assigned to oppress or hinder the manifestation of Your Creation blessings (fruitfulness, multiplication, replenishment, subduing, and dominion), expire now, to Your glory.
6. Demonic powers assigned to project into my mind lies and deceptions that oppose God's Creation blessings, the Lord rebuke you. Depart from me now, in the name of Jesus Christ.
7. Demonic powers assigned to project into my mind unbelief and doubt against God's Creation blessings, the Lord rebuke you. Be cut off from me now, in the name of Jesus Christ.

8. By the power of the Holy Spirit, I plead the blood of the Lamb to overcome inherited evil ancestral patterns that have prevented God's Creation blessings (fruitfulness, multiplication, replenishment, subduing, and dominion) from coming alive in my life, in the name of Jesus Christ.

9. Demonic pollution that has severed the link between God's Creation blessings and my divine destiny, be neutralized now, through the blood and the name of the Lord Jesus Christ.

10. Let the blessing of fruitfulness come alive now in my life and destiny, in the name of Jesus Christ.

11. Let the blessing of multiplication come alive now in my life and destiny, in the name of Jesus Christ.

12. Let the blessing of replenishment come alive now in my life and destiny, in the name of Jesus Christ.

13. Let the blessing of power to subdue come alive now in my life and destiny, in the name of Jesus Christ.

14. Let the blessing of power to take dominion come alive now in my life and destiny, in the name of Jesus Christ.

15. Thank You, Lord, for answering my prayers. Amen.

✝ PRAYERS FOR RENEWED FRUITFULNESS, MULTIPLICATION, REPLENISHMENT, SUBDUING, AND DOMINION—PART 3

BIBLE PRAYER LINKS

I have satiated the weary soul, and I have replenished every sorrowful soul (Jer. 31:25).

Joseph called the name of the firstborn Manasseh: For God, said he, hath made me forget all my toil, and all my father's house. And the name of the second called he Ephraim: For God hath caused me to be fruitful in the land of my affliction (Gen. 41:51-52).

He increased his people greatly; and made them stronger than their enemies (Ps. 105:24).

PRAYER FOCUS

- To appropriate the Creation blessings for additional areas of my life

PRAYER GUIDES

1. Father God, thank You for making me in Your image, after Your likeness, in the name of Jesus Christ (see Gen. 1:26).
2. Father God, I thank You for the blessings You granted me at Creation (fruitfulness, multiplication, replenishment, subduing, and dominion), in the name of Jesus Christ.
3. Father God, as You did for the early apostles, empower me by the Holy Spirit to tap into the divine blessings of a new beginning, unhindered by any demonic force, in the name of the Lord Jesus Christ.
4. Father God, arise now and enforce Your Creation blessing of replenishment for my grieving soul, my sick body, my failed marriage, my damaged marital destiny, my devoured finances, etc., in the name of Jesus Christ.
5. Father God, arise now and enforce Your Creation blessing of fruitfulness in my life, to make me fruitful wherever You lead me, in the name of Jesus Christ.
6. Father God, arise now and enforce Your Creation blessing of dominion in my life, so that I confront and conquer all afflictions and contrary situations, in the name of Jesus Christ.
7. O Lord, make me stronger than my enemies, as You did for the Israelites, in the name of Jesus Christ.
8. Father God, by the Holy Spirit, reconnect my divine destiny and purpose to Your Creation blessings (fruitfulness, multiplication, replenishment, subduing, and dominion) for the fulfillment of my life and destiny, in the name of Jesus Christ.
9. Father God, arise now and decree an unbreakable bond between the works of my hands and Your Creation blessings, in the name of Jesus Christ.
10. In this time of new beginning, when I ask, it shall be given me; when I seek, I shall find; when I knock, it shall be opened to me; in the name of Jesus Christ (see Matt. 7:7).

11. In this time of new beginning, whatever I put my hands to shall prosper, in the name of Jesus Christ (see Ps. 1:3).

12. In this time of new beginning, new and wonderful things shall manifest in my life and destiny, in the name of Jesus Christ.

13. Thank You, Lord, for answering my prayers. Amen.

✠ Prayers to Purge my Life and Heal My Barrenness

Bible Prayer Link

> *The men of the city said unto Elisha, Behold, I pray thee, the situation of this city is pleasant, as my lord seeth: but the water is naught, and the ground barren. And he said, Bring me a new cruse, and put salt therein. And they brought it to him. And he went forth unto the spring of the waters, and cast the salt in there, and said, Thus saith the Lord, I have healed these waters; there shall not be from thence any more death or barren land. So the waters were healed unto this day, according to the saying of Elisha which he spake* (2 Kings 2:19-22).

Prayer Focus

- To prayerfully address any polluted areas of my life and purge all forms of obstruction and hindrance
- To return all barren areas of my life to fruitfulness

Prayer Guides

1. Father Lord, I thank You for the changes that will take place in my life, destiny, finances, career, and body during this prayer program, in the name of Jesus Christ.

2. O Lord, arise and make the impossible possible in my life, destiny, and circumstances, in the name of Jesus Christ.

3. Every demonic source that has brought barrenness into my life, receive Holy Ghost fire and be banished, in the name of Jesus Christ.

4. Pollution in my family line, be cleansed by the purging fire of the Holy Ghost, in the name of Jesus Christ.

5. O Lord, arise now and purge my family foundation with Your cleansing Holy Ghost fire, in the name of Jesus Christ.

6. O Lord, arise now and cut off every evil source that has polluted my life, destiny, finances, and prosperity with bitterness, anger, pain, and failure, in the name of Jesus Christ.

7. Let the holy fire of God disconnect me from any generational curse that is hindering my glorious destiny, progress, elevation, success, promotion, and marital fulfillment, in the name of Jesus Christ.

8. O Lord, let Your holy fire possess me now and disconnect my body from any disease, sickness, or affliction, in the name of Jesus Christ.

9. My destiny, life, body, finances, and marital destiny — receive the anointing of the Holy Spirit. Begin to prosper and be fruitful, in the name of Jesus Christ.

10. O Lord, arise now. Heal my barren land and revive the dry works of my hands, in the name of Jesus Christ.

11. O Lord, bless me and my family. Cause us to be a blessing to you, in the name of Jesus Christ.

12. Thank You, Jesus Christ, for answering my prayers. Amen.

Seeking and Finding Favor

✝ PRAYERS FOR FAVOR IN THE SIGHT OF GOD AND MAN

As children of God seeking to reach our breakthroughs and sustain the fulfillment of our divine purpose, we need His favor. When we receive it, the people we meet on our life's journey will also be favorable toward us.

BIBLE PRAYER LINKS

So shalt thou find favour and good understanding in the sight of God and man (Prov. 3:4).

*Now God had brought Daniel into favour and tender
love with the prince of the eunuchs* (Dan. 1:9).

*The angel said unto her, Fear not, Mary: for thou hast
found favour with God* (Luke 1:30).

*Jesus increased in wisdom and stature, and in favour
with God and man* (Luke 2:52).

*Praising God, and having favour with all the people.
And the Lord added to the church daily such as should
be saved* (Acts 2:47).

PRAYER FOCUS
- To remove all favor blockers
- To release the flow of God's favor in my life and destiny

PRAYER GUIDES
1. I thank You, Lord God, for Your faithfulness and favor, in the name of Jesus Christ.
2. O Lord, let every bewitchment of rejection that is rooted in my foundation and is preempting favor in my life and destiny, scatter today, in the name of Jesus Christ.
3. Every satanic contractor constructing rejection for my life and destiny, be paralyzed, in the name of Jesus Christ.
4. Father Lord, by the greatness of Your power, destroy all bewitchment that is working against my receiving favor, in the name of Jesus Christ.
5. Redeeming blood of our Lord Jesus Christ, erase now every mark and spell of hatred and rejection that is marring my life and destiny and blocking favor, in the name of Jesus Christ.
6. Every evil garment upon me that is limiting my blessings, breakthroughs, and goodness, be roasted by the Holy Ghost fire of God, in the name of Jesus Christ.
7. Lord Jesus Christ, beautify my life and destiny with Your favor.
8. O Lord, generate love and favor in the hearts of my divine helpers (<u>name them</u>), in the name of Jesus Christ. (Divine

helpers are the people assigned by God to assist you in the fulfillment of your destiny.)

9. With the blood of Jesus Christ, I dismantle and destroy all manipulation of my divine helpers, (name them), against me, in the name of Jesus Christ.

10. Lord Jesus Christ, arise in Your power and destroy anything and everything working against my favor.

11. Lord God, by Your favor, arise and make my spiritual and financial mountains stand strong, in the name of Jesus Christ.

12. O Lord, from today forward, let Your favor rest and abide with me everywhere that I am and wherever I go, in the name of Jesus Christ.

13. Thank you, Lord God, for answering my prayers. Amen.

Seeking and Prophesying Restoration and Revival

✝ PRAYERS FOR THE LORD TO REVIVE ME

To revive is to restore something dead to life or consciousness. When praying, remember that we can ask the Lord to revive our finances, health, mental health, marriage, church— anything that has been adversely affected by sin or by the means of the wicked.

BIBLE PRAYER LINKS

For thus saith the high and lofty One that inhabiteth eternity, whose name is Holy; I dwell in the high and holy place, with him also that is of a contrite and humble spirit, to revive the spirit of the humble, and to revive the heart of the contrite ones (Isa. 57:15).

Wilt thou not revive us again: that thy people may rejoice in thee? (Ps. 85:6).

Though I walk in the midst of trouble, thou wilt revive me: thou shalt stretch forth thine hand against the wrath of mine enemies, and thy right hand shall save me (Ps. 138:7).

They that dwell under his shadow shall return; they shall revive as the corn, and grow as the vine: the scent thereof shall be as the wine of Lebanon (Hosea 14:7).

Note that the humble are people who are modest, but bold to confess their shortcomings. They are not proud or self-assertive, but are confident in God. The contrite are tender-hearted people who are remorseful for having done wrong to man and God.

PRAYER FOCUS

- To seek God's reviving, resurrection power for every area of my life
- To be restored to perfect wholeness and soundness

PRAYER GUIDES

1. Thank You, O Lord, for reviving me (my body, business, career, etc.) today.
2. Father Lord, let the glory of divine liberty be seen on me today and forever, in the name of Jesus Christ.
3. Fragmented bones of my life, receive the resurrection power of the Lord Jesus Christ and come together now, in the name of Jesus Christ (see Ezek. 37).
4. Resurrection power of the Lord Jesus Christ, come upon my body now and revive it to perfect functioning, in the name of Jesus Christ.
5. Resurrection power of the Lord Jesus Christ, come upon my life and destiny now and revive them to glory, in the name of Jesus Christ.
6. Father, let the resurrection power of the Lord Jesus Christ revive my life and revoke every curse (financial problems, sickness, failure, rejection, nonachievement, etc.), in the name of Jesus Christ.

7. Dead organs of my body, receive the resurrection power of the Lord Jesus Christ and return to wellness, in the mighty name of Jesus Christ.

8. O breath of God, come upon me now and revive me spiritually and physically, in the name of Jesus Christ.

9. I, (insert your name), dwell under the shadow of Almighty God. Therefore, my glory shall revive today, in the name of Jesus Christ.

10. My calling, ministry, business, career, etc.—arise and dwell under the shadow of the Almighty God and revive now, in the name of Jesus Christ.

11. Let the glory of God overshadow me now and overthrow the shadow of death that has covered my glory, in the name of Jesus Christ.

12. Holy Ghost revival power, possess my prayer/spiritual life now, in the name of Jesus Christ.

13. Thank You, Jesus Christ, for answering my prayers. Amen.

✞ PRAYERS TO RESTORE ALL THAT BELONGS TO ME

The following prayers can be used to recover everything that satanic robbers have stolen from you.

BIBLE PRAYER LINKS

When the king asked the woman, she told him [how God used Elisha to restore her dead son to life]. *So the king appointed unto her a certain officer, saying, Restore all that was hers, and all the fruits of the field since the day that she left the land, even until now* (2 Kings 8:6).

Restore, I pray you, to them, even this day, their lands, their vineyards, their oliveyards, and their houses, also the hundredth part of the money, and of the corn, the wine, and the oil, that ye exact of them (Neh. 5:11).

PRAYER FOCUS

- To reverse every theft and restore all that the enemy has stolen

PRAYER GUIDES

1. O Lord, I praise and worship You!
2. Thank You, Lord, for Your mighty acts and excellent greatness in my life (see Ps. 150:2).
3. O covenant-keeping God, arise and let Your words in this prayer program become operational instantly, in the name of Jesus.
4. I praise You, O Lord, who commands and cannot be resisted.
5. O Lord, remember me for good today. Forcibly recover all that belongs to me, but is in the hands of oppressive and demonic powers, in the name of Jesus.
6. Father Lord, command demonic confiscators to restore all that belongs to me now, in the name of Jesus.
7. Father Lord, recover and restore back to me every benefit and blessing that suddenly vanished from my life, in the name of Jesus.
8. O Lord, let the creative power of the Holy Spirit come upon my destiny and restore its glory, in the name of Jesus.
9. Demonic powers sucking away my virtues, the Lord rebuke you. Be cut off from me, in the name of Jesus.
10. Thank You, Jesus, for You have restored all to me!

✝ PRAYERS FOR THE LORD TO RAISE ME UP TODAY

BIBLE PRAYER LINKS

Come, and let us return unto the LORD: for he hath torn, and he will heal us; he hath smitten, and he will bind us up. After two days will he revive us: in the third day he will raise us up, and we shall live in his sight (Hosea 6:1-2).

Behold, the angel of the Lord came upon him, and a light shined in the prison: and he smote Peter on the side, and raised him up, saying, Arise up quickly. And his chains fell off from his hands (Acts 12:7).

We having the same **spirit of faith,** *according as it is written, I believed, and therefore have I spoken; we also believe, and therefore speak; knowing that he which raised up the Lord Jesus shall raise up us also by Jesus, and shall present us with you* (2 Cor. 4:13-14).

PRAYER FOCUS
- To appropriate the life of Christ that raises me up from all oppression

PRAYER GUIDES
1. Father Lord, I thank You for raising me up today, in the name of Jesus Christ.
2. Let the blood of Jesus Christ speak deliverance into my life and destiny, in the name of Jesus Christ.
3. Any demonic power assigned to hold me down, your assignment is canceled. Be destroyed by the power of God, in the name of Jesus Christ.
4. Let the voice of the Lord thunder now and scatter every wicked means assigned to oppress my enlargement and fruitfulness, in the name of Jesus Christ.
5. My Lord Jesus lives! Therefore, I am raised up and refreshed in His presence, in the name of Jesus Christ.
6. My Lord Jesus lives! Therefore, I am raised up from spiritual weakness to spiritual power, in the name of Jesus Christ.
7. My Lord Jesus lives! Therefore, I am raised up from the valley of poverty to the pinnacle of prosperity, in the name of Jesus Christ.
8. My Lord Jesus lives! Therefore, I am raised up from the bed of disease and sickness to the heights of healing and wholeness, in the name of Jesus Christ.

9. My Lord Jesus lives! Therefore, I am released from the grip of failure and transformed into an unbridled success, in the name of Jesus Christ.

10. O Lord, raise up my glory and let it shine forever, in the name of Jesus Christ.

11. O Lord, raise up my life and let me live in Your presence forever, in the name of Jesus Christ.

12. Thank You, Lord, for answering my prayers. Amen.

✝ PRAYERS TO REVIVE AND SHINE

BIBLE PRAYER LINKS

Wilt thou not revive us again: that thy people may rejoice in thee? (Ps. 85:6).

Come, and let us return unto the LORD: for he hath torn, and he will heal us; he hath smitten, and he will bind us up. After two days will he revive us: in the third day he will raise us up, and we shall live in his sight (Hosea 6:1-2).

They that dwell under his shadow shall return; they shall revive as the corn, and grow as the vine: the scent thereof shall be as the wine of Lebanon (Hosea 14:7).

O LORD, I have heard thy speech, and was afraid: O LORD, revive thy work in the midst of the years, in the midst of the years make known; in wrath remember mercy (Hab. 3:2).

PRAYER FOCUS

- To seek revival, restoration, and renewal to every area of my life
- To rescind any ground being accessed by the enemy

Prayer Guides

1. Thank You, Lord, for Your love for me, in the name of Jesus Christ.
2. In the name of Jesus Christ, I declare that today I shall have the divine encounter that gives me fresh life.
3. Today, by the blood of Jesus Christ, I come against and overcome the power of death that has exercised dominion over my life and destiny.
4. Today, I come against and overcome the power of death that has exercised dominion over the organs of my body, in the name of Jesus Christ.
5. Today, by the grace of God Almighty, I shall revive and shine—spiritually, physically, and financially, in the name of Jesus Christ.
6. Holy Ghost revival fire, come upon me now and revive my life and destiny, in the name of Jesus Christ.
7. By the Word of God, I come and dwell under the shadow of Almighty God. My life and destiny shall revive as the corn and grow as the vine, in the name of Jesus Christ.
8. By the Word of God, I come and dwell under the shadow of Almighty God. My business, career, calling, and ministry shall revive as the corn and grow as the vine, in the name of Jesus Christ.
9. Holy Ghost revival fire, come upon me now, and revive the works of my hands (my labor, career, and business) in the name of Jesus Christ.
10. Holy Ghost revival fire, come upon my body now and revive my blood and bodily organs, in the name of Jesus Christ.
11. In the name of Jesus Christ, my glory shall revive and shine, and I will rejoice in the Lord my God.
12. Thank You, Lord, for answering my prayers. Amen.

✞ Prayers Prophesying My Freedom to Arise and Prosper

Prayers can prophesy! Prophetic prayers are:

- Prayers of a faith as small and powerful as a grain of mustard seed (see Matt. 17:20)
- Prayers of desperation like the one prayed by Elijah to revive a dead child (see 1 Kings 17:21)
- Prayers tied to time and season, as when Elisha told the Shunnammite woman, "about this season, according to the time of life, thou shalt embrace a son" (2 Kings 4:16)
- Prayers of "thus saith the Lord God of Israel" as when Elijah told the widow of Zarephath, "The barrel of meal shall not waste, neither shall the cruise of oil fail, until the day that the Lord sendeth rain upon the earth" (1 Kings 17:14)
- Faith-filled, targeted prayers to dismantle evil blockages Faith-filled, targeted prayers to repair damages

BIBLE PRAYER LINKS

Then the prophets, Haggai the prophet, and Zechariah the son of Iddo, prophesied unto the Jews that were in Judah and Jerusalem in the name of the God of Israel, even unto them (Ezra 5:1).

The elders of the Jews builded, and they prospered through the prophesying of Haggai the prophet and Zechariah the son of Iddo. And they builded, and finished it, according to the commandment of the God of Israel, and according to the commandment of Cyrus, and Darius, and Artaxerxes king of Persia. And this house was finished on the third day of the month Adar, which was in the sixth year of the reign of Darius the king (Ezra 6:14-15).

Thou, son of man, prophesy and say, Thus saith the Lord GOD concerning the Ammonites, and concerning their reproach; even say thou, The sword, the sword is drawn: for the slaughter it is furbished, to consume because of the glittering (Ezek. 21:28).

Moreover the word of the LORD came unto me, saying, Son of man, set thy face toward the south, and drop thy word toward the south, and prophesy against the forest of the south field; and say to the forest of the south, Hear the word of the Lord; Thus saith the Lord GOD; Behold, I will kindle a fire in thee, and it shall devour every green tree in thee, and every dry tree: the flaming flame shall not be quenched, and all faces from the south to the north shall be burned therein (Ezek. 20:45-47).

PRAYER FOCUS
- To pray prophetic prayers of breakthrough

PRAYER GUIDES
1. Father Lord, I thank You for the blessings that shall be established in my life.
2. Father Lord, let the glory of divine liberty be seen on me today and forever, in the name of Jesus Christ.
3. Now, my life, receive the Holy Ghost anointing to prosper physically, spiritually, and financially, in the name of Jesus Christ.
4. Now, my body, receive the fire of divine healing and be made whole, in the name of Jesus Christ.
5. Now, my life (career, business, marriage), hear the Word of the Lord. Come out of the valley of demonic oppression and excel, in the name of Jesus Christ.
6. Now, my glory, break out of demonic detention and shine, in the mighty name of Jesus Christ.
7. Now, my destiny, hear the Word of the Lord. Come out of the shadow of death and be fulfilled, in the name of Jesus Christ.
8. Now, my calling and ministry, arise and excel, in the mighty name of Jesus Christ.
9. Now, work of my hands, arise and prosper, in the name of Jesus Christ.
10. Now, my womb, arise and receive the power to conceive, in the mighty name of Jesus Christ.

11. O God of times and seasons, arise in Your glory and beautify my life and destiny, in the name of Jesus Christ.

12. O God of times and seasons, connect me to those who will add to my life, in the name of Jesus Christ.

13. O God of times and seasons, stir my divine helpers to seek me out, in the name of Jesus Christ.

14. O Lord, frustrate the powers assigned to delay my divine purpose and neutralize their agendas, in the name of Jesus Christ.

15. Every wicked garment delaying my blessings and breakthroughs, catch fire and be destroyed, in the name of Jesus Christ.

16. Powers assigned to arrest my glory, be confused and rendered powerless, in the name of Jesus Christ.

17. O God of time and purpose, behold with Your eyes of mercy the situations in my life and cause them to change, for Your glory, in the name of Jesus Christ.

18. Thank You, Jesus Christ, for answering my prayers. Amen.

✝ Prayers Prophesying the Restoration of My Decayed Places

Bible Prayer Link

> *Thus saith the Lord, thy redeemer, and he that formed thee from the womb, I am the Lord that maketh all things; that stretcheth forth the heavens alone; that spreadeth abroad the earth by myself; that frustrateth the tokens of the liars, and maketh diviners mad; that turneth wise men backward, and maketh their knowledge foolish; that confirmeth the word of his servant, and performeth the counsel of his messengers; that saith to Jerusalem, Thou shalt be inhabited; and to the cities of Judah, Ye shall be built, and I will raise up the decayed places thereof* (Isa. 44:24-26).

Prayer Focus

- To praise, worship, and give thanks for God, my Redeemer

■   To prophesy the restoration of all good things in my life, by Almighty God

PRAYER GUIDES

1.   Lord God, I praise and worship You, my Restorer, and I thank You for Your mighty miracles, signs, and wonders.

2.   Father Lord, empower me with Your holy fire. Grant me physical, spiritual, and financial breakthroughs during this prayer program, in the name of Jesus Christ.

3.   Lord, my Redeemer, arise now in Your power to redeem my life and destiny from every form of demonic oppression, in the name of Jesus Christ.

4.   Lord, my Redeemer, arise now and redeem my past misdeeds with Your blood. Let them not come against the glory of my future, in the name of Jesus Christ.

5.   O God who makes all things, arise now and let everything that is arrayed against my divine purpose collapse now, in the mighty name of Jesus Christ.

6.   Decayed places in my life, hear the Word of the Lord God to you: "I will raise up your decayed places." Decayed places in my life, be raised up now, in the name of Jesus Christ.

7.   Decayed places of my destiny, hear the Word of the Lord God to you: "I will raise up your decayed places." Decayed places in my destiny, be raised up now, in the name of Jesus Christ.

8.   Decayed places in my marriage/marital destiny, hear the Word of the Lord God to you: "I will raise up your decayed places." Decayed places in my marriage/marital destiny, be revived now, in the name of Jesus Christ.

9.   Decayed places in my career, hear the Word of the Lord God to you: "I will raise up your decayed places." Decayed places in my career, be reactivated now, in the name of Jesus Christ.

10.   Decayed places in my business, hear the Word of the Lord God to you: "I will raise up your decayed places." Decayed places in my business, be restored to excellence now, in the name of Jesus Christ.

11. Decayed places in my ministry, hear the Word of the Lord God to you: "I will raise up your decayed places." Decayed places in my ministry, be restored now, in the name of Jesus Christ.

12. Decayed places in my progress, hear the Word of the Lord God to you: "I will raise up your decayed places." Decayed places in my progress, be reactivated now, in the name of Jesus Christ.

13. Thank You, Jesus Christ, for answering my prayers. Amen.

✝ PRAYERS PROPHESYING LIFE TO DRY BONES

BIBLE PRAYER LINKS

I will restore to you the years that the locust hath eaten, the cankerworm, and the caterpiller, and the palmerworm, my great army which I sent among you. And ye shall eat in plenty, and be satisfied, and praise the name of the Lord your God, that hath dealt wondrously with you: and my people shall never be ashamed. And ye shall know that I am in the midst of Israel, and that I am the Lord your God, and none else: and my people shall never be ashamed. (Joel 2:25-27).

Again he [the LORD] said unto me, Prophesy upon these bones, and say unto them, O ye dry bones, hear the word of the LORD. Thus saith the Lord GOD unto these bones; Behold, I will cause breath to enter into you, and ye shall live: And I will lay sinews upon you, and will bring up flesh upon you, and cover you with skin, and put breath in you, and ye shall live; and ye shall know that I am the LORD. So I prophesied as I was commanded: and as I prophesied, there was a noise, and behold a shaking, and the bones came together, bone to his bone (Ezek. 37:4-7).

PRAYER FOCUS

- To prophesy resurrection life to the dry bones in my life, destiny, and circumstances

PRAYER GUIDES

1. Father Lord, I thank You for causing my desires to prosper as I prophesy today.

2. O Lord, arise and baptize me with the spirit of prophecy. Fill my mouth with Your words of prophecy, in the name of Jesus Christ.

3. By the Word of the Lord God, I prophesy that the glory of divine liberty shall be seen on me today and forever, in the name of Jesus Christ.

4. Dry bones of my life, hear the Word of the Lord God to you: "Behold, I will cause breath to enter into you, and ye shall live." Now receive the Lord God's breath and live, in the name of Jesus Christ.

5. Dry bones of my destiny, hear the Word of the Lord God to you: "Behold, I will cause breath to enter into you, and ye shall live." Now receive the Lord God's breath and live, in the name of Jesus Christ.

6. Dry bones of my marriage, hear the Word of the Lord God to you: "Behold, I will cause breath to enter into you, and ye shall live." Now receive the Lord God's breath and revive, in the name of Jesus Christ.

7. Dry bones of my career, hear the Word of the Lord God to you: "Behold, I will cause breath to enter into you, and ye shall live." Now receive the Lord God's breath and reactivate, in the name of Jesus Christ.

8. Dry bones of my ministry, hear the Word of the Lord God to you: "Behold, I will cause breath to enter into you, and ye shall live." Now receive the Lord God's breath and prosper in God's will, in the name of Jesus Christ.

9. Dry bones of my business, hear the Word of the Lord God to you: "Behold, I will cause breath to enter into you, and ye shall live." Now receive the Lord God's breath and excel, in the name of Jesus Christ.

10. Dry bones of my marital destiny, hear the Word of the Lord God to you: "Behold, I will cause breath to enter into you, and ye shall live." Now receive the Lord God's breath and be restored, in the name of Jesus Christ.

11. Dry bones of my progress, hear the Word of the Lord God to you: "Behold, I will cause breath to enter into you, and ye shall live." Now receive the Lord God's breath and be restored, in the name of Jesus Christ.

12. Thank You, Jesus Christ, for answering my prayers. Amen.

✞ PRAYERS TO PROPHESY THAT IT SHALL BE WELL

BIBLE PRAYER LINKS

Say ye to the righteous, that it shall be well with him: for they shall eat the fruit of their doings (Isa. 3:10).

Thus saith the Lord, the Holy One of Israel, and his Maker, Ask me of things to come concerning my sons, and concerning the work of my hands command ye me (Isa. 45:11).

PRAYER FOCUS
- To prophesy that it shall be well with me
- To command the works of the Lord's hands and the restoration of my dominion

PRAYER GUIDES
1. Thank You, Lord, for restoring my dominion power today.
2. By the Word of the Lord God, I prophesy that the glory of divine liberty shall be seen on me today and forever, in the name of Jesus Christ.
3. The Lord says, "Say ye to the righteous, that it shall be well with him" (Isa. 3:10). I prophesy that regardless of the current condition of my life, it shall be well with me, in the name of Jesus Christ.

4. According to the Word of the Lord God, I say to my life and destiny that from today forward it shall be well, in the name of Jesus Christ.

5. The Lord says, "Command ye Me concerning the work of My hands" (see Isa. 45:11). I command the years of demonic damage to my life and destiny, "Be restored to me now, in the name of Jesus Christ."

6. The Lord says, "Command ye Me concerning the work of My hands" (see Isa. 45:11). I command all decayed places in my life and destiny to be repaired now, in the name of Jesus Christ.

7. The Lord says, "Command ye Me concerning the work of My hands" (see Isa. 45:11). I command that all my afflicted bodily organs be made whole by the blood of the Lord Jesus Christ.

8. Thank You, Jesus Christ, for answering my prayers. Amen.

✝ PRAYERS PROPHESYING GOD'S GLORY UPON ME

BIBLE PRAYER LINKS

Even every one that is called by my name: for I have created him for my glory, I have formed him; yea, I have made him (Isa. 43:7).

Thou shalt also decree a thing, and it shall be established unto thee: and the light shall shine upon thy ways (Job 22:28).

PRAYER FOCUS
- To acknowledge being created for God's glory
- To prophesy the resting of God's glory upon my life

PRAYER GUIDES
1. Thank You, Lord, for creating me for Your glory.
2. By the Word of the Lord God, I prophesy that the glory of divine liberty shall be seen on me today and forever, in the name of Jesus Christ.

3. According to the Word of the Lord to everyone who is called by His name—"I have created him[/her] for glory"—I speak against backwardness and failure in my life. Vanish now, for He has created me for His glory, in the name of Jesus Christ.

4. According to the Word of the Lord to everyone who is called by His name—"I have created him[/her] for glory"—I speak to all sickness and disease in my body: vanish now, for He has created me for His glory, in the name of Jesus Christ.

5. According to the Word of the Lord to everyone who is called by His name—"I have created him[/her] for glory"—my divine purpose shall be established now, for He has created me for His glory, in the name of Jesus Christ.

6. According to the Word of God, which says, "Thou shalt also decree a thing, and it shall be established unto thee: and the light shall shine upon thy ways," I command that every embargo imposed against the fulfillment of my life and destiny be lifted now. Light of God, shine upon my ways, in the name of Jesus Christ.

7. According to the Word of God, which says, "Thou shalt also decree a thing, and it shall be established unto thee: and the light shall shine upon thy ways," I decree that all wickedness fashioned against me must backfire. Light of God, shine upon my ways, in the mighty name of my Lord Jesus Christ.

8. According to the Word of God, which says, "Thou shalt also decree a thing, and it shall be established unto thee: and the light shall shine upon thy ways," I command every affliction assigned to destroy or kill me: be neutralized now by the blood of Jesus Christ.

9. Thank You, Jesus Christ, for answering my prayers. Amen.

CPSIA information can be obtained
at www.ICGtesting.com
Printed in the USA
BVOW10s1046240817

492944BV00013B/105/P